Socialism: the 100-Year-Old Misnomer

Studies in Critical Social Sciences Book Series

Haymarket Books is proud to be working with Brill Academic Publishers (www.brill.nl) to republish the *Studies in Critical Social Sciences* book series in paperback editions. This peer-reviewed book series offers insights into our current reality by exploring the content and consequences of power relationships under capitalism, and by considering the spaces of opposition and resistance to these changes that have been defining our new age. Our full catalog of *SCSS* volumes can be viewed at https://www.haymarketbooks.org/series_collections/4-studies-in-critical-social-sciences.

In an era when political labels—socialist, populist, fascist—are applied thoughtlessly, Neacșu's book challenges us to reconsider what we think we know about the meaning of the word "socialism" and its protean, resilient foil, capitalism. By turns historical, sociological, philosophical, and practical, *Socialism: The 100-Year Misnomer* offers a nuanced analysis of one of today's most vibrant political movements. Looking back at the uses and abuses of the word "socialism" over the last 100 years, Neacșu raises important questions about politics for the future, and shows that there are—and have always been—many socialisms.

– Larry Jackson, Ph.D. Associate Dean of Academic Affairs, Director of the Center for the Core Curriculum, Lecturer in Philosophy, Columbia College, New York, NY, USA

•••

It is of the nature of the intellectuals' mission that they use their own knowledge and convictions to point to a better and more just society. Dana Neacșu's *Socialism: the 100-Year-Old Misnomer*, written with passion and nourished by her twofold experience in contemporary United States and the former communist Romania, makes an ambitious and controversial argument about what I would call, paraphrasing the title of François Furet's last work, the future of an illusion. She boldly challenges the belief that capitalism is inevitable or eternal and invites her readers to demystify both socialism and capitalism. The readers are thus invited to decide whether the ideas of her book offer a new road to serfdom or a way to build a truly just society.

– Aurelian Crăiuțu, Distinguished Professor and Chair, Department of Political Science, Indiana University, Bloomington, IN, USA

•••

In our time of threatened nationalizations by President Donald Trump, Professor Neacșu's needed book reminds us that socialism appears where we least expect it. Is Trump the true Marxist after all?

– Bruce Ledewitz, Professor of Law and Adrian Van Kaam C.S.Sp. Endowed Chair in Scholarly Excellence, Thomas R. Kline School of Law, Duquesne University, Pittsburgh, PA, USA

•••

Powerful and engaging, Dana Neacșu's book is a gift to every person who believes in the lessons of the past.

– Eugene D. Mazo, Associate Professor of Law and Political Science, Duquesne University, Pittsburgh, PA, USA

•••

Brilliant scholarship can be rare but most valuable. Dana Neacșu's *Socialism: the 100-Year-Old Misnomer* is that rare scholarly gem. It delivers a powerful perspective that students and scholars in a host of disciplines will find most illuminating. Exploring "What's in a name?" Readers of Neacșu's book will come away with fresh insight into a term often used but rarely well understood.

– John V. Pavlik, Ph.D., Distinguished Professor, Journalism and Media Studies Department, School of Communication & Information, Rutgers, the State University of New Jersey, New Brunswick, NJ, USA

Socialism

The 100-Year-Old Misnomer

Dana Neacșu

Foreword by
George P. Fletcher

Haymarket Books
Chicago, IL

First published in 2025 by Brill Academic Publishers, The Netherlands

Published in paperback in 2026 by
Haymarket Books
P.O. Box 180165
Chicago, IL 60618
773-583-7884
www.haymarketbooks.org

ISBN: 979-8-88890-904-1

Distributed to the trade in the US through Consortium Book Sales and Distribution (www.cbsd.com) and internationally through Ingram Publisher Services International (www.ingramcontent.com).

This book was published with the generous support of Lannan Foundation, Wallace Action Fund, and the Marguerite Casey Foundation.

Special discounts are available for bulk purchases by organizations and institutions. Please call 773-583-7884 or email info@haymarketbooks.org for more information.

Cover design by Jamie Kerry and Ragina Johnson.

Printed in the United States.

Library of Congress Cataloging-in-Publication data is available.

Contents

G.III. 443 Definitions are not arbitrary, as Hobbes believed, and we cannot form ideas as we like, though it seems that the Cartesians are of this opinion. For it is necessary that these ideas which we undertake to form should be veritable, i.e., possible, and that the ingredients which we put into them should be compatible inter se.

Die philosophischen *Schriften* von. G.W. LEIBNIZ, herausgegeben von C.J. GERHARDT. Berlin, 1875–90

Foreword

George P. Fletcher

It is a pleasure to write this foreword to Dana Neacșu's learned and meticulously documented book, *Socialism: the 100-Year-Old Misnomer*. Rich with extensive footnotes, the book features visuals, literary analysis, and close readings of political, economic, and legal texts. It is intended to spark curiosity in both readers with established views on socialism and those open to rethinking their understanding, inviting deeper engagement with socialist theory and practice.

More than an endorsement of the book, this foreword is also personal. Like Dana, I was shaped by that alternative, otherworldly space—the former Soviet Union—first as an *advokat* (lawyer), and later, culturally, through my deep devotion to the ballet. More to the point of a foreword, however, this book—through its close reading of journalism, personal testimony, scholarly analysis, and historical reportage—invites a reevaluation of what common sense tells us about socialism. My reflections aim to offer one more layer of insight to that evolving understanding. So, here it goes.

I was born in 1939 to immigrant parents in Chicago, Illinois. This means my childhood was spent under the threat of Hitler's war against both East and West—against both capitalists and Soviet communists. Hitler's notorious antisemitism and his regime's genocide of six million Jews, along with millions of Roma and anyone perceived as opponents of the Third Reich, are well-known. I mention the Holocaust against the Jews because the Nazis blamed them for being both capitalists and true communists. And, to be sure, there were many Jewish devotees of both. Karl Marx, a secular Jew, was as much a communist as the Rothschild banking family were capitalists.

In prosecuting the war, Hitler made the classic mistake of repeating Bonaparte's disastrous invasion of Mother Russia in the winter. I always found it curious that Russians referred to their enormous stretch of land—spanning over nine time zones from Saint Petersburg (formerly Leningrad) to Vladivostok—as the Motherland, while Germans thought of their home territory as the Fatherland. I will leave it to the reader to ponder whether there is a deeper meaning latent here.

My earliest political memory, apart from the death of FDR on April 12, 1945, was my mother's work for Russian war relief, an experience that later led her to run an organization called Shelters for Israel, which I will discuss later.

I mention this because, as Neacșu makes clear, there is socialist theory and belief, communist theory and belief—and then there is ersatz theory.

In high school, I studied German, which proved invaluable in my career as a devotee of legal theory and philosophy. At Cornell University, I turned to Russian, and had the good fortune of becoming personally acquainted with Vladimir Nabokov, who at that time rode the buses of Ithaca to study the idioms of teenagers in preparation for writing *Lolita* (1955). The few of us who took the advanced Russian course all went on to significant careers, mostly shaped by our knowledge of the language. As it turns out, I was the only one who went on to law school.

At the University of Chicago, I fell under the influence of Professor Max Rheinstein, one of the many Jewish academics who fled Germany for the West and greatly enriched our understanding of comparative law. At the time, I was still interested in Marxist ideology and the supposed withering away of the state, coupled with the paradoxical idea—as Neacșu points out—of the dictatorship of the proletariat.

In law school, I wrote a research paper on comrades' courts—local lay tribunals established to handle disturbances in apartment buildings and other small communities. They represented a potential model for criminal justice functioning independently of the formal state apparatus. I read every Soviet journal I could find at the University of Chicago and Northwestern libraries and concluded that, in fact, these courts functioned more like bullies targeting the least popular members of the community. Professor Rheinstein gave me a low grade. When I asked him why, he replied, "Any hack in the State Department could have written this." That was the moment I understood the importance of creative thinking in academic work—even, one might add, for researchers in the State Department.

After graduating from law school, I studied German law in Freiburg and came under the influence of three teachers who changed my life: Hans Heinrich Jescheck in criminal law, Ernst von Caemmerer in advanced private law, and Erik Wolf in legal history. Each helped me grasp the essential difference between common law and civil law thinking. It is important to note that the former Soviet Union and contemporary Russia function as civil law systems, as Neacșu also clarifies—despite the perception that Soviet law was fundamentally different. Many scholars believe the difference lies in the reliance on case law (common law) versus statutes and codes (civil law). This is a misconception. I believe the essential difference lies in the role of academic authority—in *la doctrine*.

I grasped this truth after writing a paper for von Caemmerer's seminar. I had read all the cases and scholarly works on a dispute at the boundary between torts and contracts. I proudly argued that scholars had misread the true source of the distinction between legal systems. Von Caemmerer responded memorably: "*Recht ist das, was die Professoren sagen*" ("Law is what the professors say it is"). This, believe it or not, is the basic principle underlying all civil law thinking—and Russia inherited it from the Soviet Union, which inherited it from Tsarist Russia. The Institute of State and Law in Moscow, located at 10 Frunze Street, remains a major legal think tank.

One note about civil law countries, which include Japan and South Korea: all European languages have two words for "law." They distinguish between law as principle and law on the books—as enacted by legislatures or courts. Professor von Caemmerer referred to the higher law, law as principle. English has only one word—"law"—with which we seem to function. But honestly, I've never fully understood what people mean by "the rule of law," although Neacșu clarifies it for skeptics like me. For Neacșu, the rule of law is law as decreed by authorities, used to legitimize the government. She does not invoke any ideal law. In Russian, the distinction is between *zakon* (statutory law) and *pravo* (ideal law). Other than the fact that ideal law is typically associated with the right hand—a concept that survives in the notion of personal rights—I, too, do not see any ideal law infusing the Soviet legal system.

Now I turn to the question of whether the Soviet Union followed any rule of law. If the U.S.S.R. was a dictatorship, as Neacșu argues, then it deserved no respect. If law is simply the command of the bully (the one with the guns), then it deserves no obedience. This is a critical question when considering whether there is a duty to obey unjust laws—such as those under Nazi Germany, Soviet rule, apartheid South Africa, or Jim Crow in the U.S. Believe it or not, many states in the U.S. forbade interracial marriage prior to 1967. Did one have a duty to respect such laws?

The anti-positivists—or perhaps, the believers in natural law—would say such laws are not truly laws at all. They assert there is no moral duty to obey them, except out of fear. Neacșu engages this ambiguity through Fredric Jameson's layered textualism, which seems the most inclusive way to do so.

In addition to theoretical knowledge, I had personal experience with the Soviet legal system. In the 1970s, the Soviets required everyone to work to "build the Motherland." Unemployment was criminalized under the offense of "parasitism." Worse, applying for an exit visa led to termination and labeling as a "refusenik." This was common among Jews trying to emigrate to Israel. Most people assume a right to leave one's country, but that did not apply in the U.S.S.R.

I recall a failed hijacking by a group who sought to flee the Soviet Union and speak freely in the West. The plan was foiled on the tarmac. They were charged with treason—not for action, but for intent. Around this time, Columbia Law Professor Telford Taylor, a Nuremberg prosecutor, tapped me to assist. I had recently become friends with Alan Dershowitz, a student of Taylor's and a major figure in the Jewish community. Taylor had personal ties to Roman Rudenko, the Soviet chief prosecutor. Because I was a visiting professor at Harvard Law School, I was brought in—perhaps because, unlike more prominent Soviet law scholars like John Hazard and Harold Berman, I had no ties to protect.

Taylor asked if I could leave for Moscow immediately. My wife sent my passport. That was the beginning of one of the great adventures of my life. I had dreamt of such a journey since my Russian studies at Cornell. I traveled to Moscow many times, sometimes with Taylor, sometimes alone.

We were supervised by Intourist, the Soviet tourist agency, and housed in a hotel reserved for foreigners who could pay in *valyuta* (convertible currency). The mission began slowly, but soon we were invited to meet with officials from the Procuracy. In civil law systems, the chief prosecutor is a hybrid figure—part prosecutor, part judge. I have no illusion they sought my legal expertise. But the visit opened doors. I returned to Moscow often, and when possible, I secured tickets to the Bolshoi Ballet.

What I learned was that the Soviets took procedural law seriously—unsurprising given the size of the country. They needed consistency. But substantive law—especially in political cases—was applied arbitrarily. Possessing anti-Soviet material, for instance, was prosecuted in the same vague manner as pornography once was in the U.S. ("You know it when you see it," said Justice Potter Stewart.) In this way, Dana Neacșu's description is apt: the Soviet Union was run by bullies for their own benefit.

But the story is not simple, which is why I'm grateful Neacșu used more than legal sources in her meaning-making. Soviet influence endures—for instance, in Israel, where many immigrants came from Russia. I once attended a theater production in Jerusalem with subtitles in Hebrew, English, and Russian. One such immigrant was Anatoly (later Natan) Sharansky, who spent nine years in prison. He stayed sane by playing chess in his head. He defended himself in court, rightly suspecting any appointed lawyer would be compromised. Despite fears of harsh sentencing, we all knew he would not face the death penalty—a restraint not always observed in the U.S.

The Israeli *kibbutz* was modeled after the Soviet collective farm. Ironically, the imitation proved more genuine. Communal property, shared labor, even collective child-rearing—until personal bonds reasserted themselves, and the *kibbutz* gradually gave way to the *moshav* model. The result may be closer to real socialism.

There is much to learn from the Soviet experience—and much to learn from Dana Neacșu's magnificent book. I strongly recommend *Socialism: the 100-Year-Old Misnomer* to anyone who remembers that, despite the Cold War and today's nationalist resurgence, we still have much to learn from Marxist ideals and the Soviet experience—even, or perhaps especially, because they did not overlap.

Acknowledgments

This book was born out of love for my adopted home, America, and from the clarity that comes with having lived in a society that claimed to empower "the little people" but, in practice, offered little more than semantic gymnastics—calling the toilers "dictators" and their political terrorization "the dictatorship of the proletariat." In retrospect, I see troubling parallels between that past and today's United States: a nation increasingly governed by corporate bullies, not unlike the Politburo that once cast a long shadow over post-Tsarist Russia. We now praise a leadership model that leaves employees terrified each day, uncertain whether they will still have a job by day's end.

Few of us who still believe that ideas have practical consequences are willing to confront the uncomfortable truth: that our current political and economic present has been long foretold. Since the late 1960s and 1970s, American academia has been marked by a kind of institutional paralysis—producing little in the way of original thought beyond the confines of postmodern sectarianism. This mode of thinking has chewed up Big Theory only to regurgitate it into small, self-referential narratives—narratives that have dulled the imagination of our youth, encouraged powerlessness, and preserved the status quo. The current wave of popular discontent, rising amidst economic inequality rivaled only by Soviet-style state capitalism and its attendant repression, may well be one of the inevitable outcomes of these diminished narratives dressed in various shades of gray.

In light of this surrounding reality, this book seeks to dispel the myth of the so-called "socialist experiment"—hence its title: *Socialism: the 100-Year-Old Misnomer*. It aims to reveal its true nature: an unprecedented consolidation of monopoly power under an illiberal, dictatorial regime—legitimized through legal soundbites, often crafted with assistance from Western advisors (Ted Sorensen, for example, contributed to the drafting of Romania's 1967 Constitution).

It is my hope that the insights offered here will prompt a critical reexamination of common-sense assumptions about socialism—both in its genuine and ersatz forms—toward envisioning a society that belongs to its people, whether immigrants or not, irrespective of race, sexual orientation, age, gender, neurodiversity, or any other marker of identity. Such a theoretical project would have been risible had it not been for the example of Bruce Ledewitz and Robert Taylor and their four decades of intellectual exchange inspired by the work of Bernard Lonergan, whose theory of knowledge also informs this book. To call Bruce and Robert giants implies an aspiration to rise to their level. It is indeed desired. Robert also read my original draft, and his suggestions shaped this revised version. Thank you, Robert, for being a fountain of youth and for helping us refresh our thinking in your presence.

While working on this project, I am deeply grateful to George P. Fletcher for reminding me that life remains colorful—even when the rainbow hides behind the rain, it is still there. Thanks also to Larry Jackson for the opportunity he gave me to engage with Columbia University undergraduates. To my students in Western Civilization, this book is for you—just as it hopes to inspire my students at Barnard College and Duquesne University.

I extend heartfelt thanks to my brilliant editor, David Fasenfest, without whom this book—like its predecessor, *The Bourgeois Charm of Karl Marx* (Brill, 2020)—would never have been published. His trust in my theory of legal meaning-making five years ago, and again in this work on knowledge production grounded in Bernard Lonergan's ideas on insight and common sense, has been essential to the realization of this project.

As with everything I do, this is for my brightest stars: ZouZou and Izzie—my breath follows the light you give off, and their older sister, Absy. ZouZou, a graduate of Oxford's Hertford College, served as a sharp and incisive sounding board for my ideas and contributed her keen editorial eye—even if she occasionally raised an eyebrow at my theoretical claims. Izzie, a graduate of Pittsburgh's Creative and Performing Arts Magnet High School (CAPA), kept me grounded and inspired, as only she can. Absy, you were not yet seven when we entered each other's lives, and your kindness and generosity of spirit continue to inspire me. Annie, thank you for Lenin's fountain pen and your artistic brilliance.

Finally, I owe a special debt to Pittsburgh. This book could not have been conceived without its backdrop, nor written without my employment at Duquesne University. As I prepare to leave Appalachia, I offer my deepest thanks to this region and its people—for I could never have imagined any of you.

Figures, Maps and Tables

Figures

Maps

Tables

Socialism and Its Long Misnomer History

Words or concepts help position us within our reality. We label our experiences, which we then use as epistemic shortcuts—tools for quickly identifying and navigating our surroundings. But while they are helpful, they are not sufficient. Once we have named a phenomenon, true understanding requires empirical investigation and speculative insight to construct a durable form of common-sense knowledge.

Such insight is often grounded in existing theories that help us interpret complex events (see Figure 1). But the mere existence of a theory does not guarantee clarity or truth. Many theories come entangled with distorted, ersatz versions that share their names but not their substance.

The central concept explored in this book is socialism. Socialism is one of those concepts which have their own theoretical and practical reality.[1] Yet, the term "socialism" has come to signify not only its authentic ideological and

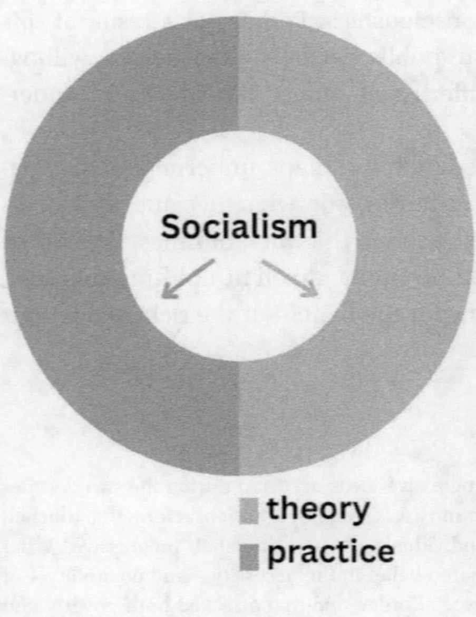

FIGURE 1
Socialism: a concept defining both theory and practice
SOURCE: NEACȘU, DANA. 2025. ORIGINAL CHART CREATED USING MICROSOFT EXCEL AND MICROSOFT PAINT

1 G.W. Leibniz. *New Essays on Human Understanding.* Book II 'of Ideas' (Peter Remnant and Jonathan Bennett, Trans. & Editors) (Cambridge, University Press, 1996), p. 109 et. seq. See also, Bertrand Russell, *A Critical Exposition of the Philosophy of Leibniz* (George Allen & Unwin, 1957).

practical expressions, but also their counterfeit counterparts. It has been used to describe both genuine efforts to construct a society grounded in principles of social justice and equality, and what this book terms "ersatz socialism"—a misappropriated label for systems that were, in fact, forms of state capitalism. In these cases, a bureaucratic elite managed the state in ways that mirrored capitalist profit structures while claiming the mantle of socialism. As such, the concept has collapsed critical distinctions, enabling false equivalencies that obscure understanding.

This book seeks to clarify that socialism has manifested in two distinct forms: one, a sincere challenge to capitalism rooted in egalitarian ideals; the other, an illiberal and hierarchical regime falsely operating under the socialist banner. Socialism, then, functions both as a framework for justice-oriented governance and as a misleading label for authoritarian practices antithetical to its foundational values.

Socialism has had its own history in the United States, mostly as a political ideology of union leaders in response to the increasing austerity of their capitalist surroundings.[2] Writers also contributed to this political awakening through literature that urged Americans to see one another with empathy. One of the most influential texts was Henry George's *Progress and Poverty* (1879), a bestseller[3] that helped shift public consciousness. Perhaps as a result of this intellectual momentum, the American public began to experience a willingness to act in solidarity with the suffering of others, not merely to understand it.[4]

Political awareness and cultural empathy perhaps undermined the rugged individualism of laissez-faire capitalism—or what became known as "business-controlled government."[5] Yet, even in the worst of times, the United States did not pivot toward a planned economy aimed at uplifting the poor. Instead, it pursued a planned economy for the benefit of the rich, and with it came the rise of corporate monopoly.

---

2 The most significant engagement with progressive ideas occurred during the two decades preceding its entry into World War I. The country was swept by a spirit of reform that touched every social stratum. A diverse array of individuals adopted the label "progressive." What united them, as Carl Resek notes, was a shared belief in the necessity—and possibility—of social progress. They envisioned a better social order, one that attacked both poverty and wasteful competition. *The Progressives* (Carl Resek, Editor, The Bobbs—Merrill Company, Inc., 1967).

3 *The Progressives* (Carl Resek, Editor, The Bobbs—Merrill Company, Inc., 1967), i–xxxiii.

4 Terri E. Givens, *Radical Empathy* (Bristol University Press, 2022) p. 15.

5 *The Progressives* (Carl Resek, Editor, The Bobbs—Merrill Company, Inc., 1967), p. xxiii.

Standard Oil, for instance, led the way in consolidating corporate power, at one point controlling 80% of the nation's refined oil production. Samuel Dodd, its attorney, devised the concept of a trust,[6] and on January 2, 1882, shareholders surrendered their company stock for trust certificates, centralizing control under a single board. J.P. Morgan followed suit in 1901 with the creation of U.S. Steel—the "world's first billion-dollar enterprise."[7]

By the late nineteenth century, capitalism had become the dominant economic model across nations. But its inherent drift toward monopoly provoked diverse political responses. World War I was one. The Bolshevik Revolution was another. Geographically insulated, the United States carved out its own response to industrial consolidation—felt across finance, law, and politics.

When monopolies began to dominate key sectors, Congress passed the Sherman Antitrust Act with near-unanimity—51–1 in the Senate, 242–0 in the House—and President Benjamin Harrison signed it into law on July 2, 1890.[8]

---

6 Under the Sherman Anti-Trust Act, a "trust" refers to any contract, combination, or conspiracy in restraint of trade or commerce among the several states or with foreign nations (15 U.S.C.A. §1). The term "trust" historically involved shareholders transferring their shares to a single trustee or board of trustees who would exercise complete control over the management of the trust, with shareholders receiving trust certificates entitling them to a share of the profits. The Sherman Act was enacted to prevent and declare unlawful any contracts and similar arrangements, or deals combinations designed to unduly restrain competition in interstate trade or obstruct the free course of trade among different states and with foreign countries (*U.S. v. Dried Fruit Ass'n of California*, 4 F.R.D. 1 (1944)). The Sherman Act condemns every contract, combination in the form of trust or otherwise, or conspiracy that restrains trade or commerce, without distinguishing between reasonable and unreasonable restraints (*Standard Oil Co. of New Jersey v. U.S.*, 221 U.S. 1 (1911)). The Act's purpose is to maintain interstate commerce on the basis of free competition and to prevent monopolistic practices that suppress competition (*U.S. v. Reading, Co*, 183 F. 427 (1910)).

7 *The Progressives* (Carl Resek, Editor, The Bobbs—Merrill Company, Inc., 1967), p. xxiii.

8 "The Sherman Anti-Trust Act authorized the federal government to institute proceedings against trusts in order to dissolve them. Any combination "in the form of trust or otherwise that was in restraint of trade or commerce among the several states, or with foreign nations" was declared illegal. Persons forming such combinations were subject to fines of $5,000 and a year in jail. Individuals and companies suffering losses because of trusts were permitted to sue in federal court for triple damages. The act was designed to restore competition, but it was loosely worded and failed to define such critical terms as "trust," "combination," "conspiracy," and "monopoly." Five years later, the Supreme Court dismantled the act in *United States v. E.C. Knight Company*, 156 U.S. 1 (1895).

The Court ruled that the American Sugar Refining Company, one of the defendants in the case, had not violated the law even though the company controlled about 98 percent of all sugar refining in the United States. The Supreme Court reasoned that the company's control of manufacture did not constitute a control of trade. The E.C. Knight ruling seemed to end any government regulation of trusts. Despite this, during President Theodore Roosevelt's "trust busting" campaigns at the turn of the century, the Sherman Anti-Trust Act was used

Yet the Act primarily served to broaden access to capitalist profits among the elite; it did little to address the conditions of wage laborers. Meaningful change came only through subsequent legal reforms that gradually improved working conditions, particularly for children[9] and mothers.[10]

The twentieth century U.S. history experienced both the fear that politically engaged workers would embrace the Bolshevik Revolution as "an ideal" which needed to be destroyed by imprisoning its leaders,[11] and a vision of a welfare society. On January 11, 1944, President Franklin D. Roosevelt, in his State of the Union Address, described what could be interpreted as a socialist vision of America—though he did not label it as such:

> *"Necessitous men are not free men." People who are hungry and out of a job are the stuff of which dictatorships are made.* In our day these economic truths have become accepted as self-evident. We have accepted, so to speak, a second Bill of Rights under which a new basis of *security*

with considerable success. In 1904, the Supreme Court upheld the government's suit to dissolve the Northern Securities Company in *Northern Securities Co. v. United States*, 193 U.S. 197 (1904). By 1911, President Taft had used the act against the Standard Oil Company and the American Tobacco Company."

Sherman Anti-Trust Act (1890). https://www.archives.gov/milestone-documents/sherman-anti-trust-act

9 The Fair Labor Standards Act of 1938, Pub. L. 75–718, addressed child labor by banning oppressive child labor practices and setting maximum work hours for all workers. For the history behind this New Deal piece of legislation, see, Jonathan Grossman, Fair Labor Standards Act of 1938: Maximum Struggle for a Minimum Wage (U.S. Department of Labor, https://www.dol.gov/general/aboutdol/history/flsa1938).

10 The Supreme Court upheld an Oregon state law that limited women's working hours to 10 hours per day in factories and laundries in *Muller v. Oregon*, 208 U.S. 412 (1908), https://supreme.justia.com/cases/federal/us/208/412/.

11 See, for instance, *Socialism on Trial* (1943) by James P. Cannon, which contains his testimony during the landmark 1941 trial of twenty-eight members of the Socialist Workers Party. This case marked the first peacetime federal prosecution for sedition in U.S. history and the first application of the Alien Registration Act, commonly known as the Smith Act. The trial concluded with prison sentences for eighteen union leaders, convicted of conspiring to advocate the violent overthrow of the U.S. government and to incite insubordination within the armed forces. For contemporary coverage, see "29 Reds Indicted in 'Overthrow Plot,'" *The New York Times*, July 16, 1941. The defendants were key figures in the Socialist Workers Party and leaders of the Minneapolis General Drivers Union 544, known for their pivotal role in the 1934 transportation strike. Each of the convicted individuals appealed; the cases were consolidated under *Dunne v. United States*, 138 F.2d 137, 139 (8th Cir. 1943), cert. denied, 320 U.S. 790 (1943), where the guilty verdicts were upheld.

> *and prosperity can be established for all—regardless of station, race, or creed.* (emphasis added)[12]

Roosevelt then listed economic rights that reflected a commitment to dignity, equality, and well-being: the right to a job, adequate food, housing, health care, education, and protection against economic insecurity. These are foundational to what socialism ought to entail.

> The right to a useful and remunerative job in the industries or shops or farms or mines of the nation; The right to earn enough to provide adequate food and clothing and recreation; The right of every farmer to raise and sell his products at a return which will give him and his family a decent living; The right of every businessman, large and small, to trade in an atmosphere of freedom from unfair competition and domination by monopolies at home or abroad; The right of every family to a decent home; The right to adequate medical care and the opportunity to achieve and enjoy good health; The right to adequate protection from the economic fears of old age, sickness, accident, and unemployment; The right to a good education. (Roosevelt, 1944)

By contrast, the twentieth century also bore witness to a so-called socialist experiment in post-Tsarist Russia. There, under Lenin's leadership, a group of men became the Founding Fathers of a society which they labeled as a proletarian dictatorship. It was a dictatorship over workers, not by them: a workers-built not a "workers' [own] state" (Levine, 1973, 86). These "necessitous" men and women became state-dependent laborers with little claim to the value of their work, living under fear and repression. The Soviet model, far from being socialism, represented a form of illiberal state capitalism—what is called here "ersatz socialism."

In this atmosphere, the Bolshevik Revolution sent shockwaves through the global order. The supposed "dictatorship of the proletariat" became a rhetorical shield for mass repression. The concept of socialism was appropriated to describe what was in fact a brutal form of state capitalism.

To capitalists worldwide, this model appeared threatening enough to suppress scrutiny.

Progressive intellectuals in the West hesitated to critique Soviet atrocities, perhaps out of guilt, strategic ambivalence, or the seductive appeal of a

12 Franklin D. Roosevelt, State of the Union Message to Congress, January 11, 1944, http://www.fdrlibrary.marist.edu/archives/address_text.html.

seemingly working-class utopia. The result was that even progressive thinkers helped rebrand Soviet state monopoly as "socialism."

Writers like Edward Upward—Cambridge-educated and torn between conscience and class—illustrated the tragic irony of this moment. In his novel *In the Thirties* (1962), he portrayed the profound alienation between privileged reformers and the working class. The character Alan admits he does not know "how to get in with them," fearing their disdain. His friend Richard reassures him that "they are rather proud of their gentlemanly friend" (Id.)—a line soaked in both irony and pathos.

From this place of guilt and condescension, it became easier to justify Soviet crimes as unfortunate but necessary steps in a grand project for "the lower orders" (Upward, 1962, 5). But Soviet state monopoly was not socialism. It was Russia's answer to capitalism's tendency toward monopolization: a monopoly of the cruelest kind. And monopoly, whether corporate or state-driven, has never been a pathway to social justice.

In fact, the Bolshevik Revolution merely changed the recipients of capitalist profit while maintaining rigid systems of extraction and control. It became a blueprint for modern authoritarian capitalism—a system perfected today by billionaires who understand that obedience thrives under monopoly, noncompetitive labor markets, and unchallengeable executive power.

Following Leibniz's insight that a concept can have only one true essence,[13] this book argues that socialism is defined by two central features that distinguish it from capitalism: First, socialism requires a democratic form of government. Second, socialism involves the redistribution of wealth to ensure collective security and prosperity for all, regardless of social or economic status. These features are only possible under a legal system committed to welfare, the separation of powers, and checks and balances.

Although the term "socialism" is widely used, it is commonly misunderstood. For some, it denotes progressive ideals centered on inclusion and human dignity. For others, it invokes failed twentieth-century regimes and unreachable utopias. But the Soviet model was never truly socialist; it was a misappropriation of the term, masking authoritarian capitalism behind a socialist facade.

---

13 Die philosophischen Schriften von. G.W. Leibniz, herausgegeben von C.J. Gerhardt. Berlin, 1875–90, in Leibniz, New *Essays on Human Understanding* (Peter Remnant and Jonathan Bennett, Translators and Editors) (Cambridge University Press, 1996), paragraph 109. See also, Bertrand Russell, *A Critical Exposition of the Philosophy of Leibniz* (George Allen & Unwin, 1957).

1 Why Now?

In his parting speech, President Biden reminded Americans of this historical fork in the road: our own democracy no longer resembles its theoretical ideals. He emphasized that democracy and oligarchy are not merely different; they are opposites. And oligarchy, as he warned, "threatens our basic rights, freedom, and a fair shot for everyone to get ahead."

> "An *oligarchy* is taking shape in America of extreme wealth, power and influence that literally threatens our entire *democracy*, our basic rights, freedom and a fair shot for everyone to get ahead," Biden said. "We must not be bullied into sacrificing the future, the future of our children and grandchildren."[14]

Echoing Dickens's famous dualism[15]—"It was the best of times, it was the worst of times ..." (Dickens, 1859, 4)—Biden juxtaposed the concepts of "oligarchy" and "democracy" to dramatize the fork in the road facing the American electorate. Yet, he wielded these concepts not strictly as analytic tools, but as emotive cues—appeals to shared intuitions rather than rigorous definitions. Still, both terms carry not only a common-sense resonance but also centuries of theoretical development and historical application.

These are concepts burdened by complexity. They encompass multiple variants and are often distorted by their false, *ersatz*, or superficial counterparts. Even Aristotle, whose *Politics* remains foundational, is not immune to interpretive ambiguity.[16] According to a simplified—but serviceable—reading of Aristotle: a form of government is "a *democracy* when the free, who are also

---

14 Adam Cancryn Biden Warns of Rising Democracy-threatening 'Oligarchy' in Grim Farewell Speech. *Politico* https://www.politico.com/news/2025/01/15/biden-oligarchy-farewell-speech-00198565 (Jan. 15, 2025, 09:51 PM EST).

15 Antithesis is a literary technique that places opposite things or ideas next to one another to highlight their contrast OED, https://www.oed.com/search/dictionary/?scope=Entries&q=antithesis.

16 "Of forms of democracy first comes that which is said to be based strictly on equality. In such a democracy the law says that it is just for the poor to have no more advantage than the rich ... There is another, in which the magistrates are elected according to a certain property qualification, but a low one; he who has the required amount of property has a share in the government, but he who loses his property loses his rights. Another kind is that in which all the citizens who are under no disqualification share in the government, but still the law is supreme. In another, everybody, if he be only a citizen, is admitted to the government, but the law is supreme as before. A fifth form of democracy, in other respects the same, is that in which, not the law, but the multitude, have the supreme

poor and the majority, govern, and an *oligarchy* when the rich and the noble govern, they being at the same time few in number" (emphasis added).[17]

Biden's language pointed to what we might call a "fake democracy"—a procedural democracy that retains the mechanics of voting while consolidating real power in the hands of the wealthy few. His cultural critique echoed what Fredric Jameson describes as "historical cultural criticism": a dialectical mode of analysis that examines how meaning is layered over time, shaped by material conditions and ideological structures.

In Biden's framing, democracy no longer means what it once did. The gap between its etymology—*demos* (the people) and *kratia* (rule)—and its lived reality has widened to the point of rupture.

Only days after Biden's farewell, that rupture deepened. The newly re-elected President Trump declared, "We're closing the border and we're drilling, drilling, drilling. After that, I'm not a dictator."[18] The remark, perhaps meant as a deflection, confirmed the fears voiced by many: that Trump's second term would discard even the pretense of constitutional constraint.

A dictator is one who governs by fiat, unconstrained by law. Trump's attempt to unilaterally amend birthright citizenship provisions—violating the Fourteenth Amendment—is a textbook example. It is not merely unconstitutional; it is despotic. His use of executive orders—26 signed on his first day in office—signals the end of a presidency tethered to checks and balances.

---

power, and supersede the law by their decrees. ... These then are the different kinds of democracy.

Of oligarchies, too, there are different kinds ... These are the different sorts of oligarchies and democracies. It should, however, be remembered that in many states the constitution, which is established by law, although not democratic, owing to the education and habits of the people may be administered democratically, and conversely in other states the established constitution may incline to democracy, but may be administered in an oligarchical spirit."

ARISTOTLE, *Politics*. Book 4. Part 4 & Part 5. (350 BC) (Translated by BENJAMIN JOWETT) https://classics.mit.edu/Aristotle/politics.4.four.html

17 Id.

18 Lindsay Kornick, CNN presidential historian claims Trump fulfilled 'promise to be a dictator on day one' with executive orders—(*Fox News*, January 21, 2025 6:30am EST, https://www.foxnews.com/media/cnn-presidential-historian-claims-trump-fulfilled-promise-dictator-day-one-executive-orders) (referencing "We're closing the border and we're drilling, drilling, drilling," Trump said. "After that, I'm not a dictator.") For more on Trump's self-described dictatorship, see also, Houston Keene, Brandon Gillespie, Here are the top moments from Trump's 'Hannity' town hall Trump touched on topics ranging from President Biden to dictatorships (*Fox News*, December 6, 2023, 4:00am EST. https://www.foxnews.com/politics/top-moments-trumps-hannity-town-hall).

What remains is governance by decree, reminiscent of the post-Tsarist rule by Politburo decree, as further discussed here.

Yet even as democracy recedes, American capitalism continues to thrive. It does not require democracy to function. Capitalism, with its remarkable elasticity, can flourish under authoritarianism as long as profits are generated and protected. It is, in fact, most efficient when dissent is minimal, labor is docile, and competition is eliminated.

Still, Americans retain the right to vote. And that vote is often cast in accordance with each individual's understanding of capitalism—what it is, whom it serves, and what kind of world it creates. This book is written in the belief that concepts matter. They shape our understanding of the world and ourselves. And they are shaped, in turn, by commonsense: that amalgam of observation, belief, education, experience, faith, alienation, and cultural inheritance through which we construct meaning and pursue justice.

Biden's speech is powerful because the forms of democracy and oligarchy he described are both possible within the United States. Our capitalist foundation is adaptable: it can be governed by the majority or by a minority without altering the essence of capitalism itself—a system centered on profit maximization.

This book argues that capitalism benefits from private property rights or basic contractual norms—such as exchanging labor for wages—but they are not essential to its function. Historically, the United States built its early wealth and capital accumulation on the backs of enslaved people. As former President Biden reminded us, capitalism does not require democracy to thrive. In fact, oligarchy, like slavery, limits the number of profit beneficiaries, thereby concentrating wealth and increasing profit levels.

Moreover, oligarchy is not the opposite of democracy, as Aristotle observed. Similarly, state corporate monopoly is not the opposite of private corporate monopoly. It is a variation, not a negation, and does not constitute an alternative to capitalism. This is one of the distinguishing perspectives this book offers—it challenges commonsense assumptions about capitalism, especially in relation to what has traditionally been seen as its antithesis: socialism. By doing so, the book opens new avenues for inquiry and offers insights to revise long-held misconceptions.

The assumption that theory influences practice runs throughout these examples, particularly in the case of Biden's January 15, 2025 speech. In religion, the connection between faith and behavior is generally accepted: believers act in accordance with their faith. In politics, ideologies like liberalism, socialism, conservatism—or even more loosely defined ones like populism—are presumed to influence political behavior. But often, that connection is illusory or fabricated. Here, however, practice is not merely behavior—it is the institutional implementation of theory, the structuring of a government or economic system in line with an ideological framework.

This book aims to uncover the obscured essence of socialism and distinguish it from the historical misnomer of Soviet socialism. Through a layered analysis of culture, law, political and economic theory, literature, film, and visual art, this work will recover the original, progressive meaning of socialism.[19] In doing so, it will also liberate ersatz socialism from uncritical and ahistorical readings, revealing that what passed as socialism in the Soviet Union was in fact its opposite: the most inhuman form of state monopoly capitalism.

Capitalism has long demonstrated its capacity to assume a variety of forms. Until recently, conventional wisdom—commonsense knowledge and understanding—tended to associate capitalism exclusively with its liberal democratic form, in which the state supported free markets and encouraged competition among capitalists (i.e., private property owners) of all scales. However, the rise of industrial monopolization—a drastic strategy adopted to secure profits in the absence of new resources or productivity gains—has made it clear that limited profit-sharing, rather than democratic governance or competition, is capitalism's most defining feature. Yet this insight marks a relatively new approach, one not developed or embraced by any of capitalism's most influential economic theorists.

Capitalism, a broad conceptual category, applies to societies as different as post-WWII liberal democracies and today's "a-democratic" or post-democratic Hayekian capitalism—a version increasingly characterized by concentrated wealth, deregulated markets, and weakened democratic oversight (Streeck, 2016, 155). Theoretically, to a large extent Karl Marx's work is related to socialism. While Marxian thought recognizes the foundational role of material reality, Marx nevertheless focused on the relationship between theory and practice, even if wrongly to bemoan that before him philosophical theories only explained reality rather than influenced human behavior accordingly. "The philosophers have only interpreted the world in various ways; the point is to change it."

Furthermore, in the 21st century, the principles of separation of powers and checks and balances have become increasingly irrelevant to capitalism's core

19 The textual analysis used in this book relies on Dana Neacșu's meaning-making theory where knowledge is negotiated between the textual instigator (author) and the textual interpellated (reader), detailed in Dana Neacșu's, *The Bourgeois Charm of Karl Marx and the Ideological Irony of American Jurisprudence* (Brill, 2020) and on Fredric Jameson's dialectical criticism developed on layered, historical textualism, developed in Fredric Jameson, *The Political Unconscious* (Cornell University Press, 1981).

function. In countries like Russia and China—two of today's most representative illiberal capitalist societies—we observe the consolidation of monopoly power in distinctly non-democratic ways. For this reason, it becomes easier to trace a logical continuity between contemporary capitalism and its most draconian form: the illiberal state-capital monopoly that existed for nearly a century in post-Tsarist Russia and its Eastern and Central European satellites (here abbreviated as "ECE"), regimes falsely branded as socialist. In the current era, those state monopolies have morphed into corporate monopolies, now governed by illiberal oligarchies—most notably in Russia, China, and Hungary. And, unexpectedly, since January 21, 2025, this same pattern has begun to emerge on our own doorstep.

Amidst this muddled embrace of totalitarian tendencies, this project offers conceptual clarity. It is structured in three parts. Part 1 offers a critical survey of socialist theories, juxtaposed with a layered analysis of testimonials about the creation of the U.S.S.R. by philosophers (e.g., Bertrand Russell), journalists (e.g., John Reed), and fiction writers (e.g., Boris Pasternak).

Part 2 continues the book's challenge to the prevailing commonsense (mis)understanding of socialism—both as concept and praxis. Conceptually, socialism is a theory about building a just society for all. In practice, however, Soviet Russia and the Eastern and Central European (ECE) countries justified their political and military coups as socialist revolutions. In doing so, they enacted a form of state capitalism which skipped over intermediary capitalist stages of accumulation and adopted the final form of capitalism—corporate monopoly—under state control.

Part 3 completes this exposé of ersatz socialism by offering a theory of knowledge grounded in commonsense and insight. It is an argument that demystifying socialism—and thus capitalism—is essential for any honest conversation about political and economic justice.

The theoretical foundation of this project is informed by the thought of Daniel C. Dennett (1996) and Bernard Lonergan (1988–2019). Dennett advanced the view that knowing is an expression of consciousness and intentionality—that people, as conscious agents, interact with their environments based on understanding or misunderstanding. Our understanding, in turn, is shaped by the subtle relationship we cultivate with the object of our inquiry. In this context, both the historical Soviet and ECE environments—and how they have been intentionally perceived and represented—fail to align with the concept of socialism, if that concept is understood as a political, economic, social, and cultural theory aimed at sustainable welfare for all.

As Dennett (1996) and Lonergan (1988–2019) both argue, understanding presupposes an intentional agent—and so does this book, which focuses on the construction of understanding. When it comes to socialism, the process of demystification requires more than historical correction; it demands recognition that "knowing" relies as much on an agent's beliefs and desires as on their conceptual and linguistic capacity to make distinctions.

To paraphrase Dennett: when someone claims, "socialism has been tried and failed," they are relying on a network of concepts—just as they would when saying, "my dish is full of beef" (Dennett, 1996, 56). To make the latter culinary statement informative, one must know what a dish is, what beef is, how it looks, how it's prepared, and what "full" implies. Similarly, to evaluate socialism meaningfully, one must understand it as both a theoretical framework and a system of political, economic, and legal organization, while also being familiar with both the experience of living under so-called socialist regimes and that of capitalist societies. Without this grounding, any blanket judgment of socialism appears uninformed or ideologically motivated.

This book assumes, following Dennett, that most people—most agents—form opinions through commonsense knowledge. This knowledge is built empirically and incrementally through observation, experience, and inference. With understanding comes knowledge, and knowledge forms the foundation for opinions, whether positive, negative, or indifferent. Changing opinions, therefore, requires altering that foundation. But only what is unknown stirs curiosity and invites deeper understanding.

Today, socialism is widely perceived as both a theory and a failed practice, manifested in the Soviet and ECE political, economic, and legal systems. Because the practice has been repudiated, opinions about socialism tend to be negative. Reframing these opinions would require a reversal—a return to ignorance acknowledged, or at least a recognition that what is commonly known about socialism may be fundamentally misunderstood. This is a difficult, but not impossible, task—provided curiosity is sparked and insight is offered. That is the aim of this book.

2 Ersatz Socialism and State Monopoly Capitalism

Both socialism and capitalism are dual concepts: they are theoretical frameworks (concepts) and historical realities (praxis). Their real-world manifestations are rooted in time, space, politics, economy, technology, society, and law. While socialism is the central misnomer interrogated in this book, capitalism—with its exceptional resilience and flexibility—emerges as the necessary point of reference. It has endured and adapted far beyond the limits envisioned by Karl Marx and Friedrich Engels, making it indispensable in

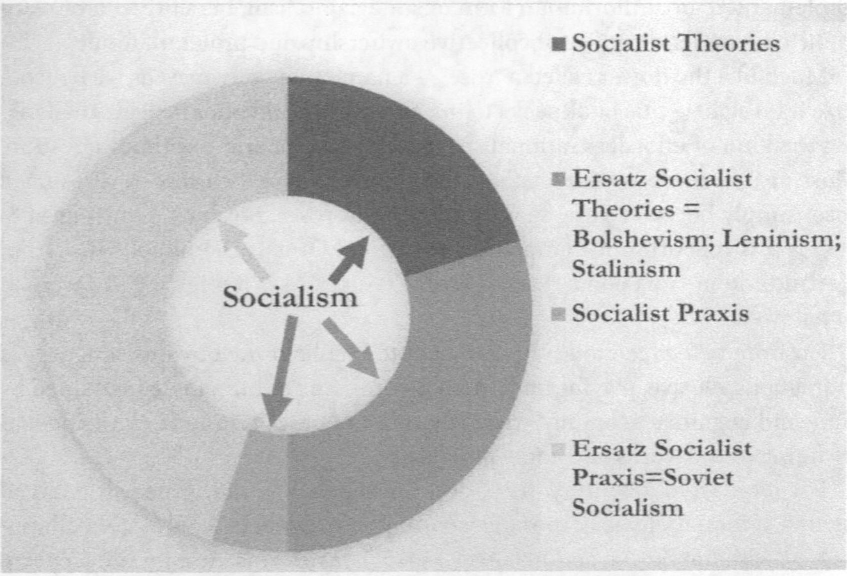

FIGURE 2 Socialism: a concept defining both authentic and ersatz theory and practice
SOURCE: NEACŞU, DANA. 2025. ORIGINAL CHART CREATED USING MICROSOFT EXCEL AND MICROSOFT PAINT

any serious effort to clarify the mislabeling and misunderstanding of socialism (see Figure 2).

This book assumes the interconnection between theory and practice, as well as that between ersatz theory and ersatz practice, much like "faith and good works" in religion (Dunn, 1969). The faith, imagined as doctrine, or theory, is often a more relatable framework of references, but it is the "good works," the actions actuating the doctrine, that demonstrate and enact the desired changes, social and individual.[20] In this way, Soviet socialism, on display in Russia for nearly a century, functioned as ersatz socialism, which

20 William Newlin Dunn, *Yugoslavia*: "Yugoslavia: National Communist Ideology and Political Integration" (1969) (Ph.D. dissertation, Claremont Graduate School). The focus of W.N. Dunn's dissertation is the relationship between what the author calls "communist ideology" (specifically in Yugoslavia) and political behavior. It rejects the idea that philosophical doctrines automatically determine specific actions. Instead, it proposes that ideology is a "union of doctrines and action programs." How does this work? Doctrines alone are not enough: Philosophical doctrines ("interpretations of the world") are different from ideology = doctrines + action programs. The author claims that doctrines provide the justification and rationale for the action programs. The action programs, in turn, prescribe and regulate specific political behavior. So, the author concludes, ideology

implemented an authoritarian form of state capitalism, benefitting a bureaucratic elite under the guise of collective ownership and proletarian rule.

Much like the flower called a "rose"—a name that convinces us we'll recognize it on sight—this book seeks to instill curiosity and offer insight, challenging the kind of effortless rationalism that accepts meaning without question. Most of us believe we understand the phrase "a rose is a rose is a rose is a rose" simply because we've seen or read about roses. But how many pause to ask: Is it a repetition for emphasis? A stutter? Or is it the famous line from Gertrude Stein's 1913 poem "Sacred Emily"? And if so, is it referring to a woman or a flower?

Far from being facetious, this is meant to highlight the obvious: language is ambiguous, elusive, playful, and often obscure. And as humans, constrained by time and cognitive economy, we rarely stop to question or unpack the deeper meaning of the words and concepts we use.

For more than a century, the world has labeled an authoritarian political regime, a monopolistic corporate economy, and a violent legal system administered without checks and balances as "socialism." This, despite the fact that socialism—at its core—is a theory of social justice for all. The confusion has been sustained by political slogans, derivative academic commentary, uncritical media narratives, and the complicity of both mainstream and marginalized intellectuals, from across the political, religious, and ideological spectrum.

Conceptually, capitalism has often been defined in a reductionist manner, in an attempt to find its essence. Capitalism has been hailed as the emergence of the "commercial society."[21] This definition reduces capitalism to a market production system, where "private" and "public" designate the independent realms of "economy" and "politics," respectively.[22] The economy is presented as a system organized into groups of participants based on ownership: capital owners, partial owners, and participants without private ownership.[23] This perspective is not monolithic. There are variations that emphasize and see capitalism arising with the accumulation of capital based on the surplus value

---

influences political behavior through the creation and implementation of specific action programs that are justified by the underlying doctrines.

21 See, e.g., Adam Smith, *An Inquiry into the Nature and Causes of the Wealth of Nations* (1776); Amy Kapczynski, "The Law of Informational Capitalism," 129 *Yale Law Journal*, pp. 1460–1515, 1481 (2020).

22 See Iversen and Soskice, *Democracy and Prosperity*, pp. 257–78.

23 E.K. Hunt, *Property and Prophets: The Evolution of Economic Institutions and Ideologies*, pp. 15 et seq.; (2003); E.K. Hunt and Mark Lautzenheiser, *History of Economic Thought: A Critical Perspective*, 3rd ed., pp. 202 et seq. (2011).

of unpaid labor[24] and developing linearly until it reaches its monopolistic and imperialist phase, defined by a hyper-concentration of capital, resources, and profit. From this perspective, capitalism is a dynamic system, whose goal is efficient capitalist production. A neoliberal view of capitalism prioritizes the concept of self-regulating markets, which are believed to promote human progress through economic growth and efficiency.

Capitalism is not just private property, nor is it merely a matter of the market, though it is often mentioned without a generally accepted definition (Neacșu, 2024b; Sonenscher, 2023). That is because capitalism, while flexible, has not been mislabeled. And today, its ability to socialize production and centralize profit distribution to secure the most cost-effective way of accumulating profit along pre-established power structures, made it fertile for even such democratically inhospitable places as Russia or China. For skeptics, Russia continues its new form of oligarchic imperialist capitalism as it engages in imperialist wars of aggression and embraces private property and profit in a more traditional manner,[25] even though it stays clear of democracy and its periodic change of political leaders. Similarly, China lives its capitalist dream[26] while being governed by an autocratic, one-party political system.

All that these examples have in common is a stable political system, whose legal system ensures the construction of property, profit, and capital.[27] Law governs the production and satisfaction of desires, the foundation of a capitalist economy, whether in liberal democratic capitalism or in state monopoly capitalism. This diversity is possible because capitalism is a flexible system. It has a dynamic social and political structure, which is technologically shaped.

This book, then, is not merely about demystifying socialism. In doing so, it also clarifies the real differences—and real similarities—between capitalism

---

24 Karl Marx, *Capital: A Critical Analysis of Capitalist Production*, Vol. 1, edited by Frederick Engels, translated by Edward Aveling and Samuel Moore, London: Swan Sonnenschein, Lowrey, & Co., pp. 156 et seq. (1887); Karl Marx and Frederick Engels, *The German Ideology*. Edited by C.J. Arthur. New York: International Publishers, p. 50 (1970).

25 See Lynne Hartnett, "The Long History of Russian Imperialism Shaping Putin's War." *The Washington Post*, March 2, 2022. https://www.washingtonpost.com/outlook/2022/03/02/long-history-russian-imperialism-shaping-putins-war/. For another perspective, see Stephen Velychenko, *Painting Imperialism and Nationalism Red* (2023); Dolgor Solongo, *Russian Capitalism and Money-Laundering*. New York: United Nations, 2001, https://www.imolin.org/pdf/imolin/rc84066e.pdf.

26 Minqi Li, *Profit, Accumulation, and Crisis in Capitalism: Long-Term Trends in the UK, US, Japan, and China, 1855–2018*, pp. 71–89 (2020).

27 Katharina Pistor, *The Code of Capital: How the Law Creates Wealth and Inequality*, pp. 205–234 (2019). (Translated in multiple languages, including Romanian, *Codul Capitalului. Cum Dreptul Creează Bogăție și Inegalitate*, translation by Dana Neacșu, 2022).

and its so-called alternatives. Soviet socialism, supposedly built on class struggle and a worker-led state, translated in practice into a system where workers labored for a state-run corporate employer, had no say in the outcome of their labor, and no deeper relationship to their work than the wage they received—much like their counterparts in capitalist economies. Does property become less "another's" simply because the constitution declares it owned by the state in the name of the people, even though any attempt at personal ownership—such as using, taking, or damaging that property—is punished just as harshly as violations of private property under capitalism?

If one cannot use, transform, or benefit from property—except as a cog in a system designed to serve a managerial elite—can it truly be called theirs? And is that system any less capitalist simply because it goes by another name?

This book answers no. Names and concepts are foundational to understanding systems of power and economy—and central to dismantling illusions that persist around them.

3 Technologically Mediated Commonsense

This book bridges the gap between reality and understanding through technology-mediated knowledge production. Philosophers such as Martin Heidegger (1997) and Bernard Stiegler (1998), have long acknowledged that knowledge is technology mediated. Technology-mediation shapes how we imagine both capitalism and socialism—sometimes to the point of erasing meaningful distinctions between them.

Incorporated in both reality and imagination, both concepts contain elements of finitude as well as infinitude, to use Martin Heidegger's vocabulary, with a legal regime (both international and domestic) defining their possibility and manifestation in finitude, in reality. Always interconnected with the advent of industry, which represents a particular type of labor that only a worker can do (Laski, 1967, 433), capitalism is a modern technological product. Capitalism did not invent technology, but it has profited from technological innovations. Technology, in turn, has helped it become a tremendously resilient economic system even in the face of government policies which, through corporate subventions, redefine the free market and tip the competitive edge in favor of increasingly fewer individuals and corporate institutions.[28]

---

28 Philip Arestis and Malcom Sawyer suggest that economic crises are due to the classic "composition fallacy" which assumes that if individual financial institutions are resilient, then the financial system as a whole is resilient" (p. 36). To the contrary, macroprudential

Imaginaries can be codified, including the potentially destructive myth of technology, which can be tamed and brought into reality as a simple tool supporting intentional global action. In philosophical and sociological literature, "imaginary spaces" have often been described as collective representations that make "common practices and a widely shared sense of legitimacy possible" (Taylor, 2003, 55). Not very different from Clifford Geertz's notion of "culture," the imaginary could be viewed as a meaning-creating tool.[29] From this perspective, social life appears as unfolding in the shadow of a background formed of codes, images, and conventions, creating networks of meaning.[30] If we add law as an identifier and speak of legal codes, images, and conventions, we might become better prepared to see capitalism as part of our legal imaginary, not too different from legal semiotics, giving meaning to our social life, with an eye on survival.[31]

Technology is fundamental to capitalism and its industrial revolution, but also to all knowledge production and dissemination about it. Below, with generative artificial intelligence, I created an image of a capitalist economy built on technologically propelled productivity (see Figures 3 and 4). Its patriarchal hierarchy makes it easier to grasp the lack of difference between ersatz socialism and capitalism. Both societies socialized work, with ersatz socialism socializing poverty. Neither socialized wealth, though western capitalism paid its workers better wages.

Capitalism after World War II was able to ensure a standard of living for the toilers far superior to the ECE. Also, the profit was more equitably shared in

---

frameworks are needed for sustainable major policy responses to the crises of capitalism. Philip Arestis, Macro-Economic and Financial Policies for Sustainability and Resilience, pp. 1–44, 18, in Philip Arestis and Malcolm Sawyer (eds.), *Economic Policies for Sustainability and Resilience*. 2022. See also, Georgescu-Roegen, N. 1971. *The Entropy Law and the Economic Process*. Harvard University Press.; Aikman, David, Jonathan Bridges, Anil Kashyap, and Caspar Siegert. 2019. "Would Macroprudential Regulation Have Prevented the Last Crisis?" *Journal of Economic Perspectives*, 33 (1): 107–30.

29 According to Clifford Geertz 1973, *The Interpretation of Cultures: Selected Essays*: culture is "the imaginative universe in which ... actions are signs" (13).

30 "Sign" is used in the broadest possible sense and in accordance with the work of Umberto Eco: "there is no other way to define semiotics except as the discipline that studies all phenomena (although they may constitute the subject of another discipline) based on a referential relationship ('referring back') to something else." Eco, Umberto, "The Influence of Roman Jakobson on the Development of Semiotics." In *Classics of Semiotics*, edited by Martin Krampen, et al., 1987. pp. 109–127, 114.

31 Eco, Umberto.1968, *La Struttura Assente. Introduzione Alla Ricerca Semiologica*. Milan: Bompiani. Signs, as Umberto Eco would say, "always open up something new. No interpreter, in adjusting the interpreted sign, manages to change its limits to any extent." Eco, Semiotics and Philosophy of Language, p. 44.

FIGURE 3 Visualizing 20th-century patriarchy west of the Iron Curtain
SOURCE: NEACȘU, DANA. 2025. ORIGINAL IMAGE DRAWN BY THE AUTHOR AND REFINED USING OPENAI'S CHATGPT (MODEL O4-MINI-HIGH)

the Western world. However, greed is capitalism's state of mind, which technology can temporarily satisfy. Ironically, scientific progress induces a sense of security that, in turn, promotes political and legal apathy on the ground of daily reality. Innovation and limitless resources have cured the crises of capitalism. But, the climate consequences of industrialization, the finitude of the resources has made greed unable to survive without a change in the profit redistribution. The easiest way to do that is to reduce the number of those accessing profit through monopoly capitalism.

Rudolf Hilferding, in his seminal work *Finance Capital* (1910), argues that capitalism had evolved into a system where finance capital, largely controlled by a few large corporations and banks, had increasingly merged with industrial capital. This led to the rise of monopoly capitalism, a stage where competition

FIGURE 4 Visualizing 20th-century patriarchy east of the Iron Curtain
SOURCE: NEACŞU, DANA. 2025. ORIGINAL IMAGE DRAWN BY THE AUTHOR AND REFINED USING OPENAI'S CHATGPT (MODEL O4-MINI-HIGH)

is increasingly limited and large corporations dominate the market. Hilferding argues that monopoly capital controls not only the economy but also the political system, creating a new elite class of financial oligarchs. In Hilferding's view, the monopolistic stage of capitalism represents a shift from the competitive, decentralized capitalism of earlier stages. In this monopoly-driven model, corporations achieve profits not primarily through competition, but through control over markets and resources.

Lenin, building on Hilferding's theories, took the concept of state monopoly capitalism and applied it to the context of Russia in the early 20th century. In backward Russia, Lenin argued, the state must take on the role of an active participant in the economy, fostering technological development and industrialization through state control and central planning. This would not only advance technological progress but also help create the profits necessary to maintain the loyalty of the working class, thus preventing revolt and the collapse of the state. By creating a system in which the state monopolizes key industries, Lenin believed that Russia could bypass the chaos of laissez-faire capitalism and move towards a more controlled, yet still capitalist, industrialization that could modernize the economy. Lenin's theory proved correct. State monopoly ensured the highest rate of investment in technological progress. Technology became a key element to profit-creation for the managerial class and improved standard of living for the toilers so they would not revolt. Again.

In addition to its role in creating and sustaining a capitalist economy, technology is intimately connected with how we position ourselves in our reality and how we make sense of it. For instance, climate change has been understood since the late 1800s,[32] and, since then, due to technological progress, whether it be techné[33] or episteme,[34] our knowledge in this area has steadily increased.[35] However, our general political will[34] refuses to acknowledge any "fault" in our governing. One may say that legal apathy seems rooted in technology.[36] How is this possible? For far too long, we have been trained to rely on technology as a mechanical savior. Technology produces "bigger and

32 See also, Clive Thompson, "How 19th Century Scientists Predicted Global Warming", *JSTOR Daily*, (December 17, 2019) https://daily.jstor.org/how-19th-century-scientists-predicted-global-warming/.

33 "Ontologically, techné made its first appearance as the earliest form of instruction offered by Greek rhetoricians. The early sophists used techné as synonymous to art or skill, when describing their knowledge-purveying activity. Protagoras, an early sophist, as imagined by Plato in the dialogue with the same title, described his instruction as techné. In the same dialogue, Plato introduces a major conceptual development of craft, art, or techné, as a practical skill which does not need to be mechanical. The knowledge and technique of using fire, under the umbrella of techné, is the beginning of humanity in its most simple and complex possibility. This is also the beginning of techné as a type of experience, similar to what we would call today know-how."

DANA NEACȘU, (2022) "Technology—Revealing or Framing the Truth? A Jurisprudential Debate", *Duquesne University Law Review*, 60: 246–270, 248 (2022)

34 In Aristotelian thought, techné means the production of something. It was the essence of technology, according to Rauno Huttunen and Leena Kakkori (2022). Heidegger's Critique of Technology and the Educational Ecological Imperative, *Educational Philosophy and Theory* 54(6): 630–641, 630. Unlike Aristotle, "Heidegger saw the essence of technology in modern times as Ge-stell (framing, enframing, structuring, exposing, universal imposition)." Id. Here, technology is presented as both techné and *Gestell*.

35 See, e.g., the work of the IPCC at https://www.ipcc.ch/.

36 J.-J. Rousseau, *Declaration of the Rights of Man and the Citizen. French: Déclaration des Droits de l'Homme et du Citoyen* (1789).

better" washing machines, cars, and airplanes, making our lives easier. But "bigger and better" machines produce "bigger and better" desires and "bigger and better" ways to satisfy them, which brings more destruction and pollution (Georgescu-Roegen, 1971), and we don't even notice the correlation with our legal, political, and economic systems.[37]

Heidegger's critique of modernity has inspired both Bernard Stiegler (1998) and Ruth Irwin's (2008) own critique of modern technology for playing with our imagination[38] and producing simplistic common understanding of complex situations. One such complex reality is capitalism, whose state monopoly iteration has been misdescribed as socialism. Stiegler argues that nowadays, technology, especially information technology, "accelerates" our reality, induces confusion, and "disorients" our sense of time, culture, and identity. In the process, we might become predisposed to engage in what Heidegger described in 1954 as "calculative thinking" rather than "reflective thinking."[39] Or, going back even further to 1927 and using Heidegger's terminology from his first book,[40] modern technology might even confuse our sense of finitude and infinitude, blurring conceptual distinctions. The confusion of two different types of capitalism, liberal and illiberal, and seeing them as capitalism and "socialism" is the gist of this book.

Knowledge occurs when we use what Daniel Dennett calls individual agency, and seek it. It also occurs because, as Leibniz would say, we have an inclination, or an aptitude for it, which does not explain much, as Bertrand

---

37 "Climate change denotes an extinction event unseen since the disappearance of the dinosaurs. We are now facing an extinction rate far exceeding the 'normal background' levels noted during the Holocene evolution. Even those who deny climate change must acknowledge the rapid rise in the planet's average temperature, which is not only measurable but also noticeable in daily life as fires intensify, cyclones wreak havoc, insect, bird, and mammal populations rapidly decline, and rivers, lakes, and ocean temperatures rise, causing toxic algae blooms and the disappearance of fish and coral reefs."

N. GEORGESCU-ROEGEN, pp. 361–2

38 Despite Heidegger's disdain for metaphysics and his critical stance toward technology, his work remains fundamental in promoting our current view of modern technology, in which we identify both danger and salvation in the face of all our faults, including the crisis generated by climate change, the most significant existential threat to human life.

39 Saul Griffith, "Scientists May Have Already Discovered a "Miracle" Fix for Climate Change. Climate scientist Saul Griffith wants you to hear him out: electrify everything." (Oct. 1, 2022) https://www.inverse.com/science/fix-for-climate-change. ("After all, the scientific theory of evolution has existed for more than 150 years, with irrefutable evidence, yet only about 35 percent of Americans believe that we evolved by natural processes.")

40 Martin Heidegger, *Being and Time* (J. Stambaugh, Trans.) (2010, orig. 1927). Martin Heidegger, *The Question Concerning Technology and Other essays*, (W. Lovitt, Trans.) (1977).

Russell noted,[41] other than to say that knowledge starts with our perceptions, whether we are consciously reflecting on them or not.[42]

When a theoretical discourse (T_1) is interpellated by an audience or interpretive community (S_2 et al.), its epistemic legitimacy is measured against the prevailing Regime of Truth, which functions as the normative filter for what constitutes "objective" knowledge. If T_1 aligns with this regime, it is readily hailed as objective; its claims pass largely uncontested, and the subjectivity of its author (S_1) becomes invisible—assimilated into dominant ideology. However, when T_1 deviates from or challenges the Regime of Truth, interpellation becomes a site of rupture, producing an oppositional negotiation of meaning that exposes the constructed and ideological nature of T_1. In such moments, S_1's subjectivity—previously submerged in hegemonic neutrality—becomes visible, and T_1 is frequently dismissed as "lacking objectivity." This is deeply ironic, as all theoretical production is already embedded in subjectivity; S_1's philosophical narrative reflects both a condition of alienation and an ideological position within hierarchical systems. Yet, this subjectivity is only problematized when it conflicts with dominant norms. Likewise, S_2's interpellation is not neutral but shaped by their own ideological standpoint. As the ideological distance between S_1 and S_2 widens, the affective and epistemic stakes of the theory become more visible and more contested. If this clash renders T_1 fundamentally incompatible with the Regime of Truth, it is excluded from the dominant Knowledge Paradigm, not on the basis of reason alone, but due to its failure to satisfy hegemonic expectations. Thus, interpellation operates not merely as a mechanism of recognition, but as a process of epistemic gatekeeping (Neacșu, 2020, 4–5, 113–119). It is against this backdrop that our understanding of socialism or any other concept is formed.

This text, too, contains insight designed to interpellate the seeker of common wisdom and a path to knowledge. As a path, it intermediates knowledge production, shaping both the insight it conveys and the reader it addresses. This dual constraint—of content and audience—is structured by the ideological forces that govern knowledge and by the technological channels through which that knowledge circulates. All images used in this work have been generated through technology, serving as representational tools for my

41 Thus, Russell states, for Leibniz "an idea is not merely something in the mind, nor must we seek to give every idea an existence somewhere else.") Bertrand Russell, *A Critical Exposition of the Philosophy of Leibniz* (George Allen & Unwin, 1937) p. 166.

42 Knowledge for Leibniz is sense-knowledge and intellectual knowledge. *Id.* This book offers insight for both.

ideas. Moreover, the final text will be disseminated either as a digital book on Brill's platform or in print via commercial vendors such as Amazon or Barnes & Noble. At every level of its production and distribution, technology appends itself to the reader's conscious engagement with the ideas herein. Since technology-mediated information forms the backbone of contemporary perception, this book inevitably adds to that stream, though it does so reflectively. We engage with technology almost mechanically—switching on a screen or swiping a device—mirroring Epimetheus, the half-wise titan who forgot humanity in the distribution of gifts. But we are also Promethean: remorseful, imaginative, and transgressive, stealing fire without a plan, hoping to remedy that initial forgetting. Like Prometheus, we may hesitate before the onslaught of information, only to succumb to its seductions out of guilt or desire. Technology feeds our imagination while shaping the contours of what we take to be reality. It bridges insight and commonsense, reflection and consumption. This text, then, may be read as an effort to bring Epimetheus and Prometheus into dialogue—an allegorical reconciliation between reflection and action in the age of technological mediation.

This book celebrates the layperson's wisdom, and it promotes a clarity of language and understanding. Knowledge reflects the limits imposed by our environment, John Dewey would have added ([1888] 2024, 21). Knowledge is complex and is built on language and concepts. Some concepts are misused to define opposite realities. That is socialism. Other concepts, like capitalism, may easily incorporate a diverse reality, a government that is democratic as well as an oligarchic government, as long as their goal is to preserve the essential element of a capitalist-based society: an ever-higher profit-return rate. In an unexpected twist of history, our understanding of capitalism in the late twentieth and now twenty-first century was conceptualized in Marxian vocabulary as the "materialist connection of people with each other, determined by their needs and mode of production and which is as old as people themselves" (Marx & Engels, [1845–46] 1970, 50). Ironically, this almost heroic version of capitalism incorporates a Marxian vision of Man versus Nature. This vision asserts that Man "has overcome a lower stage in social relations within the sphere of material life, whether they are between man and man or between man and nature" (Id.).

Socialism is commonsensically associated with a particular geographical region of the world. It covers post-Tsarist Russia (The Union of Soviet Socialist Republics, or U.S.S.R) and Eastern and Central European (ECE) countries. In addition to its spatial geography, socialism has a temporal axis as well. Socialism was believed to exist behind the militarized border called

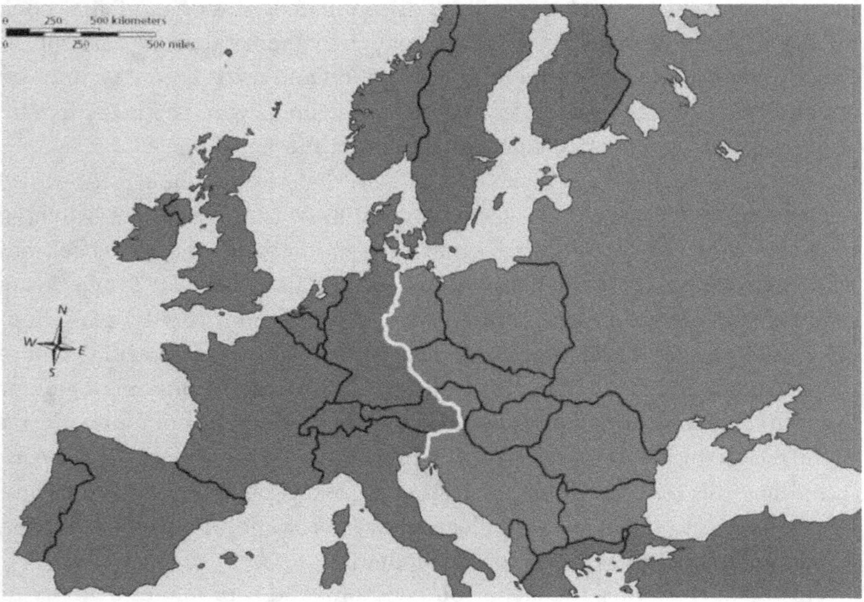

MAP 1 Countries behind the Iron Curtain
SOURCE: WIKIMEDIA COMMONS. *IRON CURTAIN AS DESCRIBED BY CHURCHILL.* 1946. IMAGE. HTTPS://COMMONS.WIKIMEDIA.ORG/WIKI/FILE:IRON_CURTAIN_AS_DESCRIBED_BY_CHURCHILL.PNG

the Iron Curtain, which included the so-called socialist countries (ECE), the non-aligned Yugoslavia, and Albania, as Map 1 shows.[43]

The socialist designation appeared in the name of many of those countries as well. A mere search engine (Perplexity[44]) inquiry brought back the following answer when asked *to spell out* U.S.S.R:

> The Union of Soviet Socialist Republics (U.S.S.R.), commonly known as the Soviet Union, was a transcontinental state that existed from 1922 to 1991. It emerged following the Russian Revolution of 1917, which overthrew the Tsarist regime and established a *socialist government* led by the Bolsheviks under Vladimir Lenin. The U.S.S.R. was the world's first

43 For another map, *see, e.g.*, Serge Berstein, Pierre Milza, 1995. *Histoire du 20e siècle.* Paris: Hatier. The Iron Curtain. (stock image).

44 Perplexity search: https://www.perplexity.ai/search/what-is-ussr-XLSl.nT2QeScneEvAZkCbg.

> *constitutionally socialist state* and was characterized by a single-party system governed by the Communist Party. (emphasis added)[45] (See Map 2)

Despite the GenAI confidence in the above definition, and the multiple use of the word "socialism", the only connection I can find between U.S.S.R.—and by extrapolation the Eastern and Central European (ECE)—reality and socialism lies in a particular kind of imaginary—an imaginary perhaps best captured by Mikhail Afanasyevich Bulgakov: absurdist, irrational, and, by today's standards, hard to follow. In *The Master and Margarita*,[46] the surreal and absurd events that unfold in Moscow—talking cats, black magic shows, bureaucrats mysteriously disappearing—capture the climate of fear, suspicion, and irrationality that defined Russia under Stalin. Bulgakov presents a society where truth is slippery, and people vanish without explanation, echoing the arbitrary power of the NKVD (direct precursor to the KGB) and the show trials of the 1930s.[47] Socialism was such a slippery concept created by Stalin.

Can this absurd association—between socialism as theory and the praxis of a paramilitary dictatorship that terrorized impoverished populations—be remedied? This book argues yes. It does so by first explaining how commonsense understanding is formed, then clarifying socialism as a knowable, definable concept, and finally offering insight into the ECE reality by analyzing its political, legal, and economic structures.

In 2023, Cambridge University Press published a two-volume compendium on socialism, defining it as "a just society in which no individual lacks the basic necessities of life and in which prosperity and knowledge are shared fairly."[48] I agree with that definition. And I also know—having grown up behind the so-called Iron Curtain, stretching from Eastern Europe across the Urals to the Pacific—that the people in that region did not live in a just society. They lived

---

45 Perplexity search: https://www.perplexity.ai/search/what-is-ussr-XLSl.nT2QeScneEvAZkCbg.

46 Mikhail Afanasyevich Bulgakov, *The Master and Margarita* (1966–67).

47 One of the most authoritative texts on Stalin's terror regime and the role of his secret police, NKVD, is the John Dewey Commission, formally known as the "Commission of Inquiry into the Charges Made against Leon Trotsky in the Moscow Trials," an independent investigation launched in 1937. It was headed by American philosopher John Dewey, and its findings are a critical part of the historical record concerning the Stalinist show trials, the NKVD, and the purges of the 1930s in the Soviet Union. *See*, Commission of Inquiry into the Charges Made Against Leon Trotsky in the Moscow Trials. 1938. *Not Guilty*. Edited by Albert Goldman and John Dewey. New York: Harper & Brothers.

48 Marcel Van Der Linden, Introduction to Volume 1, in 1 *The Cambridge History of Socialism* (Marcel Van Der Linden, ed.), 1 (2023).

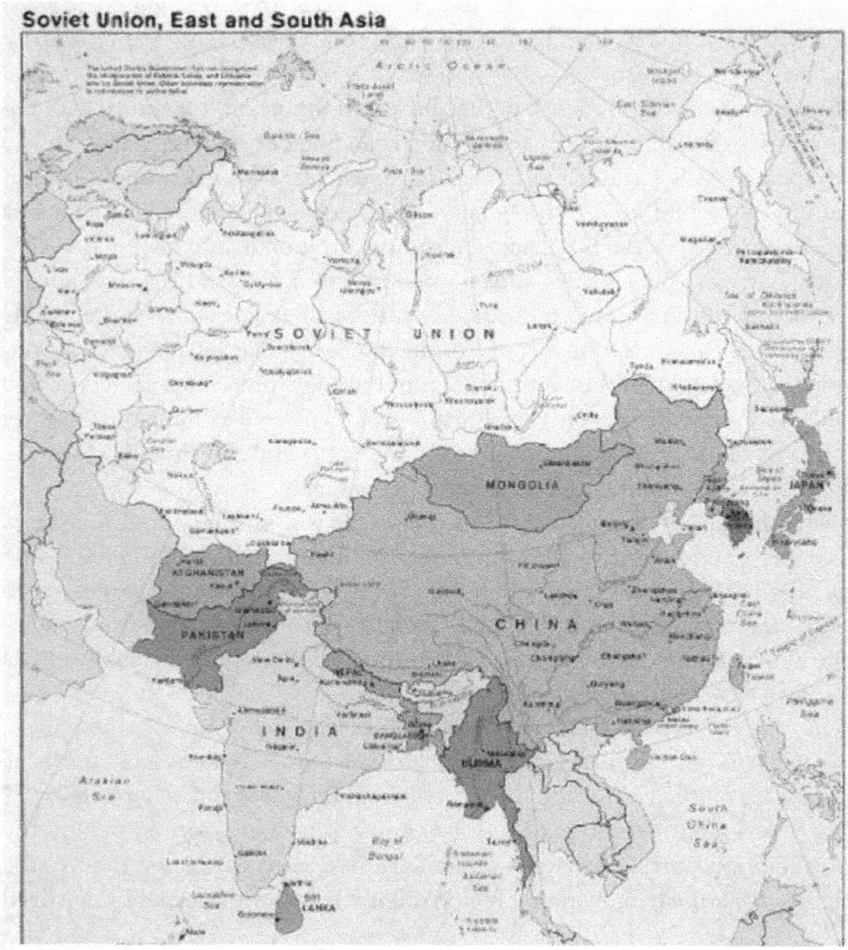

MAP 2 The Soviet Union or U.S.S.R.
Note: For other similar maps, see, e.g., Michael Ray et al. "The End of Soviet Communism", *Encyclopedia Britannica*, (Oct 28, 2024) https://www.britannica.com/event/the-collapse-of-the-Soviet-Union/The-end-of-Soviet-communism
SOURCE: UNITED STATES. CENTRAL INTELLIGENCE AGENCY, CARTOGRAPHER. 1987. *SOVIET UNION, EAST AND SOUTH ASIA*. [WASHINGTON, D.C.]: CENTRAL INTELLIGENCE AGENCY. MAP. HTTPS://WWW.LOC.GOV/ITEM/2015585743/

under military and paramilitary dictatorship, governed by a state capitalist monopoly that served the interests of 1 percent of the population.

Yet commonsense understanding often discredits such claims—not only mine but also those of respected scholars like the Cambridge contributors. Still, commonsense is not absurd. As demonstrated in this book, it is empirically grounded, dynamic, and rational. What this book seeks to do is peel away the rational veneer of what is, in fact, an absurd commonsense narrative about "ECE socialism." This task is achievable precisely because commonsense is not fixed—it evolves through insights, those spontaneous "Eureka!" or "Aha!" moments.[49]

This book is neither a theoretical defense of socialism nor a collection of annotated documents. It is not another ideologically deterministic explanation of oppression. Those interpretations tend to attribute fault to the ideology itself, framing the failure as inherent in socialism's promise of a better world. The reaction to its collapse is often quasi-religious: a rejection not of political execution, but of the ideas themselves.

Here, as in all my work, ideology is understood in its original French Revolutionary sense—as a set of ideas crafted in service of producing knowledge for political ends. The French even invented a Ministry of Ideology, and since then, that role has only expanded, dispersed across countless official roles and institutional structures. This book seeks to expose and examine these ideologically embedded roles in modern governance.

This is a journey into a much-neglected region of political theory, macroeconomics, and legal thought—one that has shaped the dominant understanding of ECE socialism outside the Iron Curtain for more than a century. I hope this exploration will resonate not only with those outside the Curtain but also with those who lived beneath its shadow. Paraphrasing Bernard Lonergan, I hope this book will start a trend of asking what precisely it is to understand to make sense of our lives.

4 Choosing the Path of Commonsense Built on Insight

This project builds on Bernard Lonergan's work on understanding, particularly Volumes Three and Five of the Collected Works of Bernard Lonergan. Like Lonergan[50]—and before him, Aristotle—I, too, believe that all human beings possess an inherent desire to know. Lonergan describes this as a conscious

49 For full transparency, I grew up behind that imaginary curtain, in a very real world filled with hope, love, crimes, music, poetry, philosophical inquiry, long walks, four distinguishable seasons, crushes, and dreams—many of them withered. It was a world shaped mostly by pedestrian wants but also suffused with surrounding lies. Our daily lives were narrated through a fictionalized lens, one that disguised systemic exploitation—a regime in which nearly everyone labored for the benefit of a powerful, unaccountable few. That multifaceted, ruthless system of oppression is well documented, and while many theories attempt to explain it, most remain incomplete.

50 Bernard Lonergan, *Volume 3: Insight: A Study of Human Understanding* (1992); and *Volume 5: Understanding and Being* (1990).

tendency toward knowledge (Lonergan, 1990, 5). We seek insight not passively but consciously, intelligently, rationally, deliberately, and methodically. A child asking questions exemplifies this tendency—the impulse to plow into the surrounding unknown. But what happens when that child stops asking questions, believing there is nothing unknown left to explore?

For more than a century, people across the globe have heard, read, and seen words and images referring to a political and economic system labeled "socialist." Over time, these words and images became internalized, and eventually accepted as true. In that moment of judgment, Lonergan writes, the goal of knowing becomes explicit: knowledge becomes objectified and self-appropriated—it becomes "ours" (Id., 14).

This book hopes to reach those whose appetite for knowing about socialism has been stirred—to encourage them to adjust their commonsense knowledge through inquiry and insight. Lonergan shows how we ask questions and generate insights, which we then use to form concepts. We assess evidence and make judgments based on it, transitioning from what he calls the "preconceptual, predicative, and prejudicial" (Id., 15) to the clarified understanding of what is. In other words, we move from words about being to an understanding of being itself. This is possible because both being and knowledge of being are dynamic.

Of course, when there is no recognition of the unknown, inquiry stalls—and without inquiry, there can be no new insights. This is perhaps the most significant obstacle this book faces. But obstacles reclaim their identity as such only when they are removed—and commonsense knowledge, when awakened by insight, offers a path to do just that.

Lonergan situates understanding in "the act of understanding," which, for him, begins with the ability to integrate evidence from multiple fields of intelligent activity into a coherent whole. This understanding is deeply subjective, but it also possesses both a public and a personal dimension. In a 2020 publication, I analyzed scholarly meaning-making as stemming from this dual subjectivity: public subjectivity—which I termed *ideology*—shapes our position within public discourse, while private subjectivity emerges from our inner experience, including feelings of alienation rooted in our personal histories (Neacșu, 2020).

Here, I expand that framework to focus on commonsense knowledge. It, too, arises from uncertainty or alienation, and it seeks to clarify the world through insight. From these insights, we formulate definitions of things—of what exists, or might exist, of what is possible. Commonsense is intuitive, because it accepts only those insights that are clear enough to support meaningful distinctions (Russell, [1900], 1957, 168). As Leibniz suggested, knowledge must

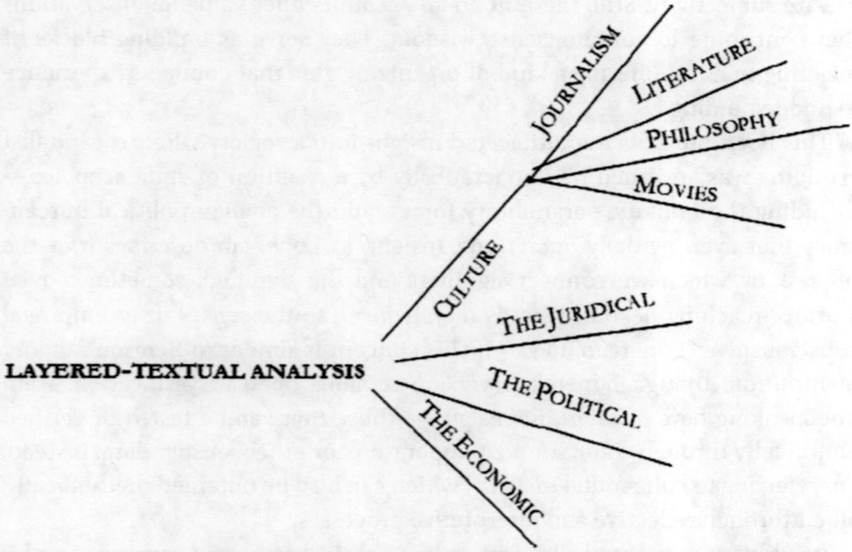

FIGURE 5 Layered textualism: the close reading method used in *Socialism: the 100-Year-Old Misnomer*
SOURCE: NEACȘU, DANA. 2025. ADAPTED FROM JAMESON, FREDRIC. 1981. *THE POLITICAL UNCONSCIOUS: NARRATIVE AS A SOCIALLY SYMBOLIC ACT*. ITHACA, NY: CORNELL UNIVERSITY PRESS, *DIAGRAM* ON P. 36

be "clear and distinct," or, at the very least, "plain and easy"[51] to understand. Capitalism is a system in which the economic structure is designed to concentrate profits in the hands of an ever-smaller group of shareholders. Socialism, by contrast, is a system in which the economic structure is designed to distribute profits for the general welfare of the population.

This shift in understanding—rooted in a deeper, clearer conceptual distinction—redefines the terms of debate. It invites a more accurate and honest evaluation of political and economic systems that have, for too long, been misrepresented, misunderstood, and conflated under the wrong names.

There are many ways to provide insight. Insight comes from many corners, including Jameson's layered-textual analysis (see Figure 5), applied to works of fiction that provide powerful insight into the historical time and space lived by people like me. Each covers one or more voices and angles, shaped by the witness's limited experience, understanding, and both public and

51 G.W. Leibniz, *New Essays on Human Understanding. Book IV—Of Knowledge* (Cambridge University Press, 1996) paragraph 453.

private subjectivity. Still, these fictional accounts offer valuable observations that contribute to commonsense wisdom. They serve as building blocks of meaning-making, offering a kind of organizing glue that connects experience to understanding.

This book presents a multifaceted insight into a society where a capitalist economy was governed undemocratically by a coalition of state agencies—including the military, paramilitary forces, and the civilian political bureaucracy that oversaw daily operations. Insight, as Lonergan describes it, is the process by which we connect signifiers and the signified, sometimes even a priori, reaching beyond what is merely given to the senses or to empirical consciousness (Lonergan, 1992, 5). This concept is similar to Bergson's theory of intuition, though Lonergan's version remains open to verification. I am not speaking here of scientific insights—those that can be tested or verified empirically through color, sound, temperature, or other sensory data. Instead, I'm referring to conceptual insights, which can also be obtained methodically, albeit through reflective and interpretive processes.

In addition to theoretical works on law, political economy, governance, philosophy, and journalism, this book incorporates fictional works—both visual and literary—as valid sources of insight. By producing understanding from a variety of sources, this book proposes a new method for generating commonsense knowledge: one that is both critical and comprehensive.

It is critical because it challenges what Lonergan called "easy flights from understanding"—those moments when we accept well-established assumptions despite their logical inconsistencies or lack of evidentiary support. And it is comprehensive because it methodically traces the origins of settled cognitive assumptions, confronts them, and encourages their reevaluation—so that, within a new reality, they can be reformed or replaced.

This book's ambition is grounded in the dynamic nature of commonsense knowledge. It seeks to spark inquiry and offer insight—insight that mirrors the reality of a specific historical time and space, without advancing a political agenda. Yes, this text is biased. As I argued in *The Bourgeois Charm of Karl Marx* (2020), all texts are inherently biased because they reflect the private and public subjectivity of their authors. Private subjectivity, encompassing emotions, desires, and personal interests, influences the author's research choices and perspective. This subjectivity, tied to creative alienation, subtly shapes the text's content. Additionally, public subjectivity—the author's ideological and social positioning—colors how they approach broader cultural and political issues.

Once published, this subjectivity persists, becoming a point of negotiation between the author and the one the text interpellates—the reader. The reader, bringing their own ideological views, interprets the text in ways that may highlight contradictions or irony. Ideology, embedded in both the creation and reception of a text, affects how it is understood. Thus, all texts are biased; they are not neutral conveyors of "objective" truth. Instead, they reflect the subjective experiences, emotions, and beliefs of their authors, shaped by the ideological context in which they are produced and consumed. Meaning is always influenced by the interplay of private and public subjectivity, ensuring that no text can be free from bias.

Therefore, the current text, which seeks to demystify the Soviet and Eastern and Central European (ECE) experiments, is also biased. My bias is not to obscure the myth, but to expose it. While I do not claim to know the true essence of socialism, I am certain that the Soviet and ECE experiments were not socialist. Russell, Reed, and Pashukanis did recognize the rot within these experiments. The bias of this text is to unveil that very rot.

The kind of understanding this book proposes is not unilateral—it is a negotiated understanding between the textual instigator (myself) and the one the text interpellates, the reader. Like a traffic officer who calls a driver to a stop, this book seeks to interpellate readers, urging them to pause, engage, and reflect. It presents historical and factual insights to stimulate curiosity and invites the reader to connect history to knowledge production through commonsense reasoning. Just as common sense tells us that a whale is not a rabbit—because a rabbit hops and whales swim—it is my hope that common sense will eventually reject the false equivalence between socialism and the paramilitary dictatorships of ECE regimes.

While rationalism and empiricism both play their roles, this book is fundamentally rooted in insight, as described by Bernard Lonergan. Insight—especially the accumulation of observations, facts, viewpoints and their signification—forms the core of this project. These insights will be made intelligible and accessible so that those interpellated by this text can identify and understand them through their own intelligence and reasonableness—capacities that, as Lonergan writes, are marks common to all of us (1992, 14).

Using examples, insights, factual analysis, and engagement with both existing theoretical interpretations and new perspectives, this book aims to become a kind of traffic light—a symbolic intervention for those passing through familiar intellectual terrain, encouraging them to stop, look, and reconsider whether what they're seeing is red, yellow, or green. Knowing is understanding. Understanding is meaning-making.

In a previous book, I addressed meaning-making more narrowly in the context of jurisprudential thought. Here, I take a broader approach: beginning with a brief history of socialism as a theory, followed by a dissection of the so-called socialist reality in Eastern and Central Europe (ECE). By examining that reality through its legal, political, and economic systems, this book seeks to counter the entrenched belief that "socialism has been tried and failed."

To be accurate, what was tried—and ultimately failed—was a ruthless form of state capitalist monopoly, ruled by an autocratic paramilitary dictatorship over the course of a century. We may not need to repeat that failed experiment here in the United States, where late-stage capitalism is increasingly cloaked in a thin democratic veneer.

This book embraces the flexibility of common sense to rethink and reframe preconceptions about ersatz socialism. Every act of knowing builds upon prior knowledge. Every act of knowing is a self-adjustment—a refinement—of what is already known, except for that of the very young child, whose knowing begins with the encounter with the unknown.

With any luck, this project is just a beginning.

PART 1

Socialism as Theory and Practice

CHAPTER 1

Socialism's 19th Century Pedigree

Socialism has been around as a school of thought, long before The Hoover Institution pigeonholed Senator Bernie Sanders, of Vermont, as owning his own brand of socialism (Gregory, 2019), or the newly re-elected US President, Donald Trump, started throwing "socialist" around at his rallies as an insult. The earliest recorded uses of the term "socialism" are often attributed to publications and discussions in the early 19th century, particularly in Britain and France.

In England, the term "socialism" was reportedly used by Robert Owen, a British industrialist and philanthropist in the 1820s. Owen engaged in social experiments in his own mills in New Lanark, Scotland. He provided workers with improved working conditions, education, and housing, believing that a nurturing environment would additionally increase workers' productivity. Owen's socialism was about improving the lives of those whose work enabled his. Owen advocated for cooperative communities as an alternative to competitive capitalism. He promoted the establishment of cooperative communities, such as the one he founded in New Harmony, Indiana, as an example of a self-sustaining, egalitarian community. In his essays collected under the title *A New View of Society*,[1] Owen argued that that improved living conditions, better education, and encouraged cooperation could lead to a more just and equitable society. He championed that "no man has a just right to the labour of any other man, without giving equal labour or value in exchange for it" (Claeys, 2023, 151). Although critics of Owen's theories remain unclear about his strand of socialism, from Owen's work it appears that his socialism is far more complex than a "utopian" minimalization. His social experiments incorporated the values of a society built on the principle of "united labour," expenditures, property and "equal privileges," while also valuing individual independence (Id., 151 et seq.).

Similarly, the French thinker, Claude-Henri de Saint-Simon laid foundational ideas for socialism as a society organized for the welfare of all. Born a French aristocrat, in 1778, he fought in the American Revolution, serving with distinction under George Washington's command at the Battle of Yorktown,

1 Robert Owen, *A New View of Society or Essays on the Principle of the Formation of the Human Character, and the Application of the Principle to Practice by* (1813–1816), https://la.utexas.edu/users/hcleaver/368/368OwenNewViewtable.pdf.

 | DOI:10.1163/9789004747210_003

and then supported the French Revolution of 1789 from its beginning and ultimately relinquished his aristocratic title chancing his name to plain Citizen Bonhomme (Jennings, 2023, 126–145). Saint-Simon emphasized the importance of industrialization and believed that society should be organized according to a rational, scientific approach. He astutely summarized the European societal crisis produced by industrialization whose first manifestation was the English Civil War and its last, the French Revolution. Engels admired Saint Simon.

In *Socialism: Utopian and Scientific* (1880) he noted that Saint-Simon correctly perceived the source of societal crises, uprisings and revolutions the antagonism between "idlers"—all who did not participate in the production and distribution of goods—and "workers" those who provided the idlers' income (Id., 138). Moreover, Saint-Simon's criticism of the French Revolution and its aftermath terror could easily be used to describe the Bolshevik Revolution: The existing political structure had already been displaced by the time of the revolution, and the existing level of civilization was in the process of scaffolding itself with new institutions. The only clear changes of the Revolution were its horrors and atrocities (Id., 130).

In his posthumously published *The New Christianity Dialogues between a Conservative and an Innovator* (1825), he explained his vision of a society built on Christian principles of brotherhood and social responsibility, centered on social justice and improving the lives of the poor. A proponent of organizing society as an "industrial system" (1821), he nevertheless believed that science and industry serve a collective good, taking care of the less fortunate.

In both instances, "socialism" described social and economic models favoring collective or cooperative organization of society's resources. Within this social engineering collective structures were distinguished from individual ownership and competition, which were viewed as core legal and economic capitalist institutions.

By the mid-19th century, "socialism" had become a widely recognized approach to social engineering. It was associated with a range of movements advocating for social and economic reforms, including workers' rights. There are many recognizable names who argued for a fairer society.[2] Louis Blanc

2 Here are additional theorists who promoted socialist principles in the 19th century: Charles Fourier (1772–1837), Pierre-Joseph Proudhon (1809–1865), Étienne Cabet (1788–1856), William Thompson (1775–1833) and John Gray (1799–1883). Fourier's most influential work is *Théorie des quatre mouvements et des destinées générales* (1808) (Theory of the Four Movements and the General Destinies). In this text, Fourier lays out his vision of a harmonious society organized into "phalanxes," self-sustaining communities where people work in roles suited to their passions. His critique of industrial society and concept of cooperative living influenced many socialists. Proudhon's foundational work, *Qu'est-ce que la propriété?* (1840) (What is Property?), is renowned for introducing his famous assertion, "Property is theft." Here,

(1811–1882), a French politician and journalist, for instance, advocated for "social workshops"—publicly funded cooperatives that would provide jobs and ensure fair wages for workers. Blanc envisioned a society where the state would establish workers' cooperatives, or "social workshops," to ensure the fair distribution of wealth and equitable treatment for all. Blanc famously promoted the idea of "From each according to his abilities, to each according to his needs / De chacun selon ses facultés, à chacun selon ses besoins," in his 1839 work, *L'Organisation du Travail* ("The Organization of Labor"), a principle associated with Marxist thought. Moreover, Louis Blanc clarified that being a proletarian was not a clamoring position, but one to leave behind, as nothing more than the modern form of slavery.

> While enduring their misery, they [the workers] studied it. To this corrupt and sick society, they [the workers] composed, full of hope, a radiant tomorrow. They [the workers] examined the law of past social transformations to see if civilization couldn't still take a step forward; and remembering that people had ceased to be slaves, then serfs, they wondered, moved by a generous hope, if they would not cease to be proletarians, because the proletariat was merely the last form of slavery. (this author's translation)[3]

Proudhon challenges capitalist property rights and promotes ideas of mutualism, where individuals exchange goods and services without state interference. This work positioned him as one of the first self-described anarchists and a major critic of state and corporate power. Cabet's *Voyage en Icarie* (1840) (Journey to Icaria) is his most important work, outlining a fictional utopia where resources are shared, and society functions collectively for the common good. Thompson's principal work, *An Inquiry into the Principles of the Distribution of Wealth Most Conducive to Human Happiness* (1824), examines economic inequalities and argues for a society based on cooperative labor and fair wealth distribution. His ideas were instrumental in early socialist and cooperative movements, particularly influencing the development of socialist economics and communal living practices collectively for the common good. Finally, Gray's *The Social System: A Treatise on the Principle of Exchange* (1831) is his key work, proposing a model for an economy without the issues he saw in capitalism. In it, he advocates for a currency system based on labor value and a state-regulated economy to prevent poverty and unemployment. Gray's proposals influenced both utopian socialism and the later development of labor-oriented socialist ideas.

3 "Tout en subissant leur misère, ils [les ouvriers] l'étudiaient. A cette société corrompue et malade ils [les ouvriers] composaient, en espérance, un lendemain radieux. Ils [les ouvriers] interrogeaient la loi des transformations sociales du passé, pour savoir si la civilisation n'avait point encore un pas à faire; et se rappelant que les hommes du peuple avaient cessé d'être esclaves, puis d'être serfs, ils se demandaient, émus d'un généreux espoir, si les hommes du people ne cesseraient pas d'être prolétaires, le prolétariat n'étant qu'une dernière forme del'esclavage."

LOUIS BLANC, *Le socialisme; droit au travail*, 9 (1849).

I will ask the reader to reflect on Blanc's view of socialism as a society devoid of poverty, *ergo* proletariat, when mentioning Lenin's "dictatorship of the proletariat"—an absurd expression and a misnomer at so many levels. Along Blanc's argument, how and why would any slaves create a million-member dictatorship where they continue as slaves? More likely a slave master would create such a dictatorship for his own benefit.

Another French thinker made famous by Karl Marx and Frederick Engels is Pierre-Joseph Proudhon, considered by Marx, a "rival socialist thinker" (Pradella, 2023, 263). Nevertheless, Proudhon's work was fraught with various limitations (mostly anti-feminism and antisemitism) and dismissive of Blanc's socialist Jacobinism (Prichard, 2023, 290, 300 et seq.).

Marx and Engels engaged with socialist theory in Section III of *The Communist Manifesto* (1888), written after the world lived through the Paris Commune. It was their theoretical answer to their search in praxis for a political structure to scaffold their vision of historical progression of the human society. Critical of socialism, Marx and Engels distinguished it into three main types: Reactionary, Conservative or Bourgeois, and Critical-Utopian. Their structuralist criticism focused on the level of wellbeing each type of socialism promoted. Furthermore, within each strand they additionally differentiated among their features. For instance, reactionary socialism was defined according to the way it rejected industrialization differently.

The first reactionary strand identified was Feudal Socialism, the product of the French Legitimists and "Young England" which Marx and Engels found too much akin to Christian Socialism. It used religious asceticism, rather than proletariat organization, to attack private property and social excesses.[4]

The second strand of reactionary socialism was called Petty-Bourgeois Socialism. While secular, like the preceding strand, it did not identify the role of the proletariat in social progress.[5]

---

4 "Feudal Socialism: half lamentation, half lampoon; half echo of the past, half menace of the future; at times, by its bitter, witty and incisive criticism, striking the bourgeoisie to the very heart's core; but always ludicrous in its effect, through total incapacity to comprehend the march of modern history. The aristocracy, in order to rally the people to them, waved the proletarian alms-bag in front for a banner. But the people, so often as it joined them, saw on their hindquarters the old feudal coats of arms, and deserted with loud and irreverent laughter." https://www.gutenberg.org/cache/epub/61/pg61-images.html#chap03

5 "dissected with great acuteness the contradictions in the conditions of modern production. It laid bare the hypocritical apologies of economists ..., the disastrous effects of machinery and division of labour; the concentration of capital and land in a few hands; overproduction and crises; it pointed out the inevitable ruin of the petty bourgeois and peasant, the misery of the proletariat, the anarchy in production, the crying inequalities in the distribution of

The third strand of reactionary socialism was the product of German intellectuals. The main critique Marx and Engels launched at it is not without irony. If the Germans adapted French socialist thought to Germany, stripping it of revolutionary energy and turning it into philosophical abstraction, that is my critique to the current myth of socialism describing the military coup that happened in every country imitating the so-called Bolshevik Revolution: stripping ideas of their revolutionary energy and turning them in ordinary palace power struggles.[6]

For the Conservative or Bourgeois Socialism, Marx and Engels used Proudhon's *Philosophie de la Misère* as an example of this form of socialism. Proudhon attempted to reconcile the class structure within bourgeois society. It aimed to alleviate social problems without challenging the underlying capitalist structure. Marx single-handedly criticized Proudhon's theory in *The Poverty of Philosophy* (1847).[7] In that sole work, socialists were the intellectu-

---

wealth, the industrial war of extermination between nations, the dissolution of old moral bonds, of the old family relations, of the old nationalities."

KARL MARX AND FRIEDRICH ENGELS, *The Communist Manifesto*, (Ed., FRIEDRICH ENGELS 1888). https://www.gutenberg.org/cache/epub/61/pg61-images.html#chap03

6 "German philosophers, would-be philosophers, and beaux esprits, eagerly seized on this literature, only forgetting, that when these writings immigrated from France into Germany, French social conditions had not immigrated along with them. In contact with German social conditions, this French literature lost all its immediate practical significance, and assumed a purely literary aspect. Thus, to the German philosophers of the eighteenth century, the demands of the first French Revolution were nothing more than the demands of "Practical Reason" in general, and the utterance of the will of the revolutionary French bourgeoisie signified in their eyes the law of pure Will, of Will as it was bound to be, of true human Will generally."

Id.

7 "Just as the economists are the scientific representatives of the bourgeois class, so the socialists and communists are the theoreticians of the proletarian class. So long as the proletariat is not yet sufficiently developed to constitute itself as a class, and consequently so long as the struggle itself of the proletariat with the bourgeoisie has not yet assumed a political character, and the productive forces are not yet sufficiently developed in the bosom of the bourgeoisie itself to enable us to catch a glimpse of the material conditions necessary for the emancipation of the proletariat and for the formation of a new society, these theoreticians are merely utopians who, to meet the wants of the oppressed classes, improvise systems and go in search of a regenerating science. But in the measure that history moves forward, and with it the struggle of the proletariat assumes clearer outlines, they no longer need to seek science in their minds; they have only to take note of what is happening before their eyes and to become its mouthpiece. So long as they look for science and merely make systems, so long as they are at the beginning of the struggle, they see in poverty nothing but poverty, without seeing in it the revolutionary, subversive side, which will overthrow the old society."

KARL MARX, *The Poverty of Philosophy* (Progress Publishers, 1955) https://www.marxists.org/archive/marx/works/download/pdf/Poverty-Philosophy.pdf, p. 56

als defending the proletarians and guiding them towards paradise on earth. A rather suspicious position for scientists who needed to make a living presumably working for some capitalist employer but whose unblemished consciousness made them work pro-bono for exploited proletarians. I do not want to make Marx's critique risible, but it is self-serving while devoid of any sense of irony.

As for the third type, the Critical-Utopian Socialism, that of Saint-Simon, and Owen, Marx and Engels opposed it because it emerged before the working class had developed a clear revolutionary potential. Politically, Marx and Engels thought them utopian because they were disconnected from the class struggle for political power.

On the other hand, Engels's work on socialism is far more nuanced. *Socialism: Utopian and Scientific* (1880), is his major contribution where "socialism" is explicitly analyzed and promoted. Engels contrasts the "Utopian Socialism" of Charles Fourier and Robert Owen, with his "Scientific Socialism," which he defined as incorporating a scientific understanding of history, particularly through dialectical materialism, rather than on utopian ideals.

This overview of socialism or socialist ideals has one goal: I just want to cover them so, when I discuss the Eastern and Central European (ECE) Soviet society, erroneously described as socialist, I can offer a meaningful insight to tear the misconception apart and encourage curiosity in reassessing common knowledge about socialism. That is why I would not define dialectical materialism more than to say that it is a perspective, an angle of analysis, whose methodology is scientific to the extent it is neither religious nor metaphysical.

A second work by Engels which contains significant passages on socialism is *Anti-Dühring* (1878). Originally written as a critique of the German philosopher Eugen Dühring, it nevertheless elaborates on the socialist transformation of society, discussing the proletariat's move toward a socialist organization of production, thus freeing the proletariat of their proletarian condition. Engels offered no blueprint for how the "lifelong uniform mechanical repetition of one and the same operation" and "this stunting of man" would be done away with, except to assume that technology would ensure a sufficient development of the productive forces of society. "The state is not abolished. It dies out," Engels wrote further alluding to socialism as an immanent technologically caused historical transition.

Nowhere the 19th century socialist thought delved into the creation of a society of paupers becoming puppets for some ideologue puppeteers who would retain the political and economic power of the newly created "socialist society." This was not what 19th century socialist thinkers advocated when they thought about a fairer society for all members. They never advocated stunting equality. Like Louis Blanc, each thought that socialism is built on equality of opportunities:

> Freedom is not merely the right but the power granted to humans to develop their faculties under the rule of justice and the protection of the law. Diversity in functions and abilities being a condition of life for society, equality consists in providing everyone with the opportunity to equally develop their unequal faculties.[8]

If Marx's work cannot be used to pinpoint a clear socialist theory, neither can Engels'. After Marx's death, Engels clarified their position favoring the violent usurpation of power from the established ruling classes for the benefit of the working-class, and a "unwavering opposition to 'opportunist' adaptations to liberal-bourgeois parliamentary politics" (Pradella, 2023, p. 282). Furthermore, Engels referenced the limited in scope and time social experiment, the Paris Commune, as the example of a proletarian dictatorship,[9] though, that example cannot have any more clarity and practical guidance than Proudhon's definition of socialism as a protest: "For us, socialism is not a system: it is, quite simply, a protest."[10]

Much more fertile for socialist theory is the work of Mikhail Bakunin. Bakunin was the only 19th theory theorist to pinpoint democratic parliamentary forms of government could be as ruthless and despotic as monarchies. The suppression of both Parisian popular movements, that of June 1848 and the Paris Commune of 1871 had been terminated in a bloodshed by republican governments (Eckhardt, 2023, 319). More interestingly, given the laughable

---

8 For more on Luis Blanc, see, e.g., Philippe Van Parijs. Yes, Freedom! *Boston Review*, (December 12, 2023) https://www.bostonreview.net/forum_response/yes-freedom/.

"Que la liberté est, non pas seulement le droit, mais le pouvoir accordé à l'homme de développer ses fa cultés sous l'empire de la justice et la sauvegarde de la loi; Que, la diversité des fonctions et des aptitudes étant pour la société une condition de vie, *l'égalité consiste dans la facilité donnée à tous dedévelopper également leurs facultés inégales*."

LOUIS BLANC, *Le socialisme; droit au travail*, 9 (1849)

9 "Well and good, gentlemen, do you want to know what this dictatorship looks like? Look at the Paris Commune. That was the Dictatorship of the Proletariat."

FREDERIK ENGELS, Introduction to Karl Marx's The Civil War in France (1891), in MECW, vol. xxvii, p. 191, quoted by LUCIA PRADELLA, KARL MARX, FRIEDERICH ENGELS, and Early Workers' Movement, in 1 *The Cambridge History of Socialism* (MARCEL VAN DER LINDEN, ed.), 283 (2023)

10 Pierre-Joseph Proudhon, Manifesto for Election, in McKay (ed.), Property Is Theft! p. 372, quoted in Alex Prichard, Pierre-Joseph Proudhon's Mutualist Social Science, in 1 *The Cambridge History of Socialism* (Marcel Van Der Linden, ed.), 290 (2023).

concept of "the dictatorship of the proletariat," as a so-called socialist form of government is Bakunin's analysis which exposes this childish nonsense of this concept. He addressed that ill-defined concept of government by workers, clarifying that such government, if ever to exist, could not be of workers, but

> of *former* workers, who, as soon as they become rulers or representatives of the people will cease to be workers and will begin to look upon the whole workers' world from the heights of the state. They will no longer represent the people but themselves and their own pretentions to govern the people.[11]

Socialism remains intrinsically connected with the 19th century[12] and the urbanization brought about capitalist technology. Cities made education and work and gender and racial equality a possibility to dream about and then seek to implement whether incrementally, through reform, or violently through social or military uprising.

This book argues that socialism is both a thing, a concept, but also a reality. This approach is similar to the one Durkheim took when he studied socialism: "Nous allons envisager le socialisme comme une chose, comme une réalité / We are going to consider socialism as a thing, as a reality, and we will strive to understand it."[13] But it adds its second real cloak, that of a living environment defined by the spirit, the principles of the concept: social justice. As any 19th century theory, socialism too has its roots in the 18th century, as Durkheim would say. As such, perhaps the best summary of socialism rests in John Thelwall's words that

> *every* man, *every* woman and *every* child, ought to obtain … some comforts and enjoyments, in addition to the necessaries of life; and to some

11 Mickhail Bakunin. Statism and Anarchy, p. 178 (1873), in Wolfgang Echardt, Mikhail Bakunin and Social Anarchism, in 1 *The Cambridge History of Socialism* (Marcel Van Der Linden, ed.), 321 (2023).

12 "Ce ne sont pas les hommes qui pensent, ce sont les siècles, et quoi qu'on fasse, le dix-neuvième siècle restera baptisé *socialisme* / There are not people, but centuries who think; and no matter what we do, the nineteenth century will always be known as the century of socialism."

LUIS BLANC is known to have said. LUIS BLANC, *Le Socialisme. Droit au travail, réponse à M. Thiers*, p. 85 (1845); http://books.google.com/books?id=fJMSAAAAIAAJ&oe=UTF-8

13 Émile Durkheim, Le socialisme Sa définition. Ses débuts. La doctrine saint-simonienne (1928), http://www.uqac.uquebec.ca/zone30/Classiques_des_sciences_sociales/index.html.

> tolerable leisure for such discussion, and some 'means of such information,' as may lead to and understanding of their *rights*; without which they can never understand their *duties*.[14]

Consequently, a reality, an environment which does not conform to its conceptual definition cannot be labeled accordingly in a meaningful way producing knowledge. The connection is faulty. It is a fake, an ersatz.

From the perspective of this book, Soviet is not socialist because its legal, political, economic systems were not socialist. They were never meant to produce anything other but illiberal capitalism, which they did. However, because one misperception addressed here is that socialism was tried and failed, the next chapter addresses the Bolshevik Revolution and its ideology.

---

14 John Thelwall, The Rights of Nature Against the Usurpations of Establishments ... p. 15–19 (1796) in Marcel Van Der Linden, Introduction to Volume 1, in 1 *The Cambridge History of Socialism* (Marcel Van Der Linden, ed.), 5 (2023).

CHAPTER 2

Ersatz Socialism as Soviet Theory and Practice

1 Capitalism and Ersatz Socialism

The main argument this book makes is that for almost 100 years the world witnessed not some cruel type of socialism, but one of the most a-democratic types of capitalism, whose atrocities needed a new name, one few could understand, and thus, more likely to be accepted. This is a challenging task, as it can be difficult to compare capitalism and socialism when capitalism is often seen as simply a market economy, while socialism is often imagined as humble servant quarters with modern amenities.

Both concepts are complex. While many interpretations of capitalism exist, one thing remains clear: at its core, capitalism is about capital accumulation. But what is the essence of capitalism beyond this? Is it simply the economic model, or does it also involve the political, legal, and social structures that sustain it? In my work, I argue that capitalism is not just an economic system; it permeates the very fabric of society, shaping everything from legal structures to cultural norms. As Marx demonstrated in *Capital: A Critique of Political Economy. Vol. 1* ([*1867*], *1965*), capitalism's defining feature is the accumulation of capital, and this accumulation is inherently tied to inequality.

Similarly, what is the essence of socialism, and what makes Soviet socialism ersatz socialism? Despite its rhetoric of revolution, the Soviet system never broke from the essential structures of capitalism. Instead, it replicated them in a new form—centralized, state-controlled capitalism that kept the masses subordinated to a new set of elites. In this way, ersatz socialism was not an alternative to capitalism but a variant of it—dressed in socialist clothing but rooted in the same mechanisms of capital accumulation.

This brings me to the central argument of my critique: ersatz socialism—a political, economic, and legal system that falsely claimed to embody the ideals of socialism—should not be confused with genuine socialism. Instead, it should be seen as a form of illiberal state capitalism that perpetuates the same fundamental inequalities of the capitalist system it sought to overthrow. Because capitalism, as I argued not long ago, in addition to its economic system, is a structure that involves political and legal scaffolding, social relations, and even a culture of innovation that sustains it (Neacșu, 2024, 112 et seq.). As such, the Soviet Union's ersatz socialism was not a break from capitalism. Instead of empowering the people, it consolidated power in the hands of a

 | DOI:10.1163/9789004747210_004

few, ensuring that the central dynamics of capitalism—inequality, exploitation, and concentration of power—remained in place.

Thus, genuine socialism requires a democratization of all aspects of life—a deeply participatory system that empowers individuals to collectively shape their world. Or, to paraphrase Dewey (1927, 143–47), socialism is a cure for the current ailments of democracy, and in that sense, it requires more, not less, democracy.

2 The Theoretical Foundation of 20th Century Soviet or Ersatz Socialism

Europe was a hotbed of revolutionary thought in the 19th and early 20th century. Russia, one of the most despotically run empires, produced a sleuth of socialist thinkers.[1] Russian theorists, despite varying interpretations of socialism, collectively contributed to the evolution of socialist ideology within Russia and globally, with influences extending from anarchism to authoritarian state socialism. There are four key figures, Trotsky, Lenin, Bukharin and Stalin,[2] who played a significant role in shaping what we now know as Soviet socialism, or what I believe has come to represent "socialism" in the collective

1 Among the Russian theorists who were highly influential in the development and interpretation of socialist thought in the 19th century are: Alexander Herzen (1812–1870); Mikhail Bakunin (1814–1876); Peter Kropotkin (1842–1921); and Georgi Plekhanov (1856–1918). Often regarded as the "father of Russian socialism," Herzen's works introduced socialist ideas to Russia. His books *From the Other Shore* (1848–1850) and *The Russian People and Socialism* (1848) critique European liberalism and advocate agrarian socialism grounded in Russian life. A founder of anarchism, Bakunin advocated for a form of socialism that rejected authoritarian state control. His works, such as *God and the State* (1882), emphasize the importance of individual freedom, anti-authoritarianism, and grassroots organization. He was an opponent of Marx, favoring decentralized, stateless socialism. A prominent anarcho-communist, Kropotkin's ideas focus on mutual aid, cooperation, and community-driven socialism. His book *The Conquest of Bread* (1892) argues for a decentralized economy based on voluntary cooperation. Kropotkin's concept of "mutual aid" opposes Darwinian competition, suggesting that cooperation is essential for human survival. Known as the "father of Russian Marxism," Plekhanov was one of the first to interpret Marx's works in a Russian context. His key texts, such as *The Development of the Monist View of History* (1895), established Marxist theory within Russia and influenced Lenin. He argued that Russia's path to socialism should follow Western Europe's industrialization model, advocating for a proletarian-led socialist state.

2 Leon Trotsky (1879–1940); Nikolai Bukharin (1888–1938); Vladimir Lenin (1870–1924) and Joseph Stalin (1878–1953) are the key intellectual figures of the Bolshevik regime, which transitioned to Stalin's socialism in Russia.

imagination of all, despite clashing differences among each theory and especially despite those theories having been abandoned or reworked into social engineering theories for the benefit of the new ruling classes of apparatchiks—or nomenklatura.

Briefly, Trotsky's call for international revolution contrasted with Stalin's nationalism, while Bukharin's mixed economic approach conflicted both with Lenin' and ultimately with Stalin's hardline collectivization. Lenin was very much invested in social engineering. He developed the idea of a vanguard party viewed as a disciplined, centralized political party whose role was to guide the workers' political coup. Given Russia's limited industrial development and small working class, the military became an organic ally as well as the agrarian workers. *What Is to Be Done? Burning Questions of Our Movement* (1901–1902) was a pamphlet which addressed the ways the industrial working class would become willing participants into a political power struggle. In *State and Revolution* (1917), Lenin focused on the role of the state in building the new society. In *Imperialism, the Highest Stage of Capitalism* (1916), Lenin analyzed socialism through the prism of the proletariat, the politically engaged industrial workers who were supposed to abolish capitalism. The problem with his analysis was that the proletariat was a capitalist by-product. The proletariat existed only as a capitalist, politically active exploited class. With the extinction of capitalism, its social hierarchy would have imploded, and with it the proletarians. Only, Lenin actively preserved proletarian exploitation, but changed its packaging. The toilers became dictators nominally. To my knowledge, this basic fallacy was never addressed by Western critics.

Perhaps understanding this fundamental error, Lenin introduced the New Economic Policy (NEP), Lenin introduced the New Economic Policy (NEP) in March 1921 at the 10th *Congress of the Russian Communist Party* (Bolsheviks). The policy was a response to the economic devastation following the Russian Civil War and the failures of "War Communism," which had caused widespread famine, economic collapse, and discontent among workers and peasants. The NEP allowed limited private trade, small-scale private enterprises, and some degree of market activity, especially in agriculture, to revive the economy and provide the Soviet state with much-needed stability. Under the NEP, peasants were permitted to sell surplus crops on the open market, and small businesses could operate under private ownership, while the state retained control over larger industries, transportation, and foreign trade. Lenin saw this as a temporary, strategic retreat from full state socialism, intending to use market mechanisms to rebuild and modernize the economy until it could transition back to a socialist model. The NEP had significant success in reviving the economy in the early 1920s but was eventually phased out under Stalin in favor of central planning and rapid industrialization.

Bukharin supported a gradual approach to socialism. *The ABC of Communism* (1922), co-authored with Yevgeni Preobrazhensky, laid out ways to enroll the proletariat's support for the Bolsheviks political struggle. His *Historical Materialism: A System of Sociology* (1921) popularized the theoretical basis for socialist economic development. His work on the New Economic Policy and economic development reflected his belief in the need for balance between state and market elements within the socialist economy. Bukharin's influence remained limited within Stalin's dictatorship.

Stalin developed the theory of "socialism in one country," as he focused on the transition from Tsarist Russia to a new form of government based on a highly centralized and authoritarian state. *The Foundations of Leninism* (1924)—was a series of talks to younger cadres—which explained his views about the new Soviet society presented incrementally, and offered ideological justification for Stalin's policies, including forced collectivization and rapid industrialization. Stalin became Lenin's political successor and the leader of the Soviet Union from 1924 until his death in 1953. He held power as General Secretary of the Communist Party of the Soviet Union (1922–1952) and Chairman of the Council of Ministers of the Soviet Union (1941–1953). Initially he promoted a collective leadership but ended by consolidating his power to become a dictator by the 1936 with the transition to Socialism. *On the National Question* (1913–14) provided a much-needed centralized view on how to continue ruling the multi-ethnic Tsarist empire in the cloak of the new regime.

Trotsky's work perhaps was the closest to any principles of socialism, understood as a society invested in its people's wellbeing. He understood that as a dictatorship, socialism in one country (Stalin's idea) was unsustainable, because globally, dictatorship tended to have a transient history. The Permanent Revolution and The Revolution Betrayed critique Stalin's policies, advocating for internationalism and criticizing the bureaucratic nature of Stalin's Soviet Union. Trotsky focused on democracy, albeit, on workers' democracy and internationalism, which were antithetic to Stalin bureaucratic dictatorship.

These thinkers aspired to shape a new social order in ways that addressed Russia's unique context. Ultimately, they created a model society that was centrally planned, state-controlled, and authoritarian, with the goal of rapidly transforming society to fit the Soviet Union's economic and political goals. Those goals aimed at positioning Russia and its new oligarchs globally in a position of power. The wellbeing of the Russian people, the goal of socialist theories, was never a primary goal of that system. The goal was regime change, which happened when a military coup produced a political void after the assassination of the Tsar. Russia was a politically unstable country, which relied on the support of a very thin layer of aristocracy, a burgeoning bureaucracy, and the exploitation of the 90 percent of the population. The regime change proved rather easy to perform given the global war, famine, and terror. The transition to a so-called socialist dictatorship took less than two decades, and then lasted quite a few more. How this age of terror became anathema to a kinder, saner, fairer society remains a mystery worth unfolding in this book.

3 John Reed's Account of 20th Century Ersatz Socialism

John Reed's *Ten Days That Shook the World* (1919) is perhaps one of the most emotionally accurate accounts of the October Revolution, which brought the Bolsheviks to power and laid the foundation for the Soviet state. Reed participated to the November events as a "representative of the American Social-Democracy, an internationalist" (Reed, 1919, 214).

Bertrand Russell's *Bolshevism: Practice and Theory* (1920), is one of its most thoughtful accounts. When engaging those texts, we need to remember that both authors regarded the revolution as heroic: it ended Russia's participation in WWI, and it fired up men's progressive hopes. Perhaps their inevitable enthusiasm clouded their observations. The revolution ultimately became a Bolshevik victory at the expense of their ideals. As Russell noted, it was "a regime of Napoleonic empire" [Russell, 1920, 4]—or, in other words, an ersatz socialism.

Reed, a journalist, was a witness to the dramatic events of October 1917, and he provides essential context for understanding the political upheaval that preceded it. The February Revolution, with its collapse of Tsarism and the rise of the Provisional Government, created a volatile political environment in which the Bolsheviks could gain support and seize power. The failure of the Provisional Government to address the pressing issues facing Russian society—such as the war, land reform, and workers' rights—paved the way for the rise of the Soviet state. Russell also visited Russia, although not during the early days of the revolution, and so did his assistant, D.W. Black (Russell, 1920, 8).

John Reed acknowledges the political landscape that led to the collapse of the Tsarist regime earlier in the year, in what became known as the February Revolution. According to Reed, the February Revolution was not a planned, palace, coup but rather a spontaneous uprising driven by a convergence of factors, including the devastating impact of World War I, food shortages, economic hardship, and the widespread disillusionment with the monarchy's inability to address these issues. By the time of the uprisings in Petrograd, Tsar Nicholas II had lost the support of key elements of Russian society, including the military. The army, traditionally a loyal pillar of the Tsarist regime, became disloyal.

Soldiers who had been sent to suppress the demonstrations ultimately joined the revolutionaries, tipping the balance of power. This breakdown of military loyalty, combined with mass protests, food shortages, and general social unrest, led to the complete disintegration of Tsarist authority. On March 2, 1917, Nicholas II abdicated in favor of his brother, Grand Duke Michael, who, upon assuming the throne, abdicated within hours, effectively ending the monarchy. This was a historic moment, marking the final collapse of the autocracy and the beginning of a new political era in Russia.

While Reed does not focus extensively on the mechanics of the Tsar's removal, he devotes significant attention to the chaos and power vacuum that followed the February Revolution. With the abdication of the Tsar, Russia was left in a state of political flux. A Provisional Government, composed of a coalition of liberals, socialists, and former Tsarist elites, led initially by Prince Georgy Lvov and later by Alexander Kerensky, struggled to establish authority. The weak and indecisive nature of the Provisional Government enabled the creation of the Petrograd Soviet—a parallel authority representing workers, soldiers, and peasants.

Furthermore, the Provisional Government was unable to resolve the key issues facing the Russian society, most notably its continued participation in World War I and its failure to address the land question, which was a central demand of the peasantry. Additionally, the parallel government, the Soviet, which held considerable power in urban centers like Petrograd, was growing increasingly sympathetic to the revolutionary ideas of the Bolsheviks, who were advocating for a radical socialist transformation of Russian society.

Lenin and Trotsky are the two most pivotal figures in the transition to the Soviet regime. Reed describes Lenin as the ideological architect and uncompromising strategist of the Bolshevik movement. Having been in exile, Lenin returned to Russia in April 1917 with a clear vision to dismantle the Provisional Government. His journey was facilitated by German authorities, who allowed him to travel through Germany in a "sealed train," hoping his return would destabilize Russia amid World War I. Once back, Lenin took control of the Bolshevik Party, articulating a clear message to workers, soldiers, and peasants that resonated deeply with their desire for "peace, land, and bread." Lenin gained legislative power for various decrees which legitimized the new regime, primarily by leveraging the support of the Petrograd Soviet, where the Bolsheviks held substantial influence, especially after the majority of soldiers and workers had shifted their allegiance from the Provisional Government. Once the Bolsheviks seized key government facilities in Petrograd, Lenin and the Bolsheviks quickly declared a Soviet government and established the Council of People's Commissars (Sovnarkom), with Lenin as its head.

This structure gave Lenin and the Bolshevik leadership the authority to issue decrees, such as those on land and peace, as they began transforming Russian society along socialist lines.

Trotsky, who had also been exiled—this time in the United States—returned to Russia separately and soon emerged as the operational leader of the revolution. Known for his powerful oratory and organizational skill, Trotsky became the head of the Petrograd Soviet and was instrumental in rallying the Red Guards and preparing the logistics for the insurrection. Reed emphasizes Trotsky's tactical brilliance, particularly in mobilizing workers and soldiers to secure key locations in Petrograd, such as the Winter Palace and other government buildings. His efforts kept revolutionary forces unified and equipped, defending against internal opposition and counter-revolutionary threats from the remnants of the Provisional Government.

All this regime change was primarily possible because of the military and financial support surrounding the October Revolution. Reed describes the role of soldiers, sailors, and the Red Guards (armed factory workers and laborers) as the primary military forces that supported the Bolshevik cause. Petrograd's garrison troops, largely composed of soldiers weary of the ongoing war and sympathetic to the Bolshevik promises of peace, played a significant role in securing the revolution. The sailors of the Baltic Fleet, particularly those stationed at the Kronstadt naval base, are also prominently featured as steadfast supporters who provided crucial naval strength, further tipping the balance in favor of the Bolsheviks. Their involvement was instrumental in taking strategic points across Petrograd.

Financial support for the revolution is less directly emphasized by Reed, but he does imply that funds came from Bolshevik control over worker and soldier councils (Soviets), who could direct resources in support of their cause. The Soviet apparatus allowed for redistribution and immediate application of resources to logistics, arms, and wages for soldiers. Additionally, Reed points out that, once in power, the Bolsheviks took control of the state treasury and banking institutions, giving them access to resources necessary for consolidating their government and paying the Red Guards. These combined military and financial supports were vital to the success of the Bolshevik uprising, as Reed illustrates through the fervent loyalty of soldiers and workers aligned with Bolshevik ideals, solidifying Lenin and Trotsky's control over Petrograd. With the Bolsheviks' seizure of power, Lenin quickly established the Council of People's Commissars (Sovnarkom), which allowed him to implement policy through decrees. This council replaced the previous government structures and asserted Bolshevik control by passing radical decrees on issues that addressed the needs of the common people—such as land redistribution to peasants and an immediate call for peace. These decrees marked the start of Soviet governance, with Lenin's Sovnarkom wielding both legislative and executive powers.

Reed's account captures Lenin's unyielding focus on ideology and Trotsky's effectiveness in organizing and rallying forces, each playing a crucial, complementary role. Together, they transformed the Bolshevik uprising into a successful coup that laid the foundations for the Soviet state. Reed's firsthand narrative illustrates not just the events, but the fervor, risks, and determination of these leaders, highlighting how their partnership and strategies drove one of the 20th century's most significant revolutions.

Lenin himself trusted Reed's book and highly recommended it, stating that

> I recommend it to the workers of the world. ... It gives a truthful and most vivid exposition of the events so significant to the comprehension of what really is the Proletarian Revolution and the Dictatorship of the Proletariat.[3]

In this section, I use *The Ten Days That Shook the World* (Reed, [1919], 1977) to make a Deweyan argument: revolutions that lack democratic substance—genuine participation, deliberation, and shared power—cannot deliver real freedom. Reed's *Ten Days* offers a vivid chronicle of the Bolshevik Revolution that, when read alongside John Dewey's democratic theory (1927), helps illuminate four critical insights. First, Reed's account reveals the disconnect between revolutionary rhetoric and political reality: while Bolshevik leaders like Lenin and Trotsky spoke in the name of socialism and popular power, they swiftly centralized authority, suppressing dissent and marginalizing the very workers and peasants they claimed to represent. Second, this supports Dewey's insight that democracy is a social, not merely political, ideal. Dewey argued that democracy must be "incarnated in human relationships," (Dewey, 1927, 143) rooted in everyday practices of mutual recognition and shared decision-making. The Bolshevik takeover, by contrast, prioritized institutional control over democratic culture, undermining its own emancipatory promises. Third, Reed's narrative clearly shows that the Bolsheviks did not dismantle the power structures of the old regime; they rebranded them, substituting new elites and revolutionary language for genuine democratic empowerment. Finally, Reed helps us see the limits of revolutions that lack a democratic culture. Without deep, participatory practices embedded in social life, even radical revolutions can calcify into new forms of domination. In Dewey's terms, what was missing was

3 Nikolai Lenin (Vladimir Ilyich Ulyanov), Introduction, John Reed, *Ten Days That Shook the World* (Penguin Books, 1977).

the cultivation of a Great Community—without which no revolution, however dramatic, can deliver enduring freedom.

Thus, the thorough review of Reed's book fits with the vary aim of this book, to be more than a critical analysis of sources—it seeks to offer material insight for readers to engage with as they develop their own commonsense understanding of the Soviet experiment. To that end, what follows is an extended account of Reed's eyewitness testimony. His day-by-day narrative captures the intensity, chaos, and, at times, hopeful spirit of the days leading up to the Bolshevik seizure of power in Petrograd in November 1917.

The first quarter of the book, its first three chapters, covers the previous history, and position the revolution historically within the Russian reality of its day. Reed begins his narrative by describing the tense atmosphere in Petrograd as Bolshevik forces prepare for their assault, and the political climate that led to that moment of political crisis. The city brimmed with workers, soldiers, and peasants disillusioned with the Provisional Government's inability to end Russia's participation in WWI and address their daily needs. Reed captures the mood of anticipation as the Bolsheviks, under Lenin's leadership, prepare to challenge the authority of the Provisional Government. The final preparations for the decisive actions to come. Lenin, in hiding, urges the Bolsheviks to move forward with their plan to overthrow the Provisional Government. The workers and soldiers in Petrograd are gearing up for the moment when they will seize control. Reed describes the general atmosphere of anticipation, with people flooding the streets and revolutionary fervor taking hold, as the Provisional Government's leader, Alexander Kerensky, failed to rally forces and mount a counter-offensive against the Bolsheviks. Kerensky, after being unable to muster support in Petrograd, flees the city. His escape marks the end of the Provisional Government's ability to mount an effective challenge to the Bolsheviks. These pages highlight the strategic importance of the upcoming events and the mobilization of Bolshevik forces for the storming of the Winter Palace.

Chapter 4. The Fall of the Provisional Government (Id., 74–111). On the night of October 25 (Julian calendar; November 7 in the Gregorian calendar), the Bolsheviks launched their final assault on the Winter Palace. By dawn on October 26, the Provisional Government had effectively fallen. The Bolsheviks declared victory, and Lenin and Trotsky issued decrees establishing the Soviet rule. This chapter marks the official beginning of Bolshevik power and the end of the Provisional Government's authority.

Chapter 5. Plunging Ahead (Id., 112–46): It describes the early stages of the revolution, as it focuses on the events of November 8, 1917. Reed captures the excitement and determination of the revolution, but also its inherent problems.

The revolution was mostly a Petrograd-based military affair. By November 8th, "the Bolsheviki had been cut out from provincial Russia and the outside world. A Military Revolutionary Committee was functioning, masses, with soldiers and workers aligning with the Bolshevik cause, while the Provisional Government struggles to maintain control" (Id., 146–47). The power struggle was playing out at multiple levels. On one hand, Lenin was using his executive power as the President of the Council of People's Commissars acted in the name of the republican government chosen by "All-Russian" deputies of "Workers," "Peasants," and "Soldiers." This government did not cover the retired and unemployed, as well as the civil servants who were not soldiers, and more tellingly, all the professional, middle class, members, such as Lenin, Trotsky, and their ilk, who could not identify with any of the social groups supposed to have elected the Government of the Republic of Russia,[4] and then, participate in the popular elections, Lenin called for November 12. Tellingly, the new political regime was meant from its inception to create a new ruling class from among the Bolsheviki, the social group who will run the country, its political, economic, and legal system. At no point was the intended social and political hierarchy obscured by Lenin. At no point was the previous society's hierarchy destroyed; only its individual had been replaced, but not their social role of a minority in charge of the electors: the peasants, the workers, and the soldiers.

Chapter 6. The Committee for Salvation (Id., 147–71): In response to the Bolshevik seizure of power, a coalition of anti-Bolshevik forces forms the "Committee for Salvation," which seeks to rally people against the new Soviet regime. Reed describes the attempts of these counter-revolutionary forces to organize resistance, but the Bolsheviks, under Trotsky's leadership, remain firm in their position, securing control over the capital.

In Petrograd, the power grab was taking place in the Mayor's Office, where representatives of all factions involved in the insurrection were present. From the Executive Committee of Peasants' Soviets, to Merchants' and Manufacturers' Association, a seemingly inclusive diversity, which nevertheless made Reed uneasy to note that "The power of the Soviet is not a democratic power, but a dictatorship—and not the dictatorship of the proletariat, but *against* the proletariat" (Id., 149, emphasis in the original). Which might explain the glaring proletarian absence: "There was not a single proletarian anywhere in sight" (Id.). Moreover, Lenin was viewed as an "usurper" and a "tyrant," whose Commissars lent him the power he sought to grab (Id., 159). More telling is the lack of socialist principles practiced by the Bolsheviks, as

4 The first decree Lenin signed called for the election of the Constituent Assembly. John Reed, *The Ten Days That Shook the World* (Penguin Books, 1977), p. 158.

noted by a member of the Duma, Vera Slutskaya. Under Lenin's leadership, the Bolshevik Party openly opposed the Socialist Revolutionary Party, and engaged in acts of retribution similar to those of any military junta: assassinating their political adversaries.

> Comrades and citizens! [said the Petrograd Mayor] I have just learned that the prisoners in Peter-Paul are in danger. Fourteen ... have been stripped and tortured by the Bolshevik guards. One has got mad. They are threatening the lynch the Ministers.' [When] Vera Slutskaya, veteran revolutionist and Bolshevik member of the Duma [said:] 'That is a lie and a provocation!' ... 'The Workers' and the Peasants' Government, which has abolished the death penalty, cannot permit such deeds. We demand that this story be investigated at once; if there is any truth in it, the Government will take energetic measures' (Id.).

The day ended with Reed requesting to see the prisoners, and the Mayor assuring him that no one had been tortured, except the threats of lynching the Ministers, but those happened as they were being brought to prison, not while they were in prison, the Mayor elucidated (Id., 163).

Chapter 7. The Revolutionary Front (Id., 172–92): Saturday, November 10, 1917, started with an attempt by the revolutionary government to emulate the Paris Commune: "all theft, brigandage, assaults, and attempts at massacre will be severely punished [as will] any looter or instigator of disorder" (Id., 164). More telling was the lack of unity, the power fragmentation, within the revolutionary government, and the prominent role of the Socialist Revolutionary party as opposed to the Bolshevik faction. That no one believed that peasants and workers can govern or be legitimate members of any government, just because they are peasants and workers seemed well-established.

Dielo Naroda said:

> A revolution is a rising of all the people ... But here what have we? Nothing but a handful of poor fools deceived by Lenin and Trotsky ... Their decrees and their appeals will simply add to the museum of historical curiosities. (Id., 165, emphasis in the original)

This dissatisfaction with the Bolsheviks stemmed from their dual position: "appealing for peace at the [war] front, and inciting for civil war in the rear."[5]

---

5 Id., p. 179 (quoting from a flier distributed by the non-Bolshevik Committee for Salvation of Country and Revolution).

Chapter 8. Counter-Revolution (Id., 193–217): The events of Sunday, November 11, 1917, focused on the impact of the counter-revolutionary movement under the leadership of Kerensky, and its impact on Moscow and Petrograd. A Revolutionary Tribunal was established to try conspirators. The Military Revolutionary Committee represented the government until a Congress of the Soviets would establish a new government. The Committee included proportional representation from the Left Socialist Revolutionaries, the Social Democrat Internationalists, the Peasants' Soviets, and the Army. Quietly, even the Bolsheviks agreed to participate. Monday, November 12, 1917, Reed described as "a day of suspense," and the battle for power played in both Petrograd and Moscow. While the major forces in that battle centered around the Bolsheviks and the Counterrevolutionaries, in the end, Lenin's Peace and Land decrees, "stolen" from the Socialist Revolutionaries,[6] conquered the day. The Red Guards proved victorious, and Trotsky, People's Commissar, issued the following statement:

> Revolutionary Russia and the Soviet Power can be proud of their Pulkovo detachment, acting under the command of Colonel Walden. Eternal memory to those who fell! Glory to the warriors of the Revolution, the soldiers and the officers who were faithful to the People! Long live revolutionary, popular, *Socialist* Russia! (Id., 199, emphasis added)

Trotsky added "socialist" as a qualifier perhaps because Lenin "stole" the Revolutionary Socialists' Land Programme. Or in a desire to prove the Military Revolutionary Committee's' ideological diversity.

Chapter 9. Victory (Id., 218–242): By Tuesday morning, November 13, 2017, the undisciplined, starving, Red Guards had morphed into something akin to an army. Thought the interim government was far from settled. The Revolutionary Socialists favored including the Bolsheviks despite the wide-spread opinion that any "agreement with the maniacs [was] impossible until they put down their arms and recognize[d] the authority of independent courts of law." This Petrograd Duma concern with the Bolsheviks opposition to the democratic administration of the law stemmed from the way their revolutionary trials were conducted in factories and barracks against those deemed adversaries.

Chapter 10. Moscow (Id., 243–259): November 14, 1917 marked the formal defeat of the counterrevolution, with a decree calling for the arrest of Kerensky.

6 Id., p. 198. (Lenin appeared for a moment to answer the accusations of the Socialist Revolutionaries: "The charge us with stealing their land programme ... It that was so, we bow to them. It is good enough for us ...").

On November 15, the White Guards and the *yunkers* in the Kremlin surrendered and a peace treaty with the counter-revolutionaries was signed. Reed and the other "American *tovarishchi*" (Id., 222, emphasis in the original) received passes to leave Petrograd for Moscow. Dense masses packed the Kremlin that day, including "the soldier who had been elected the commandant of Moscow" (Id., 228). The streets were soon filled with people caring their dead. Banners read "Long Live the Third International!" and "We Want an Honest, General, Democratic Peace!"

Reed ended this chapter which described how 500 coffins were laid in pits, full of emotions. It read as contradicting much of the observations recorded in the previous chapters, while it offered a glimpse of clarification over the original confusion regarding ersatz "socialism". Even progressives have individual ego. And the idea that they participated in any way to shaping the world for the better might obscure insights otherwise more valuable to understanding history: "I suddenly realized that the devout Russian people no longer needed priests to pray them into heaven. On earth they were building a kingdom more bright than any heaven had to often, and for which it was a glory to die" (Id., 259). Thus, perhaps Reed's emotional quote is more complex than we might like it.

Obviously, on one level, Reed is swept up in the revolutionary fervor. The image evokes a profound shift in spiritual and political consciousness: a people once dependent on religious institutions for salvation are now finding purpose in earthly, collective transformation. It's a moment of revolutionary transcendence—where political struggle takes on the intensity and devotion of religious faith, and martyrdom for the cause becomes a secular form of sainthood.

But read critically—especially against the grain of Reed's earlier, more ambivalent observations—it becomes clear that this passage may reflect less the objective truth of the revolution and more Reed's own yearning to believe in its meaning. Throughout *Ten Days*, Reed documents chaos, fragmentation, elite manipulation, and popular exclusion. So, this moment of epiphany risks romanticizing what, in practice, was a top-down seizure of power. It raises the question: is Reed seeing a genuine "kingdom on earth," or projecting revolutionary hope onto a reality already slipping into authoritarianism?

In this sense, the quote can be read as a tragic idealism: it captures how revolutions can inspire deep personal belief in the possibility of transformation—even as the social and political structures taking shape contradict that vision. It reveals how even sympathetic witnesses like Reed can be caught between critical insight and emotional investment, and how revolutionary narratives often blur the line between history and myth.

Chapter 11. Conquest of Power (Id., 260–292): It highlighted the legitimacy of the revolution. It highlighted the *Declaration of the Rights of the Peoples of Russia*, which both Stalin (as the People's Commissar for Nationalities) and Lenin (as the President of the Council of People's Commissars) signed on November 15, 1917. It incorporated progressive, internationalist, principles. It enabled the declaration of independent states, which Ukraine and Finland immediately did. It also abolished national privileges while proclaiming the "free development of national minorities and ethnographic groups" (Id., 231). The latter principle might have played a role in the West's indulgence of Stalin's nondiscriminatory murderous regime over Hitler's murderous regime focused on ethnic cleansing, and subsequent reluctance to call ersatz socialism undemocratic capitalism.

After the flight of Kerensky, on November 16, 1917, the Bolsheviks and the Socialists agreed to form a representative government. However, when the issue of the freedom of the press was raised, the Bolsheviks opposed it because the government the Bolsheviki wanted to build was not democratic, and by that very reason, it could not have been socialist.

> The civil war is not yet finished; the enemy us still with us; consequently, it is impossible to abolish the measures of represent against the press. *We Bolsheviki have always said that when we reached a position of power we would close the bourgeois press.* To tolerate the bourgeois newspapers would mean to cease being Socialist. When one makes a Revolution, one cannot mark time; one must always go forward—or go back. *He who now talks about the "freedom of the press" goes backward, and halts our headlong course towards Socialism.* (Id., 270–271, emphasis added)

Socialism represents the will of the people. What Lenin describes in this quote and the one below is the reverse. It is a prison where no disobedience was allowed. Democratic capitalism allows a "pretense of freedom," which is the freedom of the press. Lenin rejected that from the beginning. So-called Soviet Socialism was never meant as anything else but a replacement of Tsarist Russia with new players. New identities for the same political, economic and legal structure.

> Now that the insurrection is over we have absolutely no desire to suppress the papers of the other Socialist parties, except inasmuch they appeal to armed insurrection, or to disobedience to the Soviet Government. However, we shall not permit them, under the pretence of freedom of the Socialist press, to obtain through the secret support of the bourgeoisie, a

> monopoly of the printing press, ink, and paper ... These essentials must become the property of the Soviet Government, and be apportioned to the ... Socialist parties in strict proportion to their voting strength. (Id., 271)

Lenin's proposal won the day, as the Socialists resigned, and the only ones left in the government were the Bolsheviks. The press spread conspiracies and multiplied fears. Soon, "[a]lert and suspicious, the working class of the city constituted itself a vast spy system, through the servants prying into bourgeois households and reporting all information to the Military Revolutionary Committee" (Id., 278). The famine spread and the war effort needed finances. On November 22, the Petrograd banks were nationalized. On November 30, the Petrograd Duma was dissolved, but the municipal employees were encouraged to continue perform their duties.

The events which occurred in the last half of November reveal the deep contradiction between revolutionary ideals and the authoritarian realities of Bolshevik rule, exposing how revolutions can betray their own promises when power is prioritized over democratic principles. Lenin's rejection of freedom of the press under the guise of defending socialism illustrates a binary revolutionary logic—"go forward or go back"—that eliminates space for dissent, debate, or democratic pluralism. In redefining socialism as loyalty to the Bolshevik Party alone, Lenin severs it from its democratic roots, transforming it into an exclusive ideology used to silence opposition, even from fellow socialists. What results is not the destruction of the old hierarchy but its reconstitution: a new ruling class of commissars and party elites replaces the Tsarist autocrats, while the people—the supposed beneficiaries of the revolution—are reduced to passive subjects.

The resignation of non-Bolshevik socialists marks the collapse of political pluralism and the onset of one-party rule, as rhetoric about protecting the revolution justifies purges, censorship, and state control over media, finance, and governance. Meanwhile, the emergence of a widespread surveillance culture, in which workers spy on bourgeois households, signals the use of fear as a tool of political control. Rather than empowering the masses, this Bolshevik takeover constructs an authoritarian state apparatus cloaked in socialist language. Ultimately, this supports Dewey's view (1927) that democracy is not simply a matter of governmental form but must be embedded in everyday relationships and practices; without a culture of participation and mutual respect, revolutions risk becoming new tyrannies that reproduce the very systems they set out to dismantle.

Reed let his readers conclude whether the 1917 Revolution morphed into a Bolshevik takeover whose power consolidated into the Soviet government.

How was it possible for a handful of Bolsheviks to win and transfer the power into the hands of a set of rulers, as ruthless as the ones they had replaced? Reed offered the answer almost unwittingly. The state became the ultimate mafia boss. Everyone was employed by the Soviet corporation.

> The strike of Government employees ... collapsed deserted by the financial and commercial interests which had been backing it. ... The only reason for Bolshevik success lay in their accomplishing the vast and simple desires of the most profound strata of the [Russian] people, calling them to the work of tearing down and destroying the old [and paying them for that]. (Id.)

This chapter also briefly covered Trotsky's negotiations with the Allies, the negotiations and the Armistice with the Germans, sketched the "Soviet Government's attempts to consolidate its political power" (Id., 355) Eventually, those negotiations ended with the "disastrous Peace of Brest-Litovsk" (Id.).

Chapter 12. The Peasants' Congress (Id., 293–314): Very tellingly, this chapter clarified the outsized role of the peasants, "the people of Russia." If the urban population was made up of workers, servants, soldiers, and the few members of the bourgeoisie, the majoring of the rural population, the vast majority of Russians, were peasants. If the Bolsheviks succeeded in quieting the urban population either by employing them or making them enemies of the people, dealing with the peasants proved more complex, and by November 16, 1917, the Bolsheviks realized they needed to address that issue. Lenin published instructions to the thousand Provisional Emissaries sent to villages to create inventories of the confiscated land and whether the peasants working the confiscated land were able to provide the grains necessary to avoid famine.

In this chapter, Reed clearly settled the problem with the Socialist Revolution: to happen it needed people to want it. To believe in it. Unfortunately, for socialism world-wide, the Bolsheviks did not wait for the consciousness of the masses to fully develop. As Lenin's words show, the Bolsheviks compromised socialist principles to capture and then retain power. The Land Decree of November 8, read that the "Revolution of November 7, 1917 [was deemed] a social revolution." and its leaders' "unalterable will" was to be "put into operation" with "whatever modifications [were] necessary but without hesitation, the social transformation of the Russian republic" (Id., 305).

This chapter thus further reveals the fragile and contested birth of Soviet socialism, particularly through the lens of the Peasants' Congress and its complex negotiations with the Bolsheviks. While the Congress expressed fervent support for the Land Decree and the broader goals of the November 7 revolution—such as land redistribution, the abolition of wage labor, and nationalization of banks—Reed's narration underscores how much of this enthusiasm rested on promises, not realities. The Congress invoked the image of a social revolution led by "peasant-workers" and supported by the industrial proletariat, affirming the need for structural transformation across agriculture, finance, and governance. However, as the chapter unfolds, Reed documents the political maneuvering behind the scenes, particularly the secret negotiations between the Bolsheviks and the Left Socialist Revolutionaries that culminated in a backroom deal, retaining Lenin, Trotsky, and the Military Revolutionary Committee in power. This compromise highlights the gap between the democratic rhetoric of the Congress and the consolidation of one-party rule. Other influential and still popular figures among the peasantry, found themselves sidelined, and efforts to propose broader socialist coalitions were dismissed as "illegal" or naive. Reed's description of the "wedding" between the Peasants' Soviets and the Workers' and Soldiers' Soviets, met with ecstatic applause, reads as both hopeful and ironic: beneath the celebration lay a reality in which political pluralism was already being sacrificed for unity under Bolshevik control.

As Reed suggests, the Socialist Revolution could not succeed merely through decrees or state action—it needed the genuine belief and participation of the people. The Bolsheviks, however, chose to act before the masses' consciousness had fully developed, substituting party will for popular will. Thus, the chapter lays bare the paradox of Soviet socialism: a revolution proclaimed in the name of the people, yet increasingly indifferent to their actual voices, especially those of the rural majority. And this is what I call ersatz socialism, which Reed could not accept, given his political beliefs. For Reed, the promise of socialism was the promise of true, participatory democracy—an ideal that was ultimately sacrificed in favor of authoritarian centralization and political expediency. This ersatz socialism, a façade of revolutionary change masking the continuation of old power structures, was the antithesis of what Reed had hoped for from the Russian Revolution. His magnificent work exposes that naked truth for all who engage with it.

4 Bertrand Russell's Account of 20th Century Ersatz Socialism

Bertrand Russell wrote *Bolshevism: Practice and Theory*, after spending more than 30 days in U.S.S.R., from May 16 until June 11, 1920, and having multiple encounters with both Lenin (in a hour-long-tête-à-tête) and Trotsky (though only in company). As its title suggests, Russell believed Bolshevism to be a home-grown theory and practice for something different than democratic capitalism: a theory which gave hope to Western socialists while it terrorized the Russians because of its methods of implementation.

However, Russell was not deflating the theory and the practice of its implementation, as this book does. Russel believed that Bolshevism was the mistaken Russian method of implementing the ideal of communism.

Nevertheless, Russell could not contain his disdain of Bolshevism, seeing through its façade the continuation of the previous Tsarist regime with different players and different names. Conceptually, Russell limited his criticism of Bolshevism to its religious dogmatism essence:

> Bolshevism is not merely a political doctrine; *it is also a religion, with elaborate dogmas and inspired scriptures*. When Lenin wishes to prove some proposition, he does so, if possible, by quoting texts from Marx and Engels. *A full-fledged Communist is* not merely a man who believes that land and capital should be held in common and their produce distributed as nearly equally as possible. [But] *a man who entertains a number of elaborate and dogmatic beliefs*. (Russell, 1920, 6, emphasis added)

And that is the problem with the type of society the Bolsheviks were building. It was the old Tsarist regime, only renamed. After an illuminating preface, Russell detailed his understanding of the "Present Conditions of Russia" (Part I), further defined in nine chapters, and of the "Bolshevik Theory" (Part II) in seven subsequent chapters. Russell, in Marxian tradition, started with the material circumstances, the foundation of the dissemination of the "widespread hope" (Id., 13), the Bolshevik theory, previously "confined to a few" (Id.). However, Russell was not a Marxian, and as man of ideas, his writing soon reverted to ideas.

Russell visited Russia, and his work reflects the existing dichotomy between the lived reality of Bolshevism and the wishful thinking it entailed. "The effect of Bolshevism as a revolutionary hope is greater outside Russia than within the Soviet Republic" (Id., 17), especially because the paucity, "exhaustion and misery" (Id., 20), witnessed could have been caused to a large extent by the two wars, and the economic blockade.

The Book thus reflects Russell's own experience with democratic capitalism. "Its injustice was so glaring that only ignorance and tradition could lead wage-earners to tolerate it" (Id., 16). Russell's Bolshevism is a mirror to his experienced capitalism, unclear whether he meant the political, legal, or economic system:

> It may be that, through the influence of America, the [liberal, democratic] capitalist system will linger for another fifty years; but it will grow continually weaker, and can never recover the position of easy dominance which it held in the nineteenth century. ... Whether the new thing will be

> Bolshevism or something else, I do not know; whether it will be better or worse than [liberal, democratic] capitalism, I do not know. (Id.)

From a political perspective, Bolshevism was analyzed as a new form of representative government, though it was referred to as a dictatorship of the proletariat. Russell described it as a Dickensian realization of Samuel Pickwick's achievements—a source of both embarrassment and wonder. "When a Russian Communist speaks of dictatorship, he means the world literally, but when he speaks of the proletariat, he means the word in a Pickwickian sense" (Id., 27). Only certain workers were part of the dictatorship—those who proved their political worth, Communist Party members,—as well as figures like Lenin and Trotsky, who were "by no means proletarian" (Id.). While voting existed, it could not truly be called an exercise in legitimate representation.

"All real power is in the hands of the Communist Party, who number about 600,000 in a population of 120 million" (Id., 77) or 0.5 percent. The ballot functioned merely to publicize the identity of the dictator at the top in each institution, municipality, county, state, federation: one would read the name on the ballot and return it to the ballot box. Pickwickian, indeed, though it offered no comic relief to those who participated in the charade as the bottom fodder of state-owned factories, farms, and other state agencies and institutions.

"Bolshevism is internally aristocratic and externally militant" (Id., 30). Or as democratic and representative as Plato's Republic.

Russell's sharp observation and analysis was also on display when discussing the economic system he witnessed. No matter what the words used for presenting the state ownership of the means of production which produced consumer goods, Russel "I fear this is a delusion" (Id., 157) to believe that all such goods were held in common. The officials who controlled the distribution of those goods "are the repositories of power" (Id.). They controlled the army and wielded despotic power, although they were a small minority.

> It is sheer nonsense to pretend that the rulers of a great empire such as Soviet Russia, when they have become accustomed to power, retain the proletarian psychology, and feel that their class-interest is the same as that of the ordinary working man. This is not the case in fact in Russia now, however the truth may be concealed by fine phrases. The Government has a class-consciousness and a class-interest quite distinct from those of the genuine proletarian, who is not to be confounded with the paper proletarian of the Marxian scheme. *In a capitalist state, the Government and the capitalists ... hang together and form one class; in Soviet Russia, the Government has absorbed the capitalist mentality together with the*

> *governmental, and the fusion has given increased strength to the upper class*. (Id., 159, emphasis added)

Russell's last chapter is best summarized by its title that "Russian Communism Has Failed." I depart from that conclusion because what failed was not communism. What failed was liberalism.

If we hold socialist theory next to the events taken after 1917 in Russia, nothing that happened there could be said followed some socialists' blueprints. There was nothing socialist,nor communist, but that is not the focus of this book, in the Russian experiment. What eventually failed in 1991, was a ruthless dictatorship based on state capitalist monopoly of its economic resources and propped for almost a century by a legal system tolerated by the West for being socialist, on equal footing with the civil and common law system, in triumvirate which I hopefully helped demolish through a recent article (Neacșu, 2025).

5 Soviet Socialism—Actuating State Capitalist Monopoly

The brief overview of various writings offers insight which hopefully will challenge the existing 100-year-old common-sense (mis)understanding of socialism as an umbrella concept of the theory and practice of the Soviet and ECE experiment with power. This book argues that all confusions or misunderstanding can be corrected through insight if curiosity on the parts of the thinking agents exist. The previous overview of the socialist school of thought and socialist theories developed for over two centuries (Van der Linden, 2022), whose implementation or praxis has yet to happen, is meant to set the fire of curiosity to address this misconception, confusion or misunderstanding.

Russell started with the reality he encountered in Russia in 1920 to disabuse the world of the method of communist implementation. He noted that the legitimacy of that regime change—which, I argue, changed little except a reshuffling of the main actors—rested on the popularity of Marxian thought, although Leninism flaunted it, turning Marxian thought about socialism and communism on its head. Marx and Engels were the personalities behind the international workers' movement, which, given the industrialization trend of all world economies, was influential and taken into consideration by policymakers everywhere.

The political, economic and legal system the Bolsheviks implemented was flawed at every single level. It was obvious that the Bolshevik road to communism was not a road and not to communism. If transitory, then the problem was complicated theoretically because Marx himself had little to say about socialism. Socialism, in the Marxian parlance, was viewed as a transitional means, and like anything underdeveloped theoretically, it became easier to repurpose. The principles behind that regime change were principles of surviving at all cost and thus bringing, blackmailing, or employing everyone needed to reach that goal. Worse, unlike Machiavelli's Principle, the peace offered the Russian people was not a principle of governing, but a means to consolidate power. "If the Bolsheviks remain in power, it is much to be feared that their Communism will fade, and that they will increasingly resemble any other Asiatic Government—for example, [the British] Government in India" (Russell, 1920, 34).

Like Reed, Russell believed in progressive principles. He went to Russia a Communist, though he doubted Bolshevism both as theory and avowed method of implementing Communism (Id., 41). "I am at one with the Bolsheviks; politically, I criticize them only when their methods seem to involve a departure from their own ideals" (Id., 5). I too believe in the ideals of social justice for all. Unfortunately for history, the leadership of the Bolshevik movement had only one ideal: grabbing and holding onto power for their own sake. The dictatorship of the proletariat proved to be worse than what Orwell thought, a dictatorship of former proletarians. It was a dictatorship of a very tight-knit of angry, well-educated men, who thought they deserved better than being born outside the Russian aristocracy, so they appointed themselves "top dogs". Having no birth rights, nor family money, they had to invent their hierarchical position, their ruling class.

The theory legitimizing the 1917 Russian insurrection, and then, after WWII in Eastern Europe, Bolshevism, as Russell so aptly calls it, was a hodgepodge, whose main international asset was that it minimized the role of nationalism, which during the subsequent decades became the root of German fascism, a threat to democratic, liberal capitalism. Liberal democratic capitalism, with few exceptions, such as Hayek, thought they could outlive autocratic capitalism. And they did until now, when the world's capitalist economies desperately need some new means of productivity, such as the trendier GenAI, for lack of new geographical markets (or worse when soon faced with shrinking markets given the geographical impact of climate change).

It is remarkable that from its inception, ersatz socialism could have been catalogued as such, but it was not. If it were to be connected to socialist theorists, Lenin's theoretical farragoes could have been discarded easily. Similarly, the new regime did not come out of a Marxian historical progression, as Tsarist Russia had no bourgeoisie to be contended with, but a full-fledged Marxian feudalism. Russell aptly remarked that any new society has to engage the structure of the previous one:

> That Communism [or Socialism], whenever and wherever it is adopted, will have to begin by [engaging] the *bourgeoisie*, is highly probable. The important question is not whether there is to be [exertion], but how long and severe it is to be. A short [resistance], in which Communism won a rapid and easy victory, would do little harm. It is long, bitter and doubtful [fights] that must be avoidable if anything of what makes *Communism* [or Socialism] *desirable* is to survive. (Id., 185)

And as both Reed and Russell noted, the new society had to be desired by the population, especially if that society was supposed to benefit its people. To the contrary, whatever Lenin and his ilk devised and implemented only benefited their ego and the new ruling class. It was not designed for or desired by the masses. Socialism can only be a society based on social justice for all. As such, socialism requires democratic representation to express the voice of the people, and not a small percent representation—given by the members of the class in charge, in the case of Soviet Russia, that class was initially defined politically, through political loyalty. Russell noted the conceptual contradiction of pretending to build a society for the people when the people were "hostile."

> [I]t is a mistake to attempt to inaugurate Communism [or Socialism] in a country where the majority are hostile, or rather, where the active opponents are as strong as the active supporters, because in such a state of opinion a very severe civil war is likely to result (Id).

The same conclusion was reached by Reed's *Ten Days That Shook the World* (1919). Although Reed was not as direct as Russell to call the Bolshevik project a "mistake". Reed suggested a more realist approach, through the "the intellectual development of all the people:"

> If Socialism can only be realized when the intellectual development of all the people permits it, then we shall not see Socialism for at least five hundred years. (Reed, [1919] 1977, 263, italics in the original)

That popular ignorance about socialism, the Bolsheviks' intentions, and their subsequent implementation developed into classic capitalist alienation, as Marx so well described, which is the root of the mass behavioral response to Stalin's terror and assassins. "Socialism" became a warped fiction which existed at the expense of the theory itself and the lives of those affected by the content into which it morphed: Leninism and Stalinism. The dictatorship of the proletariat, as allegoric and unreachable as it seemed, became the dictatorship of the new ruling class, that of the "former proletarians"[7] and the rotating members of the Politburo, the supreme policy-making body, which "until July 1990 exercised supreme control over the Soviet government."[8]

Reed's account of the events as they were originally planned and then unveiled is as accurate as any because Reed is aware of his political biases while thoroughly noting everything around.

> There was no doubt now in anyone's mind who held the reins of power. It was the Bolsheviks, with their workers' councils and the Red Guards, who now determined the fate of Russia. … The Provisional Government was gone, and with it went the last vestiges of the old Russia. The White Guards had failed. The generals had failed. The counter-revolutionaries had failed. The workers had won.

Reed was a witness to the events. He noted how the previous political structure was replaced by a new political structure. It was undemocratic. It remained undemocratic. The White Guards had been replaced with the Red Guards. Was Reed's statement that "the workers had won" simple wishful thinking?

As Figure 6, courtesy of the Library of Congress,[9] further visualizes the Russian "masses," they were limited to those uprooted from villages: behind the banners filled with the slogans march some soldiers, sailors, women, and children. The peasants, the vast majority of Russians (in May and June 1920, they represented 85 percent of the population), were away from the centers of political power and cameras, as were the "proletarian dictators" because there

---

7 "The dictatorship of the proletariat originally was conceived by Karl Marx (1818–83) as a dictatorship by the majority class. Because Marx regarded all governments as class dictatorships, he viewed proletarian dictatorship as no worse than any other form of government. However, the Bolshevik Revolution in Russia in 1917 resulted in a dictatorship not of the majority class of proletarians but of a political party that claimed to represent proletarian interests. Contrary to Marx's vision and as George Orwell (1903–50), Mikhail Bakunin (1814–76), and others had foreseen, the *proposed dictatorship of the proletariat eventually became a dictatorship of former proletarians.* (emphasis added)."

The Editors of Encyclopedia Britannica, *Britannica* (Last Updated: Dec 27, 2024), https://www.britannica.com/topic/dictatorship-of-the-proletariat

8 The Editors of Encyclopedia Britannica, *Britannica*, https://www.britannica.com/topic/Politburo.

9 See also, *Le Point*. Fédorovski et le malentendu de l'histoire de la révolution russe (Nov. 25, 2016) https://www.lepoint.fr/video/fedorovski-est-le-malentendu-de-l-histoire-de-la-revolution-russe-25-11-2016-2085791_738.php.

FIGURE 6 "Long live the Council of Workmen's and Soldiers' Deputees!"—Revolutionary slogan and visual motif

SOURCE: LIBRARY OF CONGRESS. 1917. LONG LIVE THE COUNCIL OF WORKMEN'S AND SOLDIERS' DEPUTEES! WASHINGTON, D.C.: PRINTS AND PHOTOGRAPHS DIVISION, LIBRARY OF CONGRESS. HTTPS://WWW.LOC.GOV/ITEM/2009631818/

were too few factories in 1917 Russia. The Russian-language sign says, "Long live the Council of Workmen's and Soldiers' Deputies!"

After his 1917–1918 stay in Russia, and the publication of his opus about the Petrograd political turmoil, Reed returned to Soviet Russia to attend the 1919 Second Congress of the Communist International (Comintern) in Moscow as a delegate from the newly formed Communist Labor Party of America. This second visit was significant because Reed faced firsthand some of the challenges and realities of the new Soviet government, including tensions and authoritarian practices, which tamed his initial enthusiasm.

Reed began to recognize that the regime change was not simply a matter of broad-based democratic control by the workers and peasants—a socialist revolution—but rather the creation of a highly centralized state controlled by the Communist Party elite. Reed's growing concerns about the bureaucratic nature of the new Soviet state were highlighted by the suppression of other socialist factions, such as the Mensheviks and Socialist Revolutionaries, who had initially been part of the coalition government with the Soviets. The

Bolsheviks increasingly sidelined or eliminated these groups, consolidating power in the hands of the party.

Reed reflected on the crystallization of the new power structures of the Soviet regime in his letters and later articles in *The Liberator*. In particular, articles written after his return to Russia in 1919 capture his growing discomfort with the consolidation of Bolshevik power, marked by the activities of the Cheka and the suppression of political opposition. Emma Goldman, who was in Russia around the same time, noted in correspondence with Reed her horror at the Soviet government's brutal approach to dissent, which Reed also witnessed during this period. He documented this shift in various accounts and personal reflections, detailing how the initial ideals of freedom and justice were being overshadowed by repression and control under Lenin's leadership. He died in Moscow in October 1920 from typhus, so he did not witness the full dictatorial and increasingly militarized regime taking over Russia.

By 1921, with the repression of the Kronstadt Rebellion of 1921, the transition to an undemocratic form of government was sealed. When the Kronstadt sailors, who had been some of the Bolshevik Revolution's most ardent supporters, revolted against the stringent economic crisis and demanded an end to the increasing authoritarianism of the Soviet state, military troops under Trotsky's leadership and Lenin's direct command were sent to crush the revolt. That swift solution clarified the direction of the new regime: a dictatorship of the newly formed Communist Party elite under the leadership of Lenin.

So, what was socialist in the theory behind this regime change? What was socialist after the regime change? If socialism, to use Rosa Luxemburg's words, "is the first popular movement in the world that has set itself a goal and has established in the social life of a human being a conscious thought, a definite plan, the free will of mankind."[10] The Bolshevik Revolution lacked that blueprint. It was a power grabbing event, lacking any provision for a democratic government. Socialism demands democracy. Socialism is a democratic movement. Mankind expresses its free will to build a more ethical and sustainable society. Socialism is not and cannot be a prison.

Thus, it seems egregious when Pulitzer-prized historians talk about Stalin's gulags as representative of socialism. Stalin's terror is a representative of the dictatorship which he called socialist. At a minimum, a scientist or historian can qualify Stalin's socialism as such, instead of promoting a view of

---

10 Rosa Luxemburg, 1915, "The 'Junius' Pamphlet: The Crisis of German Social Democracy" ["Die Krise der Sozialdemokratie: Die 'Junius' Broschüre"], Dave Hollis (trans.), in [RLR], pp. 312–341, p. 320]), in *The Rosa Luxemburg Reader*, Peter Hudis and Kevin Anderson (eds.), (New York: Monthly Review Press, 2004).

socialist disillusionment and discontent. Stalin's socialism is the heir to Lenin's Soviet state.

Indeed, Lenin crushed the March, 1921, Kronstadt Rebellion in a violent confrontation, alerting observers, like Emma Goldman and Alexander Berkman, about the authoritarian direction of the Soviet government. But, in reaction to that rebellion, Lenin brought about the implementation of the New Economic Policy (NEP) later that year. It relaxed some monopolist economic policies and thus it stabilized the country. However, that capitalist reformist trend was erased when Lenin died and Stalin became his successor, only three years later. With Stalin the direction of the new regime became intimidation and terror in a police state built to ensure a dictatorship through a client state managing the wealth for the benefit of the ruling elite.

From the brief analysis of Reed's writing, his enthusiasm for the regime change in Russia is easily understandable. The Tsarist rule had been ruthless. Unfortunately, Reed's enthusiasm was misplaced as the Bolshevik regime did never embrace communal power shared in a democratic way among various social groups.

Socialism aims to be transformative. Can it be? Can mankind aspire to build a sustainable society for the benefit of all? What would that entail? I do not know.

All this book aspires to do is to plant doubt in the commonsense understanding of socialism. Socialism could not begin to encompass what Lenin with Trotsky's aid started in Petrograd. Or, using Nikolay Bukharin's words, there is nothing socialist in devising a "police state" to run the "military-feudal exploitation of the country's peasant majority" and pushing for a draconian kind of rapid industrialization to birth the industrial proletariat needed to establish a proletariat dictatorship, an impossibility in a non-capitalist society as the very existence of the proletariat is causally linked to capital and capitalism, and legitimize the new (capitalist) regime. Stalin's ruthless measures of 1929–1933, immediately after he terminated the NEP, brought in some estimated 10 million peasants to an early grave or enslavement in the Gulag of forced labor camps. Among them the former ideologue, Nikolay Bukharin, was executed after the last of Moscow's Show Trials on March 2, 1938, as Hitler was marching into Austria.

Socialism was the concept, theory and the implanting practice used by Stalin to describe, legitimize, and implement his way of governing post-Tsarist Russia. Stalin named Russia socialist in 1936.

That the Bolsheviks did not envisage building a society much different from the one they inherited is perhaps best exemplified with the prison system. Russian literature is filled with stories about the Tsarist prison system, such as

Fyodor Dostoyevsky's *Notes from a Dead House*, the semi-fictionalized account of his 1849 internment in a Siberian prison camp after he was sentenced to four years of hard labor for his involvement in a revolutionary conspiracy. Lenin made good use of the Tsarist prison system, as Solzhenitsyn, himself a direct witness of the Russian prison system, persuasively explains.

The state detention system became known as the Gulag, an acronym which comes from the Russian for "Chief Administration of Corrective Labor Camps." When the Soviet labor camps and accompanying detention camps, transit camps, and prisons metamorphosed into Stalin's societal signature, from the mid-1920s to the mid-1950s, everyone who was deemed an enemy of the system ended dead or in detention. In the West, the name of this detention system is known because of Aleksandr Solzhenitsyn's *The Gulag Archipelago, 1918–1956* (1973). The Gulag is both an epistemic short cut, a label easily understood to stand in for a terrorist form of government. They existed to keep Stalin's regime floating. I don't know how much repression is necessary to maintain a repressive society. I assume that is not theoretically imparted knowledge. It takes practice, and one day at a time. Luckily for the Russian society, Stalin eventually died.

Marx did not know much about socialism because, I believe, he was not really interested in re-writing the Bible. His best work was about observing the society in which he lived and pointing out that its economy did not need a democracy that favored the larger segments of the population to flourish, according to its laws of increased profit. A sociologist, he thought that mankind cannot reform itself to reach such an enlightened society. I don't know if Marx is right or Engels. I know that, like Bukharin wrote in 1937 in *How It All Began* (1993), while imprisoned in Stalin's Gulag system, building a new society is not like erecting a building—it cannot follow a blueprint. A society is a living organisms and, whatever theory people want to use, it has to be a dynamic vision following a particular goal. If that goal is the wellbeing of the exploited classes, or the 99 percent of the population, then the theory behind it cannot be a straitjacket. Even if those in charge spit out the Bible, the straitjacket remains. And if the insights offered in this book are not enough, then I am sure more persuasive ones are nearby.

Lenin believed in technocrats to control wealth and distribute it to a more enlightened working force, but he never thought of changing the proletariat's fate: still proletariat but better educated, in better health, and living in better conditions. A more moral capitalist democracy could reach Lenin's dream. There is nothing fundamentally anti-capitalist in Lenin's social engineering. As there is nothing fundamentally anti-capitalist in Stalin's gulags. Because, what we commonly describe as features of socialism, such as mass prison camps, are in fact staples of capitalism, think about U.S. immigration camps or German concentration camps, and should be regarded as yet another example that socialism never existed in Russia before or after 1936, when its Constitution defined that capitalist monopolist state as socialist.[11]

11 Appendix A. *Constitution (Fundamental law) of the Union of Soviet Socialist Republics*, Kremlin, Moscow, December 5, 1936, in J.V. Stalin, *Works*, Vol. 14, (Red Star Press Ltd., London, 1978) https://www.marxists.org/reference/archive/stalin/works/1936/12/05.htm ("**Chapter I: The Organization of Society. ARTICLE 1.** The Union of Soviet Socialist Republics is a socialist state of workers and peasants.") (Herein, "The Stalin Constitution," reproduced in Appendix A).

PART 2

The Political, Economic, and Legal Scaffolding of Ersatz Socialism

CHAPTER 3

Beyond the Narrative of Failed Socialism

The twentieth century witnessed the collapse of numerous dictatorships—arguably more than any other era, aside from the Middle Ages and their endemic forms of undemocratic rule. From the perspective of this project, it was also the century of historical irony: theories grounded in material conditions, such as Marxism, were paradoxically blamed for those very conditions—namely, the political and economic realities of Soviet Russia and the countries of Eastern and Central Europe (ECE). The widespread belief in a direct, irrefutable connection between Marxian theory—here argued to be only tangentially related to socialism—and the poverty and repression that characterized much of twentieth-century Soviet and ECE life was promoted by both those who lived under those regimes and outside observers.

Equally worthy of scrutiny is the way in which brief nineteenth- and early twentieth-century socialist writings were appropriated or distorted. Western theorists such as Joseph A. Schumpeter could declare in *Capitalism, Socialism and Democracy* (1942), that Marxism had, by the twentieth century, become a "message of terrestrial paradise of socialism" ([1942], 1950, 6). In truth, Marx was a relatively marginal figure in actual socialist political engineering. His work was neither the divine herald nor the demonic precursor of socialism—whether idealized or dystopian.

Marx critiqued socialist thought, but his engagement was inconsistent and theoretically limited. If socialism is understood pragmatically—as a system striving for the general welfare of all—then the sharp distinctions Marx and Engels made between "scientific socialism" and the so-called "utopian" thinkers become largely irrelevant. A more humane society might be desirable for moral, aesthetic, or practical reasons—none of which requires a "scientific" foundation. By this standard, the theoretical foundation of scientific socialism is shaky at best. What remains is Engels's articulation of socialism in *Anti-Dühring* (*1878*) and Marx's brief, transitional description in *Critique of the Gotha Program* (*1875*), where socialism appears only as a halfway stage between capitalism and communism.

The question, then, remains: What is socialism, and how can it be defined?

Following the Bolshevik—or October—Revolution, the term "socialism" began its long emancipation from the communist statist project. Within Soviet Russia, it was rendered meaningless by authoritarian rule, despite its rhetorical use. True socialism requires at least minimal democratic structures and

 | DOI:10.1163/9789004747210_005

basic economic welfare—conditions entirely absent in the Soviet regime. In the U.S.S.R, to recall John Thelwall in 1796, workers could only claim "food, and rags, and a wretched hammock with a poor rug to cover it; [while] working eight-twelve [...] hours a day, six days of seven, from six to sixty."[1] Outside the Soviet empire, however, socialism continued to evolve—as a theory of social justice and a reform-oriented party platform advocating parliamentary change as an end in itself.

Nevertheless, despite ample evidence of Stalinist atrocities, socialism came to be identified with the so-called "transitional" society that violently upheld state power while claiming to pursue future social justice. That this transitional regime functioned as a militarized dictatorship—lacking any meaningful social justice agenda—should have ended the discussion. Yet, as of this writing, the Soviet and ECE model of ersatz socialism continues to dominate public understanding of the term. A century of authoritarian rule—marked by centralized economic and political control, and absent any egalitarian outcomes—is still misrepresented as socialism.

A significant exception to this confusion is *The Cambridge History of Socialism* (2023), which offers a broad critical survey of socialist thought, movements, and practice. As its editors note, prior histories have often fallen short in at least one of four ways: by focusing almost exclusively on Europe and its settler colonies; by narrowing their scope to only a few cases; by overlooking grassroots social movements; or by neglecting gender as an analytical category. In contrast, this two-volume work draws on scholars from six continents and engages deeply with anarchism, syndicalism, social democracy, labor, the New Left, and trajectories in the Global South.[2]

Its first volume's editor, Van der Linden, is right to suggest that the history of socialism is broader and more nuanced than previously acknowledged. While *The Cambridge History of Socialism* does not explicitly frame itself as

1 John Thelwall, The Rights of Nature Against the Usurpations of Establishments ... p. 15 (1796) in Marcel Van Der Linden, Introduction to Volume 1, in 1 *The Cambridge History of Socialism* (Marcel Van Der Linden, ed.), 5 (2023).

2 "Countless historical accounts, in the form of both national case studies and international surveys, have been authored on each and every trajectory. In spite of their real achievements, these works generally suffer from at least one of four weaknesses: they focus almost exclusively on Europe and its settler colonies; they focus only on a subset of cases; they neglect the social movement aspect; and/or they neglect the gender aspect. Nor are the histories of state-negating and sate transforming socialisms usually seen holistically—unlike in the past, when memories of the 'schism' were still vivid."

MARCEL VAN DER LINDEN, Introduction to Volume 1, in 1 *The Cambridge History of Socialism*, 26 (MARCEL VAN DER LINDEN, ed., 2023)

a corrective to misinformation, its breadth and analytical depth implicitly challenge decades of academic and political distortion—particularly that promoted by Soviet regimes and echoed globally. The effect is a slow destabilization of the received narrative—much like this book seeks to do—by emphasizing that capitalism can thrive under dictatorship, and that monopolies, whether corporate or state-run, often pave the way for authoritarianism. In such systems, reflective thought flickers like a candle in a wind tunnel—present, but unsustainable.

This epistemic tension—between flattening abstraction and lived, material specificity—is also central to how Marx's metaphorical language is understood. One is reminded not just of Marx's *Gallerte*—his jarring and ironic term for undifferentiated human labor—but also of how metaphor and translation shape the very frameworks through which we interpret labor, value, and ideology.[3] In *The Bourgeois Charm of Karl Marx* (Brill, 2020), I explored how Marx used food terminology—such as *Gallerte* (gelatin)—to express key socio-economic and legal concepts. *Gallerte* is not merely metaphor; it is embedded irony. It directs the reader away from abstraction toward a sensorial, visual register. Marx's use of this term marks a deliberate critique of abstraction itself: work becomes subsistence for the lower classes and an object of bourgeois revulsion. I wrote there, "*Gallerte* indicates subsistence for the lower classes and repulsive frowning by the upper social echelons" (Neacșu, 2020, 122).

This choice of imagery reflects Marx's broader methodological insistence—elaborated by Bhikhu Parekh (1982)—that concepts like "property as such" are useless abstractions without socio-economic grounding. In this light, *Gallerte* is not an accident of diction but a necessity of critique. It expresses the transformation of labor into something consumable, processed, and indistinct—akin, I was opining in 2020 to Spam (Special Processed American Meat), which could serve as a culturally resonant English-language equivalent. Yet, as Sutherland (2011) points out, the English translation of *Gallerte* has often been sanitized, losing the pungency of its original metaphor. This flattening in translation is no mere linguistic slip—it mirrors the broader philosophical risk of rendering radical critique inert through abstraction.

Much like American jurisprudence has often turned complex European philosophical roots into conceptually gelatinous frameworks, Marx's original critique has too frequently become *Gallerte* in its own right—ironic, unrecognizable, and diluted. From that perspective the Regime of Truth that governs

3 "Abstrakt menschliche Arbeit [is a] bloße *Gallerte* unterschiedsloser menschlicher Arbeit. Human labor in the abstract [is a] mere *congelation* of human labor."
NEACȘU, 2020, 122, quoting SUTHERLAND, 2011, 39; emphasis added

academic and ideological production can only be contested by recovering any metaphor's material anchoring. In this regard, *The Cambridge History* succeeds by reintroducing texture where ideology had imposed smoothness. It challenges abstraction by recovering specificity—about power structure and political regimes, and about the material and metaphorical stakes of how we tell history itself.

The twentieth century was not the century of tried-and-failed socialism. It was the century of tried-and-failed ersatz socialism. As this book further clarifies.

CHAPTER 4

Government and Politics

All societies organize themselves politically, economically, and legally. As Wayne, MacKenzie, O'Brien, and Cole explain to American college students, the term politics originates from the Greek word *polis*—the ancient city-state, which represented the foundational unit of organized society (Wayne et al., 1997). From small municipalities to entire nations, people have devised various systems of governance to structure communal life.

Government serves as the framework—or scaffolding—through which authority is distributed and exercised to achieve the goals deemed essential for a society's survival and development. These goals vary, but most include securing borders, maintaining order, and promoting the welfare of citizens. While border security may rely on military force, national well-being encompasses broader objectives, such as education, healthcare, infrastructure, and even cultural enrichment.

Pursuing these aims requires political decision-making: the creation and implementation of policies that determine how a society's limited resources will be allocated. In this way, politics becomes the practical mechanism by which government organizes society.

One way to conceptualize the role of government—both in service to the people and as an authority over them—is through the image of Thomas Hobbes's *Leviathan*: a sovereign power created by individuals to protect them from chaos, yet powerful enough to command obedience. This metaphor remains useful when adapted to various political systems, helping us understand how different forms of governance balance authority, responsibility, and the public good.

This image is representative of an absolute monarchy, where a single individual embodies multiple institutions or governmental entities. The crown and elevated position of the sovereign reinforce the notion of centralized power, with all legislative, executive, and judicial authority concentrated in one ruler.

The towering figure, composed of countless smaller human bodies (Figure 7), visually expresses Hobbes's concept of the social contract—the idea that individuals surrender certain freedoms in exchange for collective order and protection under a sovereign power.

Symbolically, the sword in the sovereign's right hand represents military and executive authority, while the crozier in the left hand signals religious legitimacy and control over civil and spiritual life. Hobbes recognized that people

 | DOI:10.1163/9789004747210_006

FIGURE 7 Abraham Bosse, frontispiece to Thomas Hobbes's *Leviathan* (1651)
SOURCE: HOBBES, THOMAS. 1651. *LEVIATHAN*. FRONTISPIECE BY ABRAHAM BOSSE. LONDON: ANDREW CROOKE

may relinquish their freedoms, but only to a ruler whose authority they perceive as legitimate. And like all theories, concepts, or constructs, legitimacy too is dynamic—subject to cultural shifts, political change, and evolving notions of justice and governance.

1 Democracy Begins in Conversation

Commonsense understanding about democracy is perhaps best understood if we recall John Dewey's belief in democracy as a social process rooted in mutual engagement and concern for shared outcomes. Dewey did not say that "democracy begins in conversation" in his seminal *The Public and Its Problems* (1927), but the phrase captures best the essence of his thinking. For Dewey, democracy isn't just a system of government—it's a way of life. Democracy "remains barren and empty save as it is incarnated in human relationships" (Dewey, 1927, 143). It must reach into every corner of social life—family, school, work, religion—not just the ballot box. And "[i]n this sense the cure for the ailments of democracy is more democracy" (Id., 146).

This vision is essential for any meaningful democracy. It's not enough to simply refine political machinery—more elections, more bureaucracies, more voting. Dewey argues that "more democracy" means returning to the idea itself: building a society rooted in shared purpose, mutual recognition, and collective problem-solving, or exactly what the Bolshevik uprising never delivered.

Dewey's insight points toward a democracy built from the ground up—through schools, neighborhoods, and workplaces that train people not just to obey, but to actively participate. Just as democratic forms arose from changing material conditions—not from abstract doctrines—democracy must grow from lived experience, not rigid blueprints.

In short: democracy needs Dewey's vision—not as procedure, but as a culture of participation, inquiry, and care.

What makes a government democratic is citizen participation in the process of governing at the local and national levels. Civic engagement is an important feature of democracy, and it is often perceived in legal terms as the right of the people to govern themselves. This right is exercised through the right to vote and hold office. Parliamentary or presidential democracies, like democratic monarchies, which incorporated Locke's and subsequently Montesquieu's principle of separation of governmental powers, were founded on some type of civic engagement.[1]

Starting with John Locke's *Two Treatises of Government* (1690), the legislative power of the government, the branch responsible for the legal system of any government, is envisaged as both a grant from the people and separated from the executive branch:

> The power of the Legislative being derived from the People by a positive voluntary Grant ... It may be too great a temptation to human frailty apt to grasp at power, for the same persons who have the power of making laws to have also in their hands the power to execute them.[2]

1 "The Celebrated Montesquieu," as Publius referenced him in *the Federalist* No. XLVII, on The Particular Structure of the New Government and the Distribution of Power Among Its Different Parts, (Friday, February 1, 1788), Charles-Louis de Secondat, baron de la Brède et de Montesquieu's works which contain his views on the separation of powers are: *Persian Letters* (1721), *Considerations on the Causes of the Greatness of the Romans and of their Decline* (1733), and *The Spirit of the Laws* (1748).

2 John Locke, *Second Treatise*, §§ 141;143 (1689), https://www.gutenberg.org/files/7370/7370-h/7370-h.htm.

But, is that enough? For 25 centuries, democracy has been discussed, debated, supported, attacked, ignored, established, practiced, destroyed, and then sometimes reestablished. As Robert A. Dahl tells it, despite this impressive long existence, there is no agreement on some of the most fundamental questions about democracy. "Ironically, the very fact that democracy has such a lengthy history has actually contributed to confusion and disagreement, for 'democracy' has meant different things to different people at different times and places" (Dahl, 2020, 3).

The principle of separation of powers, further championed by Baron de Montesquieu (Charles-Louis de Secondat) in his seminal work, *The Spirit of the Laws* (*De l'Esprit des Lois*, 1748), has been incorporated into the U.S. Constitution, in Articles I[3] and II[4]. To those branches, add the judiciary (Art. III).[5] Thus, American democracy seems to meet all the theoretical criteria, as civic engagement is reflected in both the legislative and executive branch, whose legal foundations lay in Article I and Article II. So, can we say that the U.S. has always been a democracy from the American Revolution onward? Or even more specifically, "democracy in a republic;" as Abraham Lincoln called it, or as French aristocrat Alexis de Tocqueville referenced it in *Democracy in America*, even as some males were perceived to represent "three fifths of all other Persons,"[6] and women did not matter? And didn't the Athenians call

3 Article I. Section 1: See Appendix B. *Constitution of the United States*, https://constitution.congress.gov/constitution/article-1/.

4 Article II. Section 1: See Appendix B. *Constitution of the United States*, https://constitution.congress.gov/constitution/article-2/.

5 Article III. Sections 1–3: See Appendix B. *Constitution of the United States*, https://constitution.congress.gov/constitution/article-3/.

6 Article I. Section 2, Clause 3. See Appendix B. *Constitution of the United States*, https://constitution.congress.gov/browse/article-1/section-2/clause-3/.

"The 14th Amendment to the U.S. Constitution: Civil Rights (1868) was passed by Congress on June 13, 1866, and ratified July 9, 1868. The 14th Amendment extended liberties and rights granted by the Bill of Rights to formerly enslaved people. Specifically, section Two of the 14th Amendment repealed the three-fifths clause of Article I, Section 2, Clause 3 of the original Constitution, which counted enslaved people as three-fifths of a person for the purpose of apportioning congressional representation. With slavery outlawed by the 13th Amendment, this clarified that all residents, regardless of race, should be counted as one whole person. This section also guaranteed that all male citizens over age 21, no matter their race, had a right to vote.

AMENDMENT XIV

Section 1.

All persons born or naturalized in the United States, and subject to the jurisdiction thereof, are citizens of the United States and of the State wherein they reside. No State shall make or enforce any law which shall abridge the privileges or immunities of citizens of the United States; nor shall any State deprive any person of life, liberty, or property,

their system a democracy in the fifth century BCE? And what about the Roman republic? Both were based, like our republic until the end of the Civil War and the passage of the Fourteenth Amendment, on slavery.

In 1947, Winston Churchill, the Prime Minister of the United Kingdom during World War II, told a session of Parliament that "democracy is the worst form of government except [for] all the others that have been tried from time

---

without due process of law; nor deny to any person within its jurisdiction the equal protection of the laws.
Section 2.
Representatives shall be apportioned among the several States according to their respective numbers, counting the whole number of persons in each State, excluding Indians not taxed. But when the right to vote at any election for the choice of electors for President and Vice-President of the United States, Representatives in Congress, the Executive and Judicial officers of a State, or the members of the Legislature thereof, is denied to any of the male inhabitants of such State, being twenty-one years of age, and citizens of the United States, or in any way abridged, except for participation in rebellion, or other crime, the basis of representation therein shall be reduced in the proportion which the number of such male citizens shall bear to the whole number of male citizens twenty-one years of age in such State.
Section 3.
No person shall be a Senator or Representative in Congress, or elector of President and Vice-President, or hold any office, civil or military, under the United States, or under any State, who, having previously taken an oath, as a member of Congress, or as an officer of the United States, or as a member of any State legislature, or as an executive or judicial officer of any State, to support the Constitution of the United States, shall have engaged in insurrection or rebellion against the same, or given aid or comfort to the enemies thereof. But Congress may by a vote of two-thirds of each House, remove such disability.
Section 4.
The validity of the public debt of the United States, authorized by law, including debts incurred for payment of pensions and bounties for services in suppressing insurrection or rebellion, shall not be questioned. But neither the United States nor any State shall assume or pay any debt or obligation incurred in aid of insurrection or rebellion against the United States, or any claim for the loss or emancipation of any slave; but all such debts, obligations and claims shall be held illegal and void.
Section 5.
The Congress shall have power to enforce, by appropriate legislation, the provisions of this article. (emphasis added)"

https://www.archives.gov/milestone-documents/14th-amendment#:~:text=Section%202.,State%2C%20excluding%20Indians%20not%20taxed

Section 5 of 14th Amendment gave Congress power to pass laws to safeguard the sweeping provisions of Section 1, in particular, the 14th Amendment. Thus, it effectively altered the balance of power between the federal and state governments in the United States. Congress used this authority to pass landmark civil rights legislation, including the *Civil Rights Act of 1964*, Pub. L 88–352, and the *Voting Rights Act of 1965*, Pub. L. 89–110.

FIGURE 8 A visual paraphrase of the branches of government, synthesizing Hobbes' absolutism with Locke's division of powers
SOURCE: NEACȘU, DANA. 2025. ORIGINAL IMAGE DRAWN BY THE AUTHOR AND REFINED USING OPENAI'S CHATGPT (MODEL O4-MINI-HIGH)

to time" (Kaplan, 2014). Churchill was paraphrasing Aristotle, if we remember the preface to this book.

So, why the attraction? If visuals help, Figure 8 is an image incorporating the Hobbesian style of government and including all governing bodies mentioned by the U.S. constitution, including the press.

So, what exactly is it that we expect from democracies that tyrannies cannot offer? The attraction of democracy is that it raises possibilities for creating what the nineteenth-century British philosopher Jeremy Bentham called "the greatest happiness for the greatest number." In the Fifth Section, entitled Radical Parliamentary Reform in his *Plan of Parliamentary Reform*, Jeremy

Bentham explained his views on the role of government. He expected a democratic government based on popular representation to pave the way for the "maximum … of comfort and security" for all (1838–43, III, 452). "The ultimate advancement of the universal interest," according to Bentham, is "the state of a maximum whatsoever residuum of comfort and security" and "without any exception, all to be considered" (Id.)

Or, what Robert A. Dahl called the "principle of ordinary people" who "are capable of governing themselves," which assumes that democracy presumes people care about and trust one another enough to collectively govern and protect shared interests (Dahl, 1998). As such, "the key characteristic of democracy is its continuing responsiveness of the government to the preferences of its citizens, considered as political equals" (Id).

The assumption is that ordinary people care about all people. Exposed to diverse ideas, people reasoning together can find and promote solutions for achieving peace, justice, and social benefits for all. Democracy rests on input from most of the governed. It is not easy to maintain, as it is always close to implode from practices which always need to be updated and represent the needs of the people, always in flux. Hence, democracy is always being recreated and protected. The governed are given the responsibility to protect it and defend it from extinction.

Representative governments, given their philosophical explanation and practical implementation, are supposed to be the most conducive of social justice policies. Therefore, socialism requires representative governments, supported by understanding of politics and what is needed to implement social justice politics. American political scientists, such as Robert S. Erikson and Kent L. Tedin, would connote the actuation of political commonsense knowledge and understanding with "popular sentiment" (Erikson & Tedin, 2001, 7) or public opinion.

2 Oligarchy and Dictatorship

Our democracy rests on two Madisonian principles explained in Federalist No. 10 and Federalist No. 51: we believe in the majority deciding who governs us and in a government of checks and balances.

> It may be a reflection on human nature, that such devices [checks and balances] should be necessary to control the abuses of government. But what is government itself, but the greatest of all reflections on human nature? If men were angels, no government would be necessary. If angels

> were to govern men, neither external nor internal controls on government would be necessary. In framing a government which is to be administered by men over men, the great difficulty lies in this: you must first enable the government to control the governed; and in the next place oblige it to control itself. A dependence on the people is, no doubt, the primary control on the government; but experience has taught mankind the necessity of auxiliary precautions.[7]

Not everyone needs to participate in the works of the government, but everyone's voice needs to be heard. Democracy is both a practice and a goal, and perhaps its most basic principle is that political power is not an appendix of the economic elite, to be used according to the dictates of some dictator. That form of government would be an oligarchy,[8] or, according to the recently pundit-coined terminology, a "broligarchy,[9]" which is meant to represent, in Biden's words, "an oligarchy" of the "tech industrial complex" whose "extreme wealth, power, and influence … threatens our entire democracy.[10]" Its head would be a dictator.

While not a friend of democracies, which he viewed as promoting the interests of the poor, Aristotle, as demonstrated in his *Politics*, made a compelling case against both dictatorships, or tyranny, and oligarchy. They were both forms of government which disregarded "common advantage" (*koinê sumpheron*) or the public good, which in this book remains the main reason to promote democracy as the best form of government.[11]

---

7 James Madison, Federalist No. 51 (1788), in *The Federalist Papers*, ed. Clinton Rossiter (New York: Signet Classics, 2003), 320–322.

8 Daron Acemoglu, Oligarchic versus Democratic Societies. *Journal of the European Economic Association*, March 2008 6(1): 1–44.

9 Scott Roxborough, "Who Will Stand Up to Trump's Broligarchs?" *The Hollywood Reporter*, January 29, 2025, https://www.hollywoodreporter.com/business/business-news/trump-musk-zuckerberg-bezos-tech-bros-1236121204/.

10 Scott Roxborough, "Who Will Stand Up to Trump's Broligarchs?" *The Hollywood Reporter*, January 29, 2025, https://www.hollywoodreporter.com/business/business-news/trump-musk-zuckerberg-bezos-tech-bros-1236121204/.

11 Aristotle's Political Theory, *Stanford Encyclopedia of Philosophy* (First published Wed Jul 1, 1998; substantive revision Fri Jul 1, 2022), https://plato.stanford.edu/entries/aristotle-politics/.

"But what exactly the "common advantage" (koinê sumpheron) entails is a matter of scholarly controversy. Some passages imply that justice involves the advantage of all the citizens; for example, every citizen of the best constitution has a just claim to private property and to an education (Pol. VII.9.1329a23–4, 13.1332a32–8)."

Power is the engine that governs human society. And power by its very essence has an elitist aspect, or at least that is how Weber imagined it. Power for Weber was the capacity to create a desired outcome within a social relationship, and as such it can be concentrated in the hands of a few (the oligarchy) or one (dictatorship) or more widely shared among competing groups (democracy).[12] This type of power is integral to views of power as accumulated capital,[13] though its root is government jobs and government appointments (Cabinet appointments). That oligarchy lives in the shadow of democracies is well evidenced by the second Trump administration, where Cabinet-level advisors can bypass any democratic vetting, no matter how minimal that is. Elon Musk briefly had his own department, called DOGE, although not a Cabinet department. This book rejects this elitist conception of power as contrary to the democratic conception of power. It is a reality that Robert A. Dahl recognized that power is distributed unequally even in democracies. What makes a democracy is the opposite of unequally distributed power. A democracy is not monopolized power by an oligarchy or even a dictator. A democracy is the form of government that contests such unequal distribution of power. Democracy requires a multitude of groups and political actors. In a democracy, citizens do not feel impotent. To the contrary, they organize and engage with the political system through built-in venues: demonstrations, citizen lawsuits, and, of course, elections.

Indeed, there are differences between authoritarian regimes and totalitarian regimes. As Yale Professor Juan Linz (2000) explains, in authoritarian regimes a small group controls power with limited political pluralism, while totalitarian regimes have a monistic center of power. While taxonomic and perhaps lacking nuance, Linz's definition is easier to grasp from a commonsense perspective. The American Trumpian democracy remains a Linzian authoritarian regime, though not totalitarian, like the ECE countries and their mother, Soviet Russia. However, as history showed, Bolshevism could have replaced authoritarian tsarism with a democracy. Instead, it chose an even more authoritarian

---

12 In democracy, the people elect their leader, whom they trust. Then the elected leader says: 'Now shut up and obey.' From then on, the people and the parties are no longer allowed to meddle. Max Weber, "Eine Unterredung mit Erich Ludendorff am 30. Mai 1919" (A conversation with Eric Ludendorff on May 30, 1919), MWG I/16, 553., quoted in Hanke, Edith, 'What about Democracy? Approaches to Max Weber's Political Sociology', in Joshua Derman, and Peter E Gordon (eds), *Max Weber at 100: Legacies and Prospects* (New York, NY, 2025; online edn, Oxford Academic, 11 Nov. 2024), https://doi.org/10.1093/9780197604953.003.0013.

13 André Munro, Power. Britannica, (Last Updated: Jan 14, 2025) https://www.britannica.com/topic/power-political-and-social-science.

regime, a totalitarian dictatorship. In Ancient Rome, something more troublesome happened. The Roman Republic developed its oligarchic tendencies—its Senatorial rule—and transitioned into dictatorship.[14] Our elected president boasted that he would be a dictator in his first day as president, and no one balked at that. That perhaps is the most telling example of our weakening democratic power: when no centers of power contest such assertions or when the contesting voices are relegated to the margins.

As this book wants itself to offer insight to challenge the common misnomer of socialism, incorporating a layered textual and visual approach, here I relied on the iconic frontispiece with the original image from Thomas Hobbes's *Leviathan* (1651), created by Abraham Bosse, a French artist and engraver who worked under Hobbes's direction to visually define a democracy and then an oligarchy. Bosse showed us what a government headed by an absolute sovereign—whether a dictator or Machiavelli's *Prince*—looked like in 1651. The image of the cover of this book is a composite meant to show what Lenin, Trotsky and Stalin thought about their form of government.

If we replace those individualized heads of the government with the state, which is regarded as a corporate entity, then the approach to government is much like running a corporation. This seems to be the trend, given that Donald Trump was (re)elected U.S. President based on his corporate experience. Thus, it may be useful to use an analogy with the way Jeff Bezos described his "nascent had-line leadership strategy" in 1999, when he was Amazon's CEO, and Amazon was an online bookstore: "I asked everyone here to wake up terrified every morning, their sheets drenched in sweat,"[15] Bezos boasted more than a quarter-century ago. What is remarkable is that no one complained. And no government agency found such working conditions troublesome either. Perhaps as a result of this acquiescence, Bezos is now both part of the

14 The Roman Republic was founded in 509 BCE after the last Etruscan king that ruled Rome was overthrown. Rome's next government served as a representative democracy in the form of a republic. At the heart of the Roman Republic was the Senate, a body which had consultative but not legislative powers. Leading the republic were two consuls who were elected by legislative assemblies. They served for one year and, presided over the Roman Senate, and commanded the Roman military. Centuries later, a consul emerged as dictator for life, while previously, dictators were temporary. While this consul/dictator was subsequently assassinated, a nephew avenged him and established himself as the first Roman emperor. Thus, from a representative democracy, through centralization of power, the Roman Empire was born, an entity both maligned and imitated through history from the French Carolingians, through various German empires.

15 Chloe Berger, "Jeff Bezos Revealed His Secret to Amazon's Success 25 Years Ago: 'I asked everyone around here to wake up terrified every morning, their sheets drenched in sweat,'" *Fortune* (May 15, 2024 at 6:59 PM ED), https://fortune.com/2024/05/15/jeff-bezos-revealed-secret-drenched-terrified-sweat/.

economic and political elite of our country, an oligarch, as his presence at the second Trump presidential inauguration shows.[16]

3 Ersatz Socialism Strived as an Authoritative Political Regime

Socialism, as theory and praxis of social justice, requires a democratic government because there cannot be justice without individual agency: justice is both normatively extended at the social level and individually experienced. Otherwise, it is a prison where the prisoners are justly incarcerated.

As Joseph A. Schumpeter reminded us:

> Until about 1916 the relation between socialism and democracy would have seemed quite obvious to most people and to nobody more so than to the accredited exponents of socialist orthodoxy. It would hardly have occurred to anyone to dispute the socialists' claim to membership in the democratic club. Socialists themselves … claimed to be the only true democrats. (1942, 235)

With the Bolshevik Revolution, socialism became a praxis "above the observance of democratic procedure" (Id. 236). That leap of imagination from the realm of possibility to the one of torture was pragmatically understood by the Soviet ruling class which went along with the mandate of mass terrorization. Even the Western intelligentsia went along with equating socialism with the road to serfdom, to paraphrase F.A. Hayek (1944), who quoted de Tocqueville (1848), rather than questioning the nature of the post-Tsarist Russian government:

> Democracy attaches all possible value to each man; socialism makes each man a mere agent, a mere number. Democracy and socialism have nothing in common but one word: equality. But notice the difference: while democracy seeks equality in liberty, socialism seeks equality in restraint and servitude.[17]

16 Andrew Ross Sorkin, Ravi Mattu, Bernhard Warner, Sarah Kessler, Michael J. de la Merced, Lauren Hirsch and Edmund Lee. "The Billionaires' Row at the Inauguration." *The New York Times*, January 21, 2025, https://www.nytimes.com/2025/01/21/business/dealbook/billionaires-trump-zuckerberg-bezos-musk.html.

17 Alexis de Tocqueville, Discours prononcé à l'assemblée constituante le 12 Septembre 1848 sur la question du droit au travail, in *Oeuvres complètes d'Alexis de Tocqueville*, vol. IX, 1866, p. 546, quoted in F.A. Hayek, *The Road to Serfdom*, 25 (1944).

Soviet Russia became socialist overnight when the 1936 Constitution defined its monopoly capitalist state as socialist.[18] The first twelve articles of the Constitution defined the Russian society.[19] Only, its constitution defined its socialist character in authoritarian terms. The Soviets grew out of "the overthrow of the landlords and capitalists" to institute a "dictatorship of the proletariat" (Article 2). The power belonged not to the people, but to them "as represented" by their political representatives (Article 3). Ten articles defined the electoral system.[20] And more telling perhaps, the 1936 Constitution abolished "the exploitation of man by man" (Article 4). Nothing was said about the exploitation of man by corporations, such as the corporate state, which was the only exploitation practiced in Soviet Russia:

> **ARTICLE 2.** The Soviets of Working People's Deputies, which grew and attained strength as a result of the overthrow of the landlords and capitalists and the achievement of the dictatorship of the proletariat, constitute the political foundation of the U.S.S.R.
>
> **ARTICLE 3.** In the U.S.S.R. all power belongs to the working people of town and country as represented by the Soviets of Working People's Deputies.
>
> **ARTICLE 4.** The socialist system of economy and the socialist ownership of the means and instruments of production, firmly established as a result of the abolition of the capitalist system of economy, the abrogation of private ownership of the means and instruments of production and

18 *Constitution (Fundamental law) of the Union of Soviet Socialist Republics*, Kremlin, Moscow, December 5, 1936, in J.V. Stalin, *Works*, Vol. 14, (Red Star Press Ltd., London, 1978) https://www.marxists.org/reference/archive/stalin/works/1936/12/05.htm ("**Chapter I: The Organization of Society. ARTICLE 1.** The Union of Soviet Socialist Republics is a socialist state of workers and peasants.")

19 See, Articles 1–12 from Stalin's Constitution, Appendix A. *Constitution (Fundamental law) of the Union of Soviet Socialist Republics*, Kremlin, Moscow, December 5, 1936, in J.V. Stalin, *Works*, Vol. 14, (Red Star Press Ltd., London, 1978) https://www.marxists.org/reference/archive/stalin/works/1936/12/05.htm.

20 See Articles 134–142, Stalin's Constitution, Appendix A. *Constitution (Fundamental law) of the Union of Soviet Socialist Republics*, Kremlin, Moscow, December 5, 1936, in J.V. Stalin, *Works*, Vol. 14, (Red Star Press Ltd., London, 1978) https://www.marxists.org/reference/archive/stalin/works/1936/12/05.htm ("**Chapter I: The Organization of Society. ARTICLE 1.** The Union of Soviet Socialist Republics is a socialist state of workers and peasants.")

the abolition of the exploitation of man by man, constitute the economic foundation of the U.S.S.R.[21]

Moreover, of 145 constitutional articles, 87, or 60 percent of the constitutional articles detailed state authority at the federal and state level.[22] Of the twelve articles which contained the fundamental rights of the Russian citizens,[23] one is about the rights of foreigners to seek political asylum in Russia, and the three below (Articles 124–126) read like indoctrination of the working people to make them docile, as a condition to survival. In addition, four more defined their fundamental duties.[24]

ARTICLE 124. In order to ensure to citizens freedom of conscience, the church in the U.S.S.R. is separated from the state, and the school from the church. Freedom of religious worship and freedom of anti-religious propaganda is recognized for all citizens.

ARTICLE 125. In conformity with the interests of the working people, and in order to strengthen the socialist system, the citizens of the U.S.S.R. are guaranteed by law: a) freedom of speech; b) freedom of the press; c) freedom of assembly, including the holding of mass meetings; d) freedom of street processions and demonstrations; These civil rights are ensured

21 See Stalin's Constitution, Appendix A. *Constitution (Fundamental law) of the Union of Soviet Socialist Republics*, Kremlin, Moscow, December 5, 1936, in J.V. Stalin, *Works*, Vol. 14, (Red Star Press Ltd., London, 1978) https://www.marxists.org/reference/archive/stalin/works/1936/12/05.htm.

22 See, Articles 30–117, Stalin's Constitution, Appendix A. *Constitution (Fundamental law) of the Union of Soviet Socialist Republics*, Kremlin, Moscow, December 5, 1936, in J.V. Stalin, *Works*, Vol. 14, (Red Star Press Ltd., London, 1978) https://www.marxists.org/reference/archive/stalin/works/1936/12/05.htm ("**Chapter I: The Organization of Society. ARTICLE 1.** The Union of Soviet Socialist Republics is a socialist state of workers and peasants.")

23 See Articles 118–129, Stalin's Constitution, Appendix A. *Constitution (Fundamental law) of the Union of Soviet Socialist Republics*, Kremlin, Moscow, December 5, 1936, in J.V. Stalin, *Works*, Vol. 14, (Red Star Press Ltd., London, 1978) https://www.marxists.org/reference/archive/stalin/works/1936/12/05.htm ("**Chapter I: The Organization of Society. ARTICLE 1.** The Union of Soviet Socialist Republics is a socialist state of workers and peasants.")

24 See Articles 130–133, Stalin's Constitution, Appendix A. *Constitution (Fundamental law) of the Union of Soviet Socialist Republics*, Kremlin, Moscow, December 5, 1936, in J.V. Stalin, *Works*, Vol. 14, (Red Star Press Ltd., London, 1978) https://www.marxists.org/reference/archive/stalin/works/1936/12/05.htm ("**Chapter I: The Organization of Society. ARTICLE 1.** The Union of Soviet Socialist Republics is a socialist state of workers and peasants.")

> by placing at the disposal of the working people and their organizations printing presses, stocks of paper, public buildings, the streets, communications facilities and other material requisites for the exercise of these rights.
>
> **ARTICLE 126.** In conformity with the interests of the working people, and in order to develop the organizational initiative and political activity of the masses of the people, citizens of the U.S.S.R. are ensured the right to unite in public organizations—trade unions, cooperative associations, youth organizations, sport and defence organizations, cultural, technical and scientific societies; and the most active and politically most conscious citizens in the ranks of the working class and other sections of the working people unite in the Communist Party of the Soviet Union (Bolsheviks), which is the vanguard of the working people in their struggle to strengthen and develop the socialist system and is the leading core of all organizations of the working people, both public and state.[25]

Also, those so-called rights have long been known "to force the people to embrace something that is believed to be good ... but which they do not actually want ... is the very hallmark of antidemocratic belief" (Schumpeter, 237). Practically, the history is filled with testimonials that the Soviet regime was antidemocratic. "Stalinism is worse than fascism, more ruthless, barbarous, unjust, immoral, [and] antidemocratic," (1940, 82) wrote once noted Marxist Max Eastman.

And yet, perhaps because of those written words, the world could not agree that the Bolshevik regime was not socialist, that it was a dictatorship, an antidemocratic regime antithetic to socialism. Bolshevik theory, despite the ambiguously written words of its 1936 Constitution, was not socialist, and neither the method, "the thing," its implementation, the praxis.

There were caveats, of course. Bertrand Russell. Another exception to the rule is Michael Harrington' *Socialism. Past & Future* (1989). Harrington did not engage in the negation of the very possibility of socialism.[26] However, he brought the theory and praxis of Soviet dictatorship to is logical conclusion: the impossibility of socialist praxis in Soviet Russia and the ECE in the absence of a democratic system (Harrington, 1989). Plainer perhaps in his magnificent

---

25 See, Stalin's Constitution, Appendix A. *Constitution (Fundamental law) of the Union of Soviet Socialist Republics*, Kremlin, Moscow, December 5, 1936, in J.V. Stalin, *Works*, Vol. 14, (Red Star Press Ltd., London, 1978) https://www.marxists.org/reference/archive/stalin/works/1936/12/05.htm.

26 Harrington's "visionary gradualism" in bringing about a socialist agenda, is being contested by other scholars, such as Doug Greene, *A Failure of Vision: Michael Harrington and the Limits of Democratic Socialism* (London: Zero Books, 2022).

work *Critique & Praxis* (2020), Bernard Harcourt describes the historical "soviet conjecture" as an alternative to liberal capitalism, but given the Stalinist shadow, it could only amass to "the absence of an attractive socialist alternative" (Harcourt, 2020, 237). And the recent Cambridge University Press global overview of socialism skips over the Russian and ECE experiment.[27]

It is worth noting that even apologists such as V.S. Pozdnyakov and O.N. Sadikov could not bring themselves to say anything more about the Soviet form of government than "the USSR is a federated state which unites the sovereign Union Republics."[28]

Unfortunately, both mass media and educational outlets promote confusion between what represents the political structure of a society and its economic system, although they can coexist only because of the glue of the legal system itself. For instance, it is common knowledge to think that democracy, representative governments, and capitalism are all codependent. Thus:

> Many Americans tend to equate democracy, a political system in which people govern themselves, with capitalism. In theory, a democratic government promotes individualism and the freedom to act as one chooses instead of being controlled, for good or bad, by government. Capitalism, in turn, relies on individualism. At the same time, successful capitalists prefer political systems over which they can exert at least some influence in order to maintain their liberty. (Krutz & Waskiewicz, 2021, 8)

This confusion between the form of government and the economic foundation of society is perhaps the reason behind the ersatz socialism of Soviet Russia and its European empire in the ECE. For instance, in his Rice University endorsed OpenStax book on American Government, Professors Glen Krutz and Sylvie Waskiewicz state:

> Socialism is an alternative economic system. In socialist societies, the means of generating wealth, such as factories, large farms, and banks, are owned by the government and not by private individuals. The government accumulates wealth and then redistributes it to citizens, primarily in the form of social programs that provide such things as free or inexpensive health care, education, and childcare. (Id.)

27 Neither volume of the two-volume tome of 1–2 *The Cambridge History of Socialism* (Marcel Van Der Linden, ed., 2023) 1 *The Cambridge History of Socialism* (Marcel Van Der Linden, ed., 2023) includes the soviet dictatorships in their historical global survey.

28 O.N. Sadikov, General Characteristics of the USSR Legal System, in *USSR Contract Law*, 9 (V.S. Pozdbyakov, ed., 1982).

Krutz and Waskiewicz correctly address the property in the Soviet empire as being owned by the state, though they stop there. They might have chosen to continue their analysis with who benefited from that form of ownership. They do not. They do continue:

> In socialist countries, the government also usually owns and controls utilities such as electricity, transportation systems like airlines and railroads, and telecommunications systems. In many socialist countries the government is an oligarchy: only members of a certain political party or ruling elite can participate in government. For example, in China, the government is run by members of the Chinese Communist Party. (Id.)

Based on the quote above, it's ambiguous whether Krutz and Waskiewicz envision their socialist government as democratic or an oligarchy. This raises a crucial question: can socialism truly exist under an oligarchic system? In other words, can social justice be limited to "free or inexpensive health care, education, and childcare"? It reads more like freedoms in a prison, albeit a humane one, but I doubt that one could equate prison with social justice.

Such examples can continue.

One of the clearest, best supported, and most accessible work on socialism as a thing and concept, praxis and theory, remains Michael Harrington's *Socialism. Past & Future* (1989). Only Harrington starts from the position that "socialism is a temporary dictatorship of party-state based on nationalized heavy industry as a means of overcoming economic backwardness" (Id., 62). Indeed, the Soviet planetary system with Russia as its star and the other ECE Soviet planets basking in the same dictatorial light was supported by state monopolies. Harrington noted the "intolerable irony that societies that are anything but socialist should thus define what socialism is in the eyes of so many. It is an irony that has to be undone" (Id., 60).

Politically, antisocialist socialism was long denounced by both Marx and Engels, as briefly discussed above, when in *The Communist Manifesto*, they denounced all four types of "socialism." Only Soviet Russia did not fit any of the four types. So, what type of antisocialist socialism is the ECE and Russian "socialism"? It's own.

Fundamentally, as Harrington noted, the Soviet people were never included in the Soviet social contract in any other capacity but its workforce. Lenin and the Bolsheviks were able to maintain their power once conquered militarily by opposing the Russian World War I involvement and promising the partition of the latifundial agricultural land for the benefit of the peasants, once the war ended. Lenin himself acknowledged that the new reality was a continuation of the old society, only with new ruling classes. In 1920, Lenin explained the dissociation between power and people. For him, the socialization of poverty was possible through political oppression exercised by a vanguard of trusted representatives, the "transmission belts."

Lenin's distrust of the masses was on display when he called representative democracies illusions. For him, the backward masses could not know their true objective interest and be able to make a political choice as the voting booth (Harrington, 1989, 67). Perhaps this distrust excused both the invention of the party bureaucrats, the "transmission belts," the Soviet ruling class, helped by the military and paramilitary state agencies, and the praxis of dictatorship. Russell's *Bolshevism* clarified that Lenin equated parliamentary democracy with capitalism, and proletarian dictatorships with socialism. This equation served his power and soon Stalin's and the other Soviet dictators'.

Until four decades ago, Eastern Europe (ECE) was forced to be increasingly aware of the lengthening Russian shadow, and for most of the twentieth century, those countries fell into the Russian zone of "geographic and political security and interests" (Benes, 1969, 6). From 1945 until the fall of the Berlin Wall, "the Soviet government's security designs have clearly included all of the small Danubian-Balkan states (Id.)."[29] Poland, East Germany, Czechoslovakia, Hungary, Romania, and Bulgaria became satellite states, and their form of government matched the Soviet model.

> After WWII the Soviet influence [continued] as a slavish imitation by those aforementioned countries. During the Stalinist period of total, monolithic control (1944–1953), the U.S.S.R succeeded first in transplanting and then proliferating Soviet Russian governmental, bureaucratic, police repression, and economic patterns of operation in a wholesale manner. ... Stalin's carefully planned "revolutions from above" systematically and ruthlessly destroyed the major, native political forces, such as members of the liberal middle class or of valorous peasant groups, which might have offered resistance to Communism. ... Soviet impulses, radiated from Moscow, were promptly received and translated into local action by the Warsaw, Budapest, Bucharest, or Sofia exponents of Stalinism ... Nor did the death of Stalin interrupt this process. (Id., 10–11)

During the latter half of he 20th century, the concept of proletarian dictatorship slowly waned out from the political vocabulary, while the cult of

29 For a map of that sphere of the satellite countries, see, *Id.* p. vi.

personality expanded. It developed with the totalitarian powers reposing on one man, who shared them with various degrees of collective power given to the local ECE variations of Politburo, further appending any social contract at work.

Soviet Russia did not know democracy. Each Soviet and ECE dictator was called president but their people never voted. The people stamped over the name of the single candidate often already in power.

There is no lack of information about the authoritarian regime, the military, and paramilitary oligarchy in each Soviet country. That aspect of the common knowledge about the Soviet political regime is well documented. The only problematic nature of that common knowledge is its use. It nourishes a public sentiment about socialism as a cynical dictatorship. Instead, it should nourish a public sentiment about what happens when democracy dies and capitalism stops being governed by a democratic regime and instead it is replaced by autocratic regimes whose transmission belts are named Bezos, Musk, Trump, or any other equivalent of the Soviet state. Socialism, as theory and praxis of social justice requires political freedom for all to support civil engagement by all for all. Socialism requires democracies. And democracies require social justice.

CHAPTER 5

State Corporate Capitalism as the Most Profitable Illiberal Economic Policy

One of the reasons behind this book is the belief that our liberal or social democracy is in grave danger because of our leaders' little understanding of how integral political, legal, and economic matters truly are. This book argues that capitalism comes in many flavors, and a fundamental characteristic of its current form is the concentration of capital—monopolization—at the expense of a socialized distribution of profit. Liberal democracies have fought against the socialization of poverty, and, until recently, government programs have been able to ensure a modicum level of dignified living for all. However, capitalism is driven by profit, and more profit means less owners. The most efficient way to monopolize profit is to ensure one corporate owner. Soviet Russia and its ECE satellites have shown the way: the state is the ultimate corporate owner. Also, that ownership did not diminish the returns for those in charge. Only the producing masses suffered from extreme poverty. The trend is clear with what the American mass-media coined as "Trump's Broligarchs":[1] fewer corporate monopolies will rule the production and the market. So much centralization can only end in state monopoly under corporate capitalism.

Thinkers tend to simplify reality and bring it under one umbrella concept—and so do all capitalist economists. For Marx, the defining feature of capitalism was the extraction of surplus value, which he sees as the basis of capitalist exploitation.[2] Rudolf Hilferding, whose economic theory influenced Lenin's, stated that the aim of capitalist production is ever more profit, attainable through a capitalist contradiction: competition annihilation. For Lenin, who was both an economic and political thinker defined by conflict, takeover, domination, obliteration, and conquest—or the more romantically palatable revolution—corporate monopoly capital is the goal. The state will own

---

1 Scott Roxborough "Who Will Stand Up to Trump's Broligarchs?" *The Hollywood Reporter*, January 29, 2025, https://www.hollywoodreporter.com/business/business-news/trump-musk-zuckerberg-bezos-tech-bros-1236121204/ ("As Elon Musk and his billionaire brethren take power in Trump's second term, the lack of legal guardrails—and the fading power of Big Media—is becoming an existential crisis.")

2 Karl Marx, *The Capital*, Chapters 7–11 (Samuel Moore & Edward Aveling, Trans. Frederick Engels, Editor, 1887) https://www.marxists.org/archive/marx/works/1867-c1/index.htm.

 | DOI:10.1163/9789004747210_007

everything, "lands, natural deposits, waters, forests." Lenin shortly qualifies the state ownership: "that is, belong to the whole people."[3]

But isn't that exactly what everyone believes socialist economy is? A state-governed and planned economy? And that was the genius of Lenin and those surrounding him? They were able to understand how flexible capitalism is and how everyone takes whatever they like from it: as a concept and a system.

Or, paraphrasing a Lacan lecture on Trotsky's wishful dream about Lenin being dead and not knowing it, only Lenin seemed to know how alive capitalism is and how dead "his immense social experiment he single-handedly brought into being" was.[4]

That is, the very essence of profit or Marx's absolute value—what is created from nothing and taken away from those creating it—was the essence of Lenin's experiment. Lenin knew very well that had he worked on a socialist experiment, empowering the workers in a sustainable manner would have been its goal. Instead, as his National Economic Plan showed, authoritarianism, vituperation, and terror were the tools used to drive workers to work the hardest they could, generating sufficient profit to maintain the Bolshevik power structure in place. Profit enabled the few to terrorize the masses. Lenin paved the way and showed the Bezoses of the world how to do it.[5]

---

3 See Article 6. Stalin's Constitution., Appendix A.

4 In Lacan's lecture of January 7, 1959, he discusses Trotsky's 1935 dream about Lenin being dead without him (Lenin) knowing it. Jameson retells it:

"Lenin does not know he is dead: this will be your text and our mystery. He doesn't know that the immense social experiment he single-handedly brought into being (*and which we call Soviet communism* [sic]) has come to an end. He remains full of energy, although dead, and the vituperation expended on him by the living—that he was the originator of the Stalinist terror, that he was an aggressive personality full of hatred, and authoritarian in love with power and totalitarianism, even (worst of all!!) the rediscoverer of the market in his NEP—none of those insults manage to confer a death, or even a second death, upon him. How is it, how can it be, that he still thinks he is alive? And what is our own position here ... what is our own non-knowledge, what is the death from which Lenin shields us? (emphasis added)"

FREDERIC JAMESON, *Valences of the Dialectic* (Verso, 2009) p. 292

5 Bezos uses "terror" to drive profits. Whether it makes a difference about the reason of the terror for some, it does not for me. No worker should work in terror. For whatever reason. It affects one's mental health. And individual productivity, in the long run, therefore, that worker would have to be replaced sooner than otherwise expected.

"But there is no rest for the weary. *I constantly remind our employees to be afraid, to wake up every morning terrified.* Not of our competition, but of our customers. Our customers have made our business what it is, they are the ones with whom we have a relationship, and they are the ones to whom we owe a great obligation. And we consider them to be loyal to us—right up until the second that someone else offers them a better service. (emphasis added)"

1 How Does Non-competitive Capitalism Work?

It goes without saying that capitalism promises the highest profits for the investing capitalist. Obtaining the largest possible profit is the motive of capitalist investment. By default, each capitalist strives not simply to keep pace with the competition, but either to outstrip or destroy it. To do the first, the capitalist needs an above-the-average profit rate to afford investment, which in turn guarantees extra profit. This course of action depends on access to technological development and knowledge of the sectors of production with above average rates of profit. Thorstein Bunde Veblen explained that "the growth of business enterprise rests on the machine technology as its material foundation" (1904, 177).

In other words, the constant influx of capital is essential for profit. It ensures "machine industry," and its result is increased productivity. As Hilferding eloquently demonstrated in his 1910 opus, the image of the early capitalist factory, with its cramped working space and the workers crowded around a few small machines, gave way to the twentieth-century factory with only a few visible workers behind the gigantic frames of automatic machines. Technological development also brought a change in the component elements of constant capital. For example, that would allow the general overhead costs of a steel manufacturing factory, its administration, laboratories, or maintenance engineers, as well as expenditure on necessary reserve machines in a furnace environment, such as blast engines and air heaters, to be spread over a larger output. This is technology and the aim of capitalism: seeking the highest profits brought about the elimination of competition and the concentration of production.

Hilferding wrote about the role of capital association, or trusts. The centralization of capital demanded a mobilization of capital to broaden the extent of the capital which can be associated. Such a cycle demanded continuous reconversion of industrial capital (including fixed capital) into money capital as independent as possible from the actual reflux of capital at the end of the turnover period during which the fixed capital has to function. Technology became viewed as invested capital.

Lenin summarized Hilferding's opus—which he mentions in his introduction to *Imperialism: The Last Stage of Capitalism*[6]—"free competition gives

---

JEFF BEZOS, 1999 letter to Amazon shareholders in JEFF BEZOS and WALTER ISAACSON, "Invent and Wander: The Collected Writings of Jeff Bezos" (2020), available at https://media.corporate-ir.net/media_files/irol/97/97664/reports/Shareholderletter98.pdf

6 "In 1910, there appeared at Vienna the work of the Austrian Marxist, Rudolf Hilferding, *Finance Capital*. In spite of a mistake on the part of the author in the theory of money, and

rise to the concentration of production which, in turn, at a certain stage of development, leads to monopoly" (Lenin, 1917, 16). Lenin incorporated Hilferding's findings and analysis of the centralized stage of capitalism, of the role of trusts and monopolies. He continued Hilferding's work and applied it to Tsarist Russia.

Lenin focused on the historical aspect of economic capitalist centralization and its impact on the development of various capitalist economies.

> [The] development of [capitalist] monopoly commenced with the international decline of industry from 1870 and lasted until just after 1890. [F]rom a European point of view, the end of the development of free competition occurred in the decade 1860–1870. [By then] England completed the construction of its capitalist edifice in the old style. (Id., 19)

From Hilferding Lenin understood the role of centralization of capital, as the most efficient way to ensure the constant influx of capital needed to introduce technology and thus increase productivity. Lenin's work clearly shows his understanding of how centralized capitalism, trusts, cartels, and monopolies work. The higher the concentration of capital, the higher the return of productivity. The mystique of capitalism as free-market economy was dispelled a century ago, and with it, Soviet socialism as the most efficient way to ensure profit returns absent a long phase of capitalist accumulation.

> "The great change commenced with the financial crash of 1873 [and] the ensuing depression ... During the short period of boom from 1880–1890, the system of cartels was widely used to take advantage of the favourable conditions. [T]his short-sighted policy raised prices even quicker and higher ... and nearly all these cartels perished ingloriously in the financial smash. Five years of bad trade and low prices followed, but a new spirit reigned in industry: the depression [was] seen no more than a phase before a new era of prosperity." The movement of 'cartels' entered into its second phase [of] no longer transitory appearances. (Id.)

Lenin viewed monopolies—production and capital concentrated in a small number of firms or a single entity which controls an entire sector or market—as a solution to a lack of capitalist accumulation at a slower rate. Monopolies

---

in spite of his tendency to conciliate Marxism and opportunism, this work is a very valuable attempt at a theoretical analysis, as its sub-title tells us, of "the latest phase of capitalist development.""

LENIN, *Imperialism: The Last Stage of Capitalism* (London, 1917) p. 9

marked a qualitative shift in capitalism from competitive markets to oligopolistic or monopolistic structures. Monopolies exercised a significant control over prices, resources, and production, creating barriers to entry for smaller competitors.

> Cartels have become one of the basic principles of economic activity. One after another they win the realms of production, and first and foremost the working up of raw materials. At the beginning of 1890, the system of cartels had already acquired in the constitution of the coke syndicate on the pattern of which was created the coal syndicate—a technique which it never surpassed. (Id., 21).

Hilferding saw monopolies as the inevitable outcome of capitalism's internal dynamics, where the drive for accumulation and efficiency leads to the consolidation of economic power. Lenin viewed them as a tool to implement a more technologically advanced society. Rather than wait for generations, using legal instruments, his own decrees, small economic entities could be concentrated in mammoth entities producing the technological advancement needed for the success of the new societal organization.

> The remarkable development of industry at the close of the nineteenth century and the crisis of 1900–1903, followed each other in the mining and iron industries at least entirely under the ægis of cartels. And if then it appeared something novel, it has now become evident to the social consciousness that important parts of economic activity are ... no longer in the domain of free competition. (Id.)

In his work on the stages of capitalism, Lenin quotes the report of the American Government Commission on Trusts (H.Doc. 57–182) explaining the reason for cartel-creation: "Their superiority over their competitors finds its cause in the enormous dimensions of their enterprises and in their remarkable technical efficiency."[7] Lenin continues his explanation of the monopolization of the

7 Lenin's quote from *Imperialism*, p. 19, is from the U.S. Industrial Commission (also known as the "American Government Commission on Trusts") which was established in 1898 to investigate the growing power of trusts and monopolies in the American economy: "Their superiority over their competitors finds its cause in the enormous dimensions of their enterprises and in their remarkable technical efficiency." The comprehensive report on trusts and industrial combinations, including recommendations for further federal regulation, which was submitted to Congress in 1901, and it is known as the "Report of the Industrial Commission". H.Doc. 57–182, https://www.govinfo.gov/app/details/SERIALSET-04343_00_00-001-0182-0000.

American economy with examples of the superiority of cartels in creating and implementing technology.

> The tobacco trust has devoted all its efforts to the substitution of mechanical for manual labour. With this end in view, it bought all the patents bearing on the preparation of tobacco and spent enormous sums. There were many patents of no use as they stood, which the engineers of the trust had to study and modify. At the end of 1906, two subsidiary companies were constituted solely to acquire patents. With the same object in view, the trust built its machine shops, casting shops and repair shops. One of these establishments, that at Brooklyn, employs 300 workmen; there experiments are carried out on machines for making cigarettes, cheroots, smoking tobacco, tin sheets for packing, boxes, etc. Inventions are perfected there. (Id., 21)

Hilferding opened the possibility of state monopoly when he stated that centralization was limited in its achievements, unless it was done on a society-wide scale, rather than among a certain number of continually changing individual capitalists. Imagine this constant reconvertibility of capital into money which endows this capital with the fluidity of loan capital, that is, of money capital which is advanced for a certain period and then returns as a sum of money enhanced by interest. This constant cycle of money suitable for industrial investment is at the same time idle when invested temporarily as pure loan capital and thus tied up. The continual changes in this sum of money are expressed in the continual changes in the ownership of shares. Its conversion into industrial capital, of course, occurs only once and once for all. Idle capital is converted definitively into money capital, and this, in turn, into productive capital. The fresh sums of money which flow out of this fund of idle capital function as means for purchasing shares and then as means of circulation for the turnover of shares.

> For the owners of the money, which was initially converted into industrial capital, they make possible the return of their money, which can now be applied to other purposes, after having served them in the meantime as capital. It should be noted that when share prices rise, more money will be required, ceteris paribus, for the turnover of shares, and more money can then enter circulation than was originally converted into industrial capital. (Id. 185)

Hilferding also clarified that the mobilization of capital had no effect upon the process of production. Lenin incorporated that observation into his work, too. It affected only property, "only creates the form for the transfer of property which functions in a capitalist way, the transfer of capital as capital, as a sum of money which breeds profit. Since it leaves production unaffected this transfer is in effect a transfer of property titles to profit. *The capitalist is concerned only with profit, and is quite indifferent to its source. This is finance capitalism*" (Id., emphasis added).

Finance capital is a commodity, namely profit. One share is, therefore, just as good as another if, all else being equal, it brings the same profit.

Hilferding was the first to explain how finance capital evolved from centralized capitalism. His explanation made it clear to, let's say, Lenin that state monopoly is better than industrial trusts, which are limited to specific sectors of production. Using Hilferding's theory, Lenin's state (Soviet) capitalism was a consequence of the new stage of global capitalism and its new commodity: finance capitalism. The centralization of capital was essential for the mobilization of capital to introduce technology. Lenin figured out how to streamline the production and ensure the fastest way of producing and introducing technology into the manufacturing industry, to create more capital to be invested. When that investment became profitable, the profit was shared by the managerial class Lenin imagined, and his lieutenants developed.

2 Non-competitive State Capitalism Is Capitalism

Non-competitive state capitalism remains capitalist because its profits benefit only the few. Furthermore, as Hilferding demonstrated in his 1910 opus, a capitalist economy does not demand "free" competition. A capitalist economy demands profits. And profits do not necessarily depend on competition. For instance, until the market is saturated with cannoli, a Napolitano dessert that many love, the best cannoli will command the highest price. For a while that would fluctuate, because what constitutes "the best" cannoli is rather subjective, so competition would be possible. However, when the market becomes saturated with every conceivable type of cannoli, competition becomes undesirable. It produces a lack of demand, and profits stagnate and then fall. Crises appear. Then, trusts, cartels, or any other tools providing concentration of capital and thus of profit distribution are welcome. One cannoli provider for the entire market becomes the best way to achieve the most profit in that economic sector. Thus, monopolies become essential for the survival of capitalism. And whether they are private, public, or a hybrid of the two, becomes irrelevant. What matters in capitalism is that profit increases. Under an illiberal, capitalist, regime, this translates into profits being concentrated in fewer hands. Ersatz socialism is a type of despotic capitalism (Figure 9).

FIGURE 9 The ersatz socialist economy: a visual interpretation
SOURCE: NEACȘU, DANA. 2025. ORIGINAL IMAGE DRAWN BY THE AUTHOR AND REFINED USING OPENAI'S CHATGPT (MODEL O4-MINI-HIGH)

In a backward country like Russia, ersatz socialism was achieved in two ways: production was socialized among the peasants (Kolkhozniks) and proletarian "dictators," while profit was concentrated in the hands of the apparatchiks, the loyal Soviet bureaucrats. The only redistribution in post-Tsarist Russia (and ECE countries) was the socialization of work. The people (mocked as dictators) only owned their income, savings, and whatever inheritance did not threaten the state economy. However, in the realm of linguistic gymnastics, their position highly improved: from servants, the masses became either factory wage-earners or kolkhoznik.

> **ARTICLE 10.** The right of citizens to personal ownership of their incomes from work and of their savings, of their dwelling houses and subsidiary household economy, their household furniture and utensils and articles

> of personal use and convenience, as well as the right of inheritance of personal property of citizens, is protected by law. (See Appendix A)[8]

The profit created by their work belonged to the state, whose managerial class uses it for the military, the internal security forces, and foremost "public wealth," which is not profit redistribution to each worker because that would have been eventually mentioned expressly in the 1936 Constitution, which was the fundamental document establishing a socialist economy. Only it was never mentioned, because the Soviet economy was state monopoly capital, determined and directed by the state, in the same way a cartel's economic plan is directed by the trustees for the benefit of the shareholders, who can be as anonymous as the Soviet political, military and paramilitary elite.

> **ARTICLE 11.** The economic life of the U.S.S.R. is determined and directed by the state national economic plan with the aim of increasing the public wealth, of steadily improving the material conditions of the working people and raising their cultural level, of consolidating the independence of the U.S.S.R. and strengthening its defensive capacity. (Id.)

That capitalism is a system of ever concentrated private distribution of ever increasingly socialized work was long explained by Adam Smith in *The Wealth of Nations*. There, Smith recognized that certain industries require government intervention to prevent the inefficiencies of private monopolies in cases of high infrastructure costs (e.g., roads and bridges).[9] That is why when this book argues that Lenin implemented his views about state monopoly as the

---

8 See Appendix A. *Constitution (Fundamental law) of the Union of Soviet Socialist Republics*, Kremlin, Moscow, December 5, 1936, in J.V. Stalin, *Works*, Vol. 14, (Red Star Press Ltd., London, 1978) https://www.marxists.org/reference/archive/stalin/works/1936/12/05.htm.

9 "The third and last duty of the sovereign or commonwealth is that of erecting and maintaining those public institutions and those public works, which, though they may be in the highest degree advantageous to a great society, are, however, of such a nature that the profit could never repay the expense to any individual or small number of individuals, and which it therefore cannot be expected that any individual or small number of individuals should erect or maintain. The performance of this duty requires, too, very different degrees of expense in the different periods of society.

After the public institutions and public works necessary for the defence of the society, and for the administration of justice, both of which have already been mentioned, the other works and institutions of this kind are chiefly those for facilitating the commerce of the society, and those for promoting the instruction of the people. The institutions for instruction are of two kinds: those for the education of youth, and those for the instruction of people of all ages. The consideration of the manner in which the expense of those different sorts of public, works and institutions may be most properly defrayed will divide this third part of the present chapter into three different articles."

FIGURE 10 The capitalist market economy: a visual interpretation
SOURCE: NEACȘU, DANA. 2025. ORIGINAL IMAGE DRAWN BY THE AUTHOR AND REFINED USING OPENAI'S CHATGPT (MODEL O4-MINI-HIGH)

foundation of the Bolshevik economic system, this claim is not as exotic as it might seem. Since the late 1800s, capitalist economies (Figure 10) have promoted a combination of public and private monopolies whenever the rules of profit demanded such interplay.[10]

ADAM SMITH, An *Inquiry into the Nature and Causes of The Wealth of Nations* (1776), Book V: On the Revenue of the Sovereign or Commonwealth, Chapter I: On the Expenses of the Sovereign or Commonwealth, Part III: On the Expense of Public Works and Public Institutions, https://www.marxists.org/reference/archive/smith-adam/works/wealth-of-nations/book05/ch01c.htm

10 In many capitalist economies, public monopolies have been established to address specific challenges where private monopolies might by more harmful. For instance, in the UK, Canada, Australia healthcare systems operate as public monopolies to ensure equitable access and avoid the inefficiencies or exploitation associated with private monopolies

Going back to Russia, where ersatz socialism started and the reign of the absolute monopoly was created, more can be learned about the cohabitation of public and private economy, the economy which in fact is present in all capitalist countries around the world.

---

in healthcare. The UK's National Health Service (NHS) is a public monopoly, providing healthcare free at the point of service. It was created to prevent the exclusion of the poor from essential medical care that often occurred under privately dominated systems.

Nowadays, Joseph Stiglitz and other economists argue that private monopolies often lead to inefficiencies and inequitable outcomes in sectors vital to public welfare. In *The Price of Inequality: How Today's Divided Society Endangers Our Future* (2012), Stiglitz discusses how monopolies distort markets by exploiting their power to charge higher prices and reduce output, ultimately harming consumers and widening inequality. This idea if further developed in his book, *In People, Power, and Profits: Progressive Capitalism for an Age of Discontent* (2019), Stiglitz criticizes the dominance of private monopolies in critical sectors, such as healthcare, education, and technology, arguing that they lead to inefficiencies and fail to serve the public interest.

Another instance of a public monopoly is when the service or industry is considered a public good, such as electricity, water, and sewage because these are considered public goods necessary for the functioning of society. In France, for instance, the water supply used to be operated as a public monopoly because of its essential nature. Even in cases of privatization, heavy regulation is often required to ensure fair access. In the United States, the government established the Tennessee Valley Authority (TVA) as a public monopoly to provide electricity to rural areas during the Great Depression, because no private providers found it profitable. Established in 1933 as a federally owned corporation, TVA continues to operate as the sole provider of electricity across its designated service area, which includes Tennessee and parts of six surrounding states. It supplies power to approximately 10 million people through a network of local power companies and direct industrial customers. As a public monopoly, TVA operates without competition within its service region. This status has been maintained over the decades, with federal regulations reinforcing its exclusive control over transmission lines and power distribution in the area. For instance, in 1959, Congress passed legislation Public Law 86–137, also called the Tennessee Valley Authority Act Amendments of 1959, prohibiting TVA from selling or delivering power to customers outside its primary service area, effectively eliminating external competition. In addition, this legislation allowed it to raise funds through selling revenue bonds to the public, essentially removing the need for direct federal appropriations to operate its power system. While maintaining its monopoly status, this amendment signed into law on August 6, 1959, by President Dwight D. Eisenhower changed TVA's funding. However, TVA remains a government-owned and regulated monopoly, as its nine-member board of directors appointed by the President and confirmed by the Senate shows. For more information, go *to Built for the People*, https://www.tva.com/about-tva, https://www.tva.com/.

Similarly, Amtrak operates as a public monopoly to ensure essential rail transportation in areas where private companies exited due to lack of profitability. Amtrak was established in 1971 under the Rail Passenger Service Act signed into law by President Nixon. The Rail Passenger Service Act of 1970, Public Law 91–518, was designated to take over failing private passenger rail services. Private companies, such as the major freight railroads, were unable to profitably maintain passenger rail services. Amtrak is owned by

Trotsky, one of Lenin's foremost lieutenants, further developed the understanding of the economic process taking place in Russia. He explained Lenin's New Economic Policy. "Lenin put the gist of the position clearly in his historic question 'Which is going to score?'"[11]

Trotsky did not have a good handle on economics. His understanding of capitalism was purely behavioral, based on Marx's description of early nineteenth-century capitalism. Trotsky only asked:

> "Are we going towards socialism or capitalism?" we must, first of all, properly formulate the question itself. It naturally divides into three subsidiary questions: (a) Are our productive forces developing? (b) What are the social forms of this development? (c) At what rate does the development proceed? (Trotsky, 2024, 23)

He never thought about asking who the owner of the means of production is, or how profit is distributed. As a good lieutenant, Trotsky summarized the reality.

> We are well aware, of course, that the social form of our economic development is dual, being founded both on collaboration and on the

---

the federal government, with its board of directors appointed by the President and confirmed by the Senate. https://railroads.dot.gov/passenger-rail/amtrak/amtrak.

However, trusts, which are a combination of businesses or corporations formed to reduce competition and control prices, and which are often created through contracts or agreements among companies to fix prices, limit production, or regulate transportation of products, are prohibited by state constitutions in the United States. For example, the Constitution of the State of Washington explicitly prohibits monopolies and trusts, stating that no company or association of persons shall combine for the purpose of fixing prices or limiting production (West's RCWA Const. Art. 12, § 22) [1]. Similarly, 15 U.S.C.A. § 1 declares illegal any contract, combination, or conspiracy in restraint of trade or commerce among states or with foreign nations (15 U.S.C.A. § 1). Similarly, under U.S. law, a monopoly exists when a single company or a group of companies acting together has the power to control prices and exclude competition in a particular market. The Sherman Anti-Trust Act defines monopolizing as acquiring or maintaining the power to exclude competitors from any part of trade or commerce, with the intent to exercise that power (*American Tobacco Co. v. U.S.*, 328 U.S. 781 (1946)). The Supreme Court has defined "monopoly power" as the power to control prices or exclude competition, and it can be inferred from a firm's dominant market share protected by entry barriers (*United States v. Google LLC*, —F.Supp.3d— (2024)). Additionally, monopolies are considered odious and contrary to the principles of commerce and free government (MD Constitution, Declaration of Rights, Art. 41). But these examples seem to be the exception to the rule that capitalism as an economic system, does not need free competition, as defined by various legal norms, it needs to create profit.

11 Leon Trotsky, "Towards Socialism or Capitalism". *The Labour Monthly*, (November 1925, Vol. 7 No. 11), p. 20. https://www.marxists.org/archive/trotsky/1925/11/towards.htm.

> struggle between capitalist and socialist methods, forms and aims. ... We can, however, no longer be satisfied by such a general conception of the contradictory forces of our development. We need and demand the most accurate coefficients for our economic contradictions, not only the dynamic coefficients of our general development, but the relative coefficients of the weight of the one or other tendency. (Id., 24–25)

And what was Trotsky's solution? "To avoid the final expansion of individualistic tendencies among the peasants might prove fatal, turning our development definitely in the direction of capitalism" (Id.). But it is not individualistic tendencies that are the hallmark of capitalism. Capitalism is flexible. Capitalism can be state capitalism. And thus, Trotsky's assumption that state economy is socialist economy is either a total lack of knowledge or mere propaganda. "On the contrary, were the State, i.e. socialist economy, to prevail in the general economic life of the country, then a more or less considerable "liberation" of individualistic tendencies among the peasantry would enter the channel of a definite correlation of forces and would become purely a matter of expediency, resolving itself into such questions as, How, when, and for how long?" (Id.). To put it differently, Hilferding noted the highest productivity possible because all the productive forces were at the disposition of the socialist state. This monopolization secured "all the higher commands grow not only rapidly but more rapidly than the individualistic, capitalistic productive forces of the town and the rural districts" (Id.).

So-called socialist state economy is tantamount to corporate capitalist monopoly. In fact, given the state of the economy and the political goals of Lenin and his ilk, state capitalism was the only way to ensure the fastest circulation of capital and invest it where it was necessary. Lenin understood that from Hilferding.

Thus, whether we accept Lenin's use of Hilferding's economic findings and understand that Bolshevism introduced state capitalism to Russia or whether we look at Trotsky's explanation of socialism as state economy, disregarding the lack of profit distribution in a planned way to everyone, what should become clear is that Soviet Russia was nothing more but a capitalist state monopoly. In other words, ersatz socialism.

3 Democratic Capitalism Boosts Free Enterprise; Ersatz Socialism Fosters Corporate Monopoly

Free enterprise is the hallmark of a specific type of capitalist society, democratic capitalism. Bernard Lonergan put it more eloquently when he stated that there is a connection between the supply of consumer goods and services and the accumulation of capital, so democracy is preserved (1957). Democracy stands on a very delicate balance, requiring either that those who accumulate capital restrain their greed or that the legal system effectively checks it. Politics is often experienced by people as an arbiter of sheer power. The politics of taxation and the laws and regulations thus required are one way to control the creation of new pots of capital for the enrichment of the many or, to the contrary, of the few.

However, commonsense understanding is often burdened by confusion and misunderstanding. For instance, untaxed wealth accumulates in the hands of the few and rots our democracy, eventually corroding our civilization as we know it.[12] Similarly to public opinion regarding the estate tax, which many oppose even though most people will never be affected by it, commonsense understanding depends on mass media outlets framing issues according to their private interests. As such, the estate tax, for instance, is rejected by voters who view it as a burden on the average American rather than a tax on wealth.[13]

Like many other thinkers, Bernard Lonergan views free enterprise as the staple of democratic capitalism. Lonergan was intimately equating free enterprise with self-government, defined by James Madison in *The Federalist Papers* as "the capacity of mankind for self-government."[14] Lonergan opposed self-government with a bureaucratically managed economy, which he equated with the Soviet economy.[15] Furthermore, Lonergan bemoaned that "the proletariat today include almost everyone." His solution to this socialization of poverty was free enterprise: "Free enterprise is a setup in which individuals are free to figure out what can be done, whether they will do it; and if they so decide they take upon themselves the risk of doing it" (Lonergan, 1941, 3).

But, while acknowledging that people in the West refrained from engaging in free enterprise, Lonergan never said that the West stopped being capitalist. (Id.) He only thought we were becoming "too indolent and too stupid" (Id.),

12 See Michael J. Graetz, *The Power to Destroy: How the Antitax Movement Hijacked America* (2024) (explaining how the opposition to taxation propelled the increased deficit which threatens the government's ability to provide needed social services).

13 Michael J. Graetz '61GS Explores the Rise of the Antitax Movement in New Book: "The Power to Destroy" (September 20, 2024), at https://www.gs.columbia.edu/news/michael-j-graetz-61gs-explores-rise-antitax-movement-new-book-power-destroy.

14 James Madison, *Federalist* No. 39, *New York Packet* (January 18, 1788) at https://avalon.law.yale.edu/18th_century/fed39.asp.

15 Frederick G. Lawrence, Editors' Introduction, xxxiii, in *Collected Works of Bernard Lonergan. The Robert Mollot Collection, Volume 15: Macroeconomic Dynamics: An Essay in Circulation Analysis (1999)*.

assessments which go beyond the purpose of this book. Given the context of Lonergan's analysis, I read it to mean that for him, free enterprise is fundamental only to democratic capitalism and not to capitalism, generally speaking. Consequently, state capitalism and its high level of corporate monopoly is only a sign of undemocratic capitalism.

When the 1917 Bolshevik Revolution happened, capitalism reached its highest levels of concentration of the means of production in the hands of the fewest people and the highest levels of socialization of labor among the largest number of people. Theoretically, it made sense to think that by changing property from the hands of the few to the Soviet state, the economic structure of Tsarist Russia would change. Only the state did not hold title over the means of production for the interest of the proletarian masses, which in Russia did not exist, given the preponderance of the peasants. But the state provided the capital necessary for those means of production to incorporate the highest levels of technology. Thus, Lenin's decrees nationalizing factories had the effect Joan Robinson called "an alternative means of carrying out industrialization."[16]

The economic structure of a society, irrespective of its type, either encourages social justice for all or for the few. F.A. Hayek saw liberal capitalism[17] as the culmination of greater freedom, justice, and prosperity. But then socialism for Hayek was the Soviet nightmare, which here I argue, along the lines of Joseph A. Schumpeter, had nothing socialist in its economic structure.[18]

Capitalism, as an economy, as a thing, finds its conceptual explanation in political economy and its basic categories of value (capital) is understood as financial resources, profit, or rent. Those categories pre-existed the Soviet economy and continued under the Soviet regime. Those resources had either been "transferred" to the Soviet state or had been created by Soviet decree. The State became the sole employer of the working class who continued to use those means of production as wage-earners. The Soviet economic forces, as Pashukanis noted in 1930, stopped having "capital entrepreneurs" as their "bearers."[19] Statism or state monopoly was the economic foundation of the Soviet economy, in addition to Kolkhozes or agricultural collectives. Most people represented the workforce and a few former workforce members became the new managerial class (the apparatchiks).

16 Joan Robinson. *Freedom and Necessity. Introduction to the Study of Society*, 76 (1971).
17 *Id.*, at 10.
18 Joseph A. Schumpeter, *Capitalism, Socialism and Democracy* (1942).
19 Pashukhanis' 1930 Speech on the Soviet State and the Revolution Law, quoted in Robert Conquest, *Justice and the Legal System in the USSR* 16 (1968).

4 Non-Democratic Capitalism Encourages State-Planned Corporate Monopolization

One benefit of any planned economy is the planned allocation of capital or investment. The allocation of investment in Soviet Russia and the ECE countries happened in a centralized manner across multiple industries. In other types of capitalist economies, that centralized investment happened through cartels usually within an industry, such as the steel or financial industry, for instance.[20] However, the result of planned allocation of capital or investment in both the Soviet countries—the illiberal capitalist countries—and the capitalist countries has never benefitted the people, only those in charge of the planification.

The Soviet experiment with planification as clearly explained by Joan Robinson further supports the thesis of the socialization of poverty as the only socialization achieved in Russia and the ECE countries in the twentieth century:

> To carry through the whole programme required strong central control, which hypertrophied into the tyranny of Stalin. The relations of productions were adjusted to fit the forces of production with a painful wrench.[21]

---

20 For a historical record, *see, generally*, Josephson, Matthew. *The Robber Barons; The Great American Capitalists, 1861–1901* (1934). For a more recent example of planned investment within a specific industry, the beef industry in the United States. see, for instance, Competition Issues in the U.S. Beef Industry, 44(3) *Applied Economic Perspectives & Policy*, 1340–1358 (2022). The empirical evidence suggests that beef production, the farm, wholesale, and retail values of beef, and marketing were carefully planned in the cartel period (2015–2019), as compared with a prior period (2010–2014). Thus, the wholesale beef pricing by beef packers shifted from being consistent with a perfectly competitive industry pricing in the pre-cartel period to being consistent with the oligopoly and monopoly pricing in the cartel period.

21 "This system was set to work to modernize and industrialize the whole empire inherited from the Tsar at the most rapid rate possible. … But there were certain serious drawbacks in the Soviet system. First, industrialization was launched before the agricultural revolution which had preceded it in the Western world. In the course of the Revolution and the civil war in which it was established, the peasants in Russia had taken possession of the land; and in central Asia tribal leaders had resumed their ancient powers. Rent, which formerly syphoned off the agricultural surplus, was not being paid, and, while industry could offer nothing to buy, the peasants had no interest to produce a surplus for sale. Stalin cut his way through this impasse by setting up collective farms, servicing them with machine-tractor stations. … The murderous brutality with which the collectivization was carried out alienated the peasants and few of the managers sent to run the farms could find a way to make them work. … Finally, being surrounded by the hostility of the [liberal] capitalist nations, which treated even Fascism as a lesser evil, the Soviet government was obliged to gear industry primarily to defense and to keep a sharp eye on internal dissent."

TABLE 1 Czechoslovakian people living in poverty (1958–1988)

Year	Workers	Employees	Peasants in cooperatives	Pensioners	Others
1958	27.2	13	12.5	23.2	24.1
1965	45.6	7.8	4.5	31.3	10.8
1970	49.2	10.7	2.4	33.9	3.8
1973	48.1	10.2	1.4	37.5	2.8
1976	50.7	11.7	1.6	33.3	2.7
1988	48.3	25.5	1.9	21.7	2.6

SOURCE: LIBOR ZIDEK, *CENTRALLY PLANNED ECONOMIES: THEORY AND PRACTICE IN SOCIALIST CZECHOSLOVAKIA*, P. 33 (2019)

Robinson's description of the state of the Russian economy can be extrapolated for all ECE countries. That economy, an alternative to industrialization, was capitalist in the sense that the owner was not a collective or the people at large. The Soviet state as a corporate entity was the owner and its manager class the beneficiaries.[22]

Furthermore, that Soviet Russia and ECE countries did not experience socialism is proven by socialization of poverty rather than the socialization of socio-economic justice. For instance, as Libor Zidek's data about Czechoslovakia (Table 1) shows, as the number of years under ersatz socialism increased, so increased the number of the proletariat or the working class who lived in poverty by the standards of that society, already known for its frugality.[23]

Adding the state employees, who were not part of the managing bureaucratic class and the pensioners, it looks like most of the 15 million residents of

ROBINSON, *Freedom and Necessity. Introduction to the Study of Society*, 80–81

22 There are many types of state capitalism. There are nations where the government owns a majority stake in some companies but the entire stake as in soviet Russia or the ECE countries in the same historical period. For instance,

"Mexico's government owns the state oil giant, Pemex. Canadian provincial governments own energy companies HydroQuebec, BCHydro, and several others. Yet none of these countries have state- capitalist economies. Their governments may be more interventionist than those of, say, the United Kingdom, which has privatized nearly all its former state companies, but they are not state capitalists—the Mexican and Canadian governments own only a tiny portion of their countries' corporate sectors."

JOSHUA KURLANTZICK, *State Capitalism: How the Return of Statism Is Transforming the World* 10 (2016)

23 Libor Zidek, *Centrally Planned Economies: Theory and Practice in Socialist Czechoslovakia*, p. 33 (2019).

Soviet Czechoslovakia, one of the better off Soviet countries, lived in poverty. That socio-economic reality did not amount to socio-economic justice for all, as a socialist society would require.

To clarify, socio-economic justice does not equate to rigid economic equality. That is not the theory and possible praxis of socialism. It is the lack of staggering inequality between individuals who are billionaires, for instance, and individuals on less than $12 a month.[24] Socialism requires an economic

---

24 Here is a brief survey of the threshold of poverty for the United States and Canada in the Americas, and France and Finland, in Europe, and Japan and India, in Asia.

"**1. United States: Poverty Line (2024)**: The U.S. defines poverty using a set of income thresholds, which vary by family size and composition. For example: **1 person**: $14,580/annually; **2 people**: $19,720/annually; **3 people**: $24,860/annually; **4 people**: $30,000/annually. These thresholds are updated annually based on inflation and the Consumer Price Index (CPI). Note that the poverty line is lower in certain areas, such as rural regions, and higher in metropolitan areas, like parts of California. *See., U.S. Department of Health and Human Services (HHS) Poverty Guidelines*. https://aspe.hhs.gov/poverty-guidelines.

2. Canada: Low Income Measure (2024): In Canada, the poverty threshold is often measured using the *Low Income Measure (LIM)*, which is 50% of the median income. This varies by province and household size. For example, **1 person**, the LIM is about CAD 22,000–24,000 annually (this varies by the cost of living in each province). For **4 people**: the threshold is higher, around CAD 45,000–50,000 annually. Canada also uses the *Market Basket Measure (MBM)*, which is based on the cost of a set of goods and services (e.g., food, clothing, shelter, transportation). The threshold for this is **approximately CAD** 30,000 for a single person in major urban areas. *See, Statistics Canada—Poverty and Income Inequality* https://www.statcan.gc.ca/eng/start. For specific information about poverty measures such as LIM and MBM, you can explore reports and articles under "Income Statistics" or "Poverty and Income Inequality."

3. Finland: Poverty Line (2024): Finland uses **relative poverty**, which is defined as an income below 60% of the median income. In **2024**, the threshold for **1 person**: €1,300–1,400 per month, depending on regional differences. For 4 **people**, this could be around €2,800–3,000 per month. The Finnish poverty threshold varies based on household size and the income distribution of the population. *See*, Statistics *Finland—Poverty and Income Distribution*. https://www.stat.fi/index_en.html. You can find information on income distribution, relative poverty, and related statistics in their "Income, wealth, and living conditions" section.

4. France: Poverty Line (2024): France defines poverty as earning less than **60%** of the median national income. The official poverty line in 2024 for **1 person** is around €1,100–1,200 per month. For **3 people**, the poverty line is approximately €2,300–2,400 per month. These figures are adjusted based on family size and cost of living, and the French government monitors this through INSEE (National Institute of Statistics and Economic Studies). *See, INSEE (National Institute of Statistics and Economic studies)*, https://www.insee.fr/en/statistiques. INSEE publishes reports on income and poverty, including detailed information about poverty thresholds based on 60% of the median income.

5. Japan: Poverty Line (2024): The relative poverty line in Japan is typically set at 50% of the median income. For **1 person**, the poverty threshold is estimated to be

system which does not undermine human dignity. Socialists do not think that all people are of the same height or gender or hair color or appetite or general needs. But socialists do believe in equal opportunity to satisfy those needs, which means socialism requires a system of planning and resource allocation for everyone's education, health care, housing, and transportation, so that everyone can become engaged citizens politically, socially, economically and culturally. Socialism abolishes marginalization. Everyone becomes an integral part of society.

For such hefty goals, socialism requires a just resource distribution for the use of everyone, to promote and support a democratic sense of equality. Socialism does not raise Buffets, Musks, Bezoses, and their ilk. The political and economic scaffolding of socialism has an ethical coding where individuals cannot be wealthier than the entire economic output of a country. Worse, each one of those individuals is worth more than a few dozen. For instance, as of 2024, Elon Musk's net worth is approximately $376 billion, making him wealthier than the Gross Domestic Product of around 55 countries.[25]

Additionally, if what makes capitalism is private property over the means of production, then the question becomes one of percentage, because all capitalist societies have known state monopolies, and no one doubts their nature.

If socialism were to follow capitalism and build on its economic structure, which is a monopolist economy, would the mere transfer of ownership from corporate non-state entities to the state change the monopolist nature of the economy? Think about a person changing from her bathing suit into a business

---

¥1,200,000–1,300,000 per year (roughly $8,000–9,000 USD). For **4 people**, it would be approximately ¥2,500,000–3,000,000 per year (roughly $16,500–20,000 USD). *See, Ministry of Health, Labour and Welfare (Japan) Statistics Bureau of Japan (Provides data on income and poverty)*, https://www.stat.go.jp/english/index.html, and *Ministry of Health, Labour and Welfare (Japan) (Provides social welfare and poverty-related data)*, https://www.mhlw.go.jp/english/.

6. India: Poverty Line (2024): Poverty Line (2024): Based on the most recent estimates, poverty thresholds in India are calculated using the *Tendulkar Poverty Line or the Tendulkar Committee Methodology*. The National Poverty Line is approximately: for **1 person** it is ₹1,000–1,200 per month for rural areas (roughly $12–15 USD); and ₹1,500–1,800 per month for urban areas (roughly $18–22 USD). India's poverty statistics and methodologies can be found on the websites of *Ministry of Rural Development* (India) *National Statistical Office (India)* (Responsible for poverty alleviation programs and related data) https://rural.nic.in/; *National Statistical Office (India)* (Publishes poverty and income statistics) http://www.mospi.gov.in/.

25 Based on World Bank GDP database or IMF Global Economy Report for 2024 updates, countries with smaller economies with GDPs in the range of $100 mil, are on all five continents, e.g., Kosovo and Montenegro (Europe); Barbados, Belize, Dominica, et al. (The Americas), Tajikistan, Kyrgyzstan, et al. (Asia), Rwanda, Niger, et al. (Africa), and Tuvalu, Samoa, et al. (Australia and Oceania).

suit. That change would not impact the person's age, gender, sexual preferences, or race. Finally, if it is the imagined competition in the marketplace, often described as antithetical to a planned economy, then, again, a more in-depth analysis is needed because no capitalist society is based on some happenstance individual behavior of bringing apples or geese to the market and hoping for the best offer. Most market players have some corporate shell, and all employ highly educated Chief Economic Officers supported by a Board of Directors, in addition to other chief officers. Planning the economic input and output of their corporations is expected. As much fun one has reading F.A. Hayek as proof in the market happenstance, the message of his book which equates socialism to serfdom is an ode to the information acumen of the market participants and their ability to predict the market and plan their actions. Hayek disliked planning by ill-informed bureaucrats working for a corrupt state, not planning itself.[26]

Similarly, capitalism is not inimical to nationalization, and socialism is not antithetical to competition. Real-life examples of state monopolies in capitalist societies include the British Gas Corporation, the United States Postal Service (or the recent Intel "partial nationalization," with the U.S. federal government acquiring a roughly 10% stake in the company), or the Saudi Aramco.[27]

---

26 F.A. Hayek, *The Road to Serfdom*, 13 (1944).

27 Here are some real-life examples of state monopolies in capitalist societies:

a. Public Utilities (Electricity, Water, Gas): In many capitalist societies, the state has a monopoly over essential services like electricity, water, and gas. For example, in the United Kingdom, before The Gast Act of 1986, which privatized the British Gas Corporation (BGS), BGS was a state-run monopoly. Similarly, the British Electricity Authority (BEA), established as the central British electricity authority in 1948 under the nationalization of Great Britain's electricity supply industry enacted by the Electricity Act 1947, was privatized by the Margaret Thatcher's government. However, both decisions brought such disastrous consequences, that in 2022, another conservative government announced it would bring a division of the privately owned National Grid back into public ownership to better meet net zero targets. "In its place, a publicly owned 'Future System Operator' is being set up to operate energy grids from 2024 onwards. The new public body will be responsible for managing the planning and distribution of Britain's electricity system to prevent supply interruptions."

b. Postal Services: In many countries, the state has a monopoly on postal services. The United States Postal Service (USPS), for example, is a government-owned entity that has historically enjoyed a monopoly on certain postal services, though it now faces competition from private companies in some areas.

c. Public Broadcasting: In many capitalist societies, national public broadcasters enjoy a state-supported monopoly or near-monopoly in their regions. BBC (British Broadcasting Corporation) in the UK is an example of a state-funded broadcaster that has historically had a dominant position in British media.

d. Natural Resources and Energy: Oil and Gas industries in many countries are monopolized or tightly controlled by the state. Saudi Aramco, the state-owned oil company of

These state monopolies, as well as any corporate entity, rely on what Hayek disparages as a "socialist" method: economic planning, for being "consciously directed to serve particular ends in a definite way."[28] Although he does admit this is rather ordinary if we expect rational behavior from economic agents, Hayek is a myth-maker playing loose with history. No corporate entity in the United States brags about a lack of strategic planning. No capitalist government brags about a lack of policymaking. Governing requires planning. Thus, there was nothing essentially socialist in economic planning and likewise there is nothing socialist in state monopolies.

Moreover, socialism is not inimical to private property to the extent that Locke connected individual freedom and creativity to property. Lenin himself noted that very connection when he decreed that private property and not corporatization is the way for the Soviets to end famine during World War I.

But socialism is inimical to state monopolizations deemed ersatz nationalizations. Nationalization in the name of the proletariat is a mere pretense if the proletariat continues to be salaried workers with no oversight role, and occupy the same subordinate economic position as before the so-called nationalization. Moreover, as only the management class benefits from that transfer of property, the mere suggestion that state monopolization is anything else becomes risible.

As Harrington noted, factories were taken away from their private owners in Soviet Russia and each of the ECE countries under the guise of popular

---

Saudi Arabia, is an example of a massive state monopoly that plays a central role in the global capitalist economy.

e Transportation (Railroads, Airlines): In some countries, the state either owns or heavily regulates transportation monopolies. In France, SNCF (Société Nationale des Chemins de fer Français) is the state-owned national railway company, controlling the majority of rail transport within the country.

f. Military-Industrial Complex: All capitalist states maintain a monopoly on defense and military production. Even military contractors, such as Lockheed Martin, or Northrop Grumman have close relationships with governments, and operate within a framework dictated by state policy and funding.

g. Healthcare Systems (National Health Service): Some capitalist countries have public healthcare systems that operate as monopolies. The National Health Service (NHS) in the UK is an example where the state dominates healthcare provision, alongside the existence of private healthcare in the system.

h. Education Systems: In many capitalist societies, especially those with a strong public sector, the state provides a monopoly on primary and secondary education. Public schools in countries like the United States, Canada, and France are examples where state control is dominant, though private schools also exist in parallel.

i. Tech Services: Intel is a US-based semiconductor firm, and the U.S. federal government just acquired 10% of its shares in exchange for federal grants.

28 F.A. Hayek, *The Road to Serfdom*, 36 (1944).

nationalization.[29] Only the people had no control over the economy they theoretically owned!

> The state that possesses those means of production is virtually the private property of a bureaucracy that manages them in the name of the people. Power is thus determined by the position of an individual, or a class, in the dictatorial political structure rather than, as under *capitalism*, in the economic and social structure. *I call this system bureaucratic collectivism and argue that it is neither capitalist nor socialist.* (Harrington, 1989, 61, emphasis added.)

If the essential elements of a socialist economy are nationalization and planned economy, I contend that these elements are insufficient if they remain in the realm of mere process and appearance rather than substance. Nationalization as state monopolization and a planned economy which curtails competition to support the state monopoly are tantamount to state capitalism not to socialism absent socio-economic justice based on profit redistribution to the workers. If the distinction is social, then, again, the Soviet society was as stratified as the capitalist society. Harrington correctly identified the proletariat as workers and the apparatchiks as managers.

In her book *Freedom and Necessity. An Introduction to the Study of Society* (1971), Joan Robinson, whom the *New York Times* described as the "woman who shattered the myth of the free market," mentions the cohesive role of mythology.

> No doubt it is important for the cohesion of a society to have its own myths, but the particular content of the myth was not bound by necessity; it was free to take whatever form imagination chose to build or inner needs suggested. (Robinson, 1970, 23)

Levi-Strauss observed the same value of mythmaking, as well as Freud. But only Robinson added, immediately after, that:

---

29 For instance, in the Soviet Union, nationalization began immediately after the 1917 revolution and was formalized in the early Soviet period with key decrees and laws: Decree on Land (1917); Decree on Nationalization of Industry (1918) and The Law on the State Industry (1920). The next country where state monopolies were created was Poland, where nationalization took place through the 1946 decree under Soviet influence. In Bulgaria, nationalization occurred in 1947, following the consolidation of the soviet-backed regime, which in Czechoslovakia, and Romania happened a year later, in 1948 under the same circumstances. Finally, in 1949, Hungarian nationalization laws brought industry and agriculture under state monopoly.

> Similarly in many species of birds the males display brilliant plumage of a particular pattern to which alone the females will respond; it does not matter what colours are, so long as they are the colours of that species and no other. Psychologists observe a number of common themes in mythology which appear to correspond to elements in the emotional life of the individual. (*Id.*, 23–24.)

Mythmaking is rather impressive. For one, myths need to have the right ingredients: the right colors to attract the right behavior—patriotism—whether manifested in fighting for one's country against others or accepting one country's socio-economic, political, and legal structures for fear of living in the other country.

The myth of socialism, the society the Russians built under Stalin and then implemented by every other country behind the Iron Curtain, unified those who came within its spell. Its colorfulness, its red flag, made it easy to notice. It gave the right umbrage to those identified within its shade. From the Red Scare to the 2024 U.S. presidential elections, when Presidential Candidate Kamala Harris was called a Marxist—though no one could point to anything Marxian she did—the socialist label continues its epistemic journey.

The unifying 100-year myth carries on in part because, as Robinson noted in 1971, people do not use scientific knowledge to promote understanding. Instead, myths, superstitions, and slogans satisfy people's understanding. Robinson is not condescending when she makes that observation. She explains it rather pertinently when she states: "Logic, inquiry by experiment and a rationalist view of history were highly developed in Athens, but since they were the occupations of gentlemen, methods of production were not much affected by them" (Id, 60). In other words, Robinson believed in knowledge for the elites and knowledge for the masses. Myths bridge that gap. Myths unify everyone. Therefore, I would add, they need to satisfy everyone's unsettled thirst for understanding. They are not slogans or superstitions, necessarily, but they could be summarized in slogans.

That socialism has a mythical value which envelopes an entire society runs parallel with Karl Marx's conceptualization of David Ricardo's explanation of capitalist economy provided in *Capital, Vol. 1*. In his *Preface to Principles of Political Economy*, Ricardo defined "capitalism" as a society organized into "three classes of the community; namely, the proprietor of the land, the owner of the stock or capital necessary for its cultivation, and the labourers by whose industry it is cultivated." Those classes were not viewed in a reductionist manner—they included their families, too. They were dynamic, as they could move easily from the country to the city. This is not a comprehensive formula because not every social class was included: the bureaucracy, for example, or the members of the military, paramilitary, or police forces, whose salary came from the taxes the other three classes paid were not mentioned. Ricardo's theory valued the "productive" classes that sustain the society, the community in its entirety, and he speculated on how the "whole produce of the earth" was "to be allotted" to each class. Ricardo's assumption that there is no society without the productive classes might explain why capitalism has come to define both the economic organization of a society and the society itself. Perhaps this conceptual confusion expanded to socialist misnomer.

5 Ersatz Socialism Strives on the Socialization of Production and Centralization of Profit

Economic policy is constituted either in a conscious, planned manner, or by happenstance, Rudolf Hilferding summarized in his pioneering work, *Das Finantzkapital* (*1910*). The problem with his summary and all the other similar economic analyses is their underlying assumption that capitalism is a competitive economic system which strives on free markets. Indeed, Karl Marx's *Capital vol 1* influenced all capitalist economists to think capitalism was revolutionary. This unadulterated influence aside, such an assumption denotes a lack of legal education: all markets exist only within some legal framework, and all legal frameworks contain some power struggle among powerful interests deciding what is legal and encouraged and what is not. That being said, predicting, planning, and estimating are tools of all state-organized activities. The U.S. Congress has a roll call. All courts of justice have a roll call. The president of the United States has a calendar and schedule.

Planning is not what separates ersatz socialism from capitalism. In itself, a planned economy represents nothing remarkable. What is remarkable is that both Hilferding and Lenin in his *Imperialism, the Highest Stage of Capitalism* (written in 1916), influenced by Hilferding's work, incorporated monopoly into the body of Marxian capitalist economic theory. But neither raised the alarm of the collusion between ersatz socialism and capitalism once Lenin's and then Stalin's bolshevism were implemented. Hilferding made it obvious that capitalism does not require competition. Concentration and centralization of capital produces monopoly capitalism. This is a different type of capitalism. Ersatz socialism is a type of monopoly capitalism.

> The ideas which Hilferding formulated … about the role of *organized capitalism* as a stage in the movement towards socialized economy, *the growth of the interventionist state with its inherent potentiality for becoming*

> *a system of total power* ... are all highly relevant in the analyses of recent and current economic and political trends.[30] (Emphasis added.)

The lack of competition cannot be inherent to capitalism if finance capitalism thrives in its absence. It is the gist of this book's economic argument that the essence of capitalism is the drive for ever-increasing profit. When the economic production is socialized to the maximum, and the majority participates as a value- or capital producer, the profit further increases when it is concentrated in the hands of an ever-shrinking number of beneficiaries.

In a very interesting manner, ersatz socialism paved the way for Western finance capitalism to reach the staggering level of centralization we are currently witnessing. Currently, we observe capital centralization bypassing laws and regulations, thereby undermining the very institutions that facilitated its accumulation. This coincides with what was, until recently, the widespread illusion of globalized free trade. The latter was perceived as the only option to minimize regulatory oversight: by outsourcing production. The Trump administration is currently destroying all regulatory oversight with the hope of making outsourcing unnecessary.

The mere concentration of finances in a national bank, for instance, is not socialism. Socialism, as Hilferding explains, would require "the conscious control of the economy *not by* and for the benefit of capitalist magnates *but by* and for society as a whole" and would involve a stance that is "neither protectionism nor free trade." (Hilferding [1910], 1981, 366) (emphasis added). Now, as argued here, indeed the magnates in ersatz socialism are not known as "capitalist magnates" but as elite members of the Politburo of the U.S.S.R. and its satellite countries. Moreover, the control of the economy was not "to ensure the independence of working-class politics and to demonstrate its superiority in the defense of proletarian interests," (Id., 367) as Hilferding so clearly demonstrated. The political control of the economy was to promote the interests of those in power, which were, at the risk of repeating myself, the elite members of the political party from each country east of the Berlin Wall.

Those ersatz socialist countries were not highly industrialized economies. Their finances never reached the financial concentration the players of the global market command. But, nationally, within the borders of each country, their finances ensured that the state—as the corporate entity—and its subsidiaries—various economic organizations—controlled the economy.

30 T. Bottomore, Introduction to the first English translation of Finance Capital, in Rudolf Hilferding, *Finance Capital A Study of the Latest Phase of Capitalist Development* (London: Routledge & Kegak Paul, 1981), p. 16–17.

Thus, the model those ersatz socialist economies offered the global capital was how to socialize production to the extent possible and concentrate its control into smaller number of entities.

Another lesson global capital learned from ersatz socialist economies was how to separate the management of production from ownership: while the state is the sole owner of finances, means of production, etc., the management of all those nationalized assets are obviously people who work for state organizations. Those managers are not members of the proletariat. Moreover, if traditionally the limits of capitalist socialization were established by the division of the world market into national economic territories of individual states, "a division which can only be overcome partially and with great difficulty through international cartelization, and which also prolongs the duration of the competitive struggle which the cartels and trusts wage against one another with the aid of state power," (Id.) the world of ersatz socialism has paved a new way. Regional collaboration annihilated all wage struggle through complete pauperization of the proletariat, now marginalized and unprotected. What ersatz socialism showed the world is how to destroy the proletariat in the name of the proletariat and ensure total control for an ever-smaller managerial class working for an ever-smaller number of capitalists, so disconnected from the market or any place of struggle that struggle itself has been crushed. It seems that American capitalism has learned that lesson.

Like any capitalist economy, ersatz socialism established social control of production antagonistically from socialization since the control of social production remained vested in an oligarchy. Had ersatz socialism been anything other than a form of capitalism, then the world would have witnessed the struggle to dispossess each country's political oligarchy as "the ultimate phase of the class struggle between bourgeoisie and proletariat" (Id.). Only that never happened. Ersatz socialism created its own oligarchy from the disposed elite classes or by producing its own elites—educated children of the disposed classes, or the proletariat—and it crushed all opposition by never discussing its oligarchy. Once the new rulers brought under their political control the most importance branches of production, they ensured control over everyone's ability to make a living. Whatever the governing political party in each ECE country and the U.S.S.R. decided, that was going to be the political economy of that country.

> Since all other branches of production depend upon these, control of large-scale industry already provides the most effective form of social control even without any further socialization. A society which has

> control over coal mining, the iron and steel industry, the machine tool, electricity, and chemical industries, and runs the transport system, is able, by virtue of its control of these most important spheres of production, to determine the distribution of raw materials to other industries and the transport of their products. (Id., 367–368)

Some remnants of economic competition continued to exist in all ECE countries as well as in Soviet Russia. Not all means of production were nationalized. Not all the land was nationalized. Some small businesses, such as cobblers or itinerant Romani making pots or jewelry, continued. The state monopoly determined the political economy. And that flexibility is a credit to capitalism, especially as Hilferding, the "first European Marxist to analyze systematically the changing character of capitalism," (Zoninsein, 1990, 5) explained in his groundbreaking *Das Finanzkapital*:

> There is no need at all to extend the process of expropriation to the great bulk of peasant farms and small businesses, because as a result of the seizure of large-scale industry, upon which they have long been dependent, they would be indirectly socialized just as industry is directly socialized. It is therefore possible to allow the process of expropriation to mature slowly, precisely in those spheres of decentralized production where it would be a long drawn out and politically dangerous process. (Hilferding, [1910], 1981, 367–368)

The lesson in political economy of monopoly capitalism was thus conducted first in Soviet Russia and everywhere else subsequently, as Hilferding first noticed. It is obvious that whoever controls the means of production controls mass media and the narrative about how society works. Bertrand Russell was among the few witnesses to explain why the hundreds of millions of Russians obediently followed their dictatorship cruelest rules without any sign of revolt. Revolt was tantamount to losing the only means of survival, state employment. While in the Western world the principals of liberal democracy were holding at bay the greed of capital concentration at the state corporate levels, now, with the dismantling of liberal democracies, there is nothing to restrain greed and concentration of capital, especially finance capital. Or as Hilferding explained:

> In other words, since finance capital has already achieved expropriation to the extent required by [wage survival], it is possible to dispense with a sudden act of expropriation by the state, and to substitute a gradual

> process of socialization through the economic benefits which society will confer. (Id.)

Given the second Trump administration and the power of monopoly capitalism in government, it is easier to opine that ersatz socialism has taught our American capitalist magnates how to minimize any meaningful struggle against its ever-illiberal rules. Ersatz socialism minimized all the class contradictions by calling the toilers dictators. And it worked. Similarly, we witness today a total abdication to illiberal capitalism. There is no Rule of Law of checks and balances. The American president signs executive orders amending the U.S. Constitution.[31] No one ever dared to imagine this level of illegality. Moreover, there is no class struggles in today's capitalism. Whether out of fear of missing out on wage survival jobs or whether because mass media propaganda works, everyone seems to see themselves somehow above the economic position of a mere proletariat. Or perhaps this is the result of the concentration of finances which produced a socialization of debt.

The burden of extra profit imposed new burdens on every voter, stripped of class consciousness, but filled with the pride of citizenship marred in debt. The rise in the cost of living brought about by the trusts reduced living standards, and all the more so because the upward trend in food prices increased the cost of the most essential necessities of life. Despite populist promises, only the very rich benefit from tax cuts, while the burden of them hit everyone else, like the middle classes, who could be in revolt, if not for the fear of losing the last remnants of their middle-class privileges or because they too are marred in debt.

The citizenship of debt has replaced consumerism as citizenship. And instead of regarding themselves more and more as exploited proletariats, the debt incurred by middle-class aspirants brought them to a silo racially self-segregated. Any social trust is being eroded by mass impoverishment and the battle to escape it, which is becoming less and less possible, and only in smaller and smaller numbers.

What ersatz socialism taught Western capitalism is that economic power also means political power. The Politburo had all the power in U.S.S.R. Its

---

31 Donald Trump, Executive Order No. 14160, Protecting the Meaning and Value of American Citizenship, 90 Fed. Reg. 8449 (January 20, 2025), https://www.federalregister.gov/documents/2025/01/29/2025-02007/protecting-the-meaning-and-value-of-american-citizenship. See also, the definition of dictator, Encyclopaedia Britannia. 2024. *Dictator*. Last modified April 8, 2024. https://www.britannica.com/topic/dictator-ruler. https://www.britannica.com/topic/dictator-ruler).

counterparts had all the power in the ECE countries. The total domination of the economy's total control of the instruments of power were in the hands of very small elites who acted with impunity under the cover of state legitimacy. The U.S.S.R. and ECE countries had only state property administered by managers in the name of the people. Only the people received the crumbs the managerial class decided to let fall and reach them.

The second Trump administration has learned the lesson of state monopoly capitalism practiced by Putin's Russia in a more transparent manner than the Politburo. The greater the degree of concentration in the economic sphere, the more unbounded is the control of the state by the economic elites. The rigorous concentration of all the instruments of state power takes the form of an extreme deployment of the power of the state, which becomes the invincible instrument for maintaining economic domination. At the same time, the conquest of political power becomes a precondition of economic liberation. At the second Trump inauguration, the world witnessed the transformation of economic monopoly into illiberal, *trumped* dictatorial, capitalism. Nothing is ersatz nowadays. Everything is clear monopoly capitalism.

Capitalism has experienced a long and variegated history. The bourgeois revolution only began when the absolutist state, having overcome the autonomous regional power of the large landowners, had concentrated in its own hands all the means of power. A new elite replaced the old elite. If the absolute monarchy required concentration of political power in the hands of the largest landowners, the bourgeois revolution opened both economic and political power to non-hereditary ambition.

The Bolshevik Revolution promised to scatter the concentration of economic power and take it away from the hands of a few capitalist magnates, or associations of magnates, and give it to the workers, thus undermining the domination of the state by the few magnates. Only this did not happen. If the bourgeois revolution brought with it some democratizing of the power structures, economic and political, and some individual freedoms, the Bolshevik Revolution brought with it a replacement of the power structures and a loss of freedoms and liberties. It became the claims of the dictatorship of state monopoly.

Outside the U.S.S.R. and ECE borders, finance capital, as Hilferding noted, matured itself and reached the highest stage of the concentration of economic and political power in the hands of the capitalist oligarchy. The most visible form taking place currently in the United States. "It is the climax of the dictatorship of the magnates of capital" (Hilferding, [1910], 1981, 267–68). It is going to be interesting to follow the second Trump administration and note whether, as Hilferding prophesized, "the dictatorship of the [American] capitalist lords [becomes] increasingly incompatible with the capitalist interests of other countries" (Id.). We will be able to testify if the attraction of liberal democracy is stronger than a dictatorship of the capitalist lords for capitalist sustainability. Whether the interest of concentrated capital will grow to become irreconcilable with the interests of lower-level capitalists or whether crass environmental destruction will rein in the greed of the capitalist lords remains to be seen. Because the other lesson of ersatz socialism is its violent metamorphosis into a quasi-democratic capitalism. For a while it had to open its gates to include outsiders. Much like the bourgeois revolution.

6 So, What Is the Connection between Socialism and Capitalism?

Marx, imbued with Hegelian rationalism and technological determinism, viewed history as a linear class struggle leading to the dictatorship of the proletariat (1852), which Lenin defined as socialism in *State and Revolution* (1917). Benefitting from technological development, those owning capital will continue to accumulate capital and profit from its investment, only to witness under the laws of profit a centralization of the capital and a socialization of labor. As there will be always fewer owners and more wage-earners, the struggle will ensue.

Unfortunately, Marx was a romantic before he was a historian. He also believed in brotherly love among the wage-earners who somehow would organize themselves to do something rather magical and extraordinary: become well educated, well fed, well rested, and devoid of any conflicts and contradictions, while still heavily polluting the earth until its self-destruction, presumably. In lesser words in Chapter XXXII, of Capital Vol. I, he nevertheless stated that due to all technological gains, the "expropriators are expropriated" (1867). Only property demands owners to exercise dominion and agency and decide what needs to be done with the expropriated property. Thus, as shown here, the masses might have become factory and farm wage-earners, but never Marx's "expropriators." They remained the toilers, albeit under a different name.

That is why Robinson is so much clearer as a theoretician when she defines Russian socialism as a mere alternative capitalist society than any other theoretician. Though I would further clarify that it was a capitalist society where the state became the monopolist owner, whose managerial class ripped the benefits of that type of ownership, having expropriated the expropriators.

> It turned out that socialism [read the economic system built by Stalin and company] was not a stage beyond capitalism but an alternative

> means of carrying out industrialization. After some fumbling about the Soviet authorities realized that their task was to industrialize the economy that had come into their hands. Without capitalists to do the job and the profit motive to hide them, the State had to develop new organs for the planning and administration of all economic activities. Within twenty years, the U.S.S.R. had overtaken the greater part of the investment which had been accumulating in the Western world over 200 years. (Robinson, 1973, 76–77)

Again, the same dual nature of the concept of "capitalism" and that of "socialism" is on display in Robinson's magnificent analysis. And like Ricardo and Marx, she too regards society as a whole, the end goal of any economic system, whether be it capitalist or socialist. Today we use socialism or socialist as a deprecatory identifier because it denotes one's interest in the wellbeing of everyone. But that is the very reason to engage in any speculative thinking, in participating in politics or in any form of government-backed activity: for the societal wellbeing. And only the alternative should be deprecatory. The obtuse small-minded individualism, where the entire planet is burned into nothingness for the benefit of a single "rubber baron," whom all should have sung the requiem for a long time ago. Socialism is a theory worth investigating into praxis. It has never been tried, and thus never failed. Or, using Jameson's words, socialism has only presented itself as a "sketch or possibility of collective or cooperative production" (Jameson, 2009, 295).

CHAPTER 6

The Rule of Law in Ersatz Socialism

At its most basic level, all societies are an association of humans. Their eternal hostility to one another requires that order and freedom be maintained by government. That is done with the help of a specific linguistic tool called law. Law is the normative tool organizing all societies, as long as it emanates "from places of authority," (Kelsen, 1961, 78) and it reflects the political goals of the ruling government within the limits of what the governed is willing to accept. Law is thus both dynamic because its object—the behavior of people within communities—changes, and it is also somehow vague, as H.L.A. Hart often explained, because social order needs stable law (2012).

Throughout history, law has transformed from the decree of a single despotic will into the collective expression of diverse "imaginations, interests and visions" (Unger, 1996, 65). This evolution reflects the broader transition of sovereign political authority—from autocratic rule to the liberal state characteristic of Western political culture.

The liberal state itself has evolved. It traces its historical roots to the Glorious Revolution of 1688.[1] That revolution represented the victory of a multi-member legislative body, the English Parliament, over one legislative will, the king's. The Glorious Revolution stands for the victory of "impersonal rules" over the king's whimsical desires, expressed as subjective language, i.e., "because I say so." While this victory of the multitude over despotism is more than a Pyrrhic victory,[2] it is rather fragile.

1 Brief Definition of the Rule of Law in a Liberal Democracy

In its almost five centuries of history, our liberal society has embraced a specific approach to social order, defined as the Rule of Law. This is a principle of governance in which everyone, all people, institutions, and entities, public

1 John Miller, *The glorious revolution* (Longman, 1997); Larry Kramer. "Putting the Politics Back". 100 *Colum. L. Rev.* 215 (2000).

2 Plutarch in Life of Pyrrhus (Part of *Parallel Lives*, written in the 1st–2nd century CE), described King Pyrrhus' costly victory over the Romans at the Battle of Asculum (279 BCE). According to legend, after the battle, Pyrrhus supposedly said: "If we are victorious in one more battle with the Romans, we shall be utterly ruined." Thus, the expression of Pyrrhic victory.

 | DOI:10.1163/9789004747210_008

and private, including the state itself, are accountable to laws. Laws need to come from legitimate sources of authority, publicly promulgated, equally enforced, and independently adjudicated. Thus, everybody's conduct—what we "may do, ought to do, or ought not to do" (Unger, 1975, 69)—is the province of law. In a liberal society like ours, Roberto M. Unger would say that law limits "the pursuit of private ends" and facilitates mutual collaboration. More specifically, it is the job of the law to guarantee the supreme good of social life, order, and freedom. (Id.). Equality before the law, accountability to the law, fairness in the application of the law, separation of powers, participation in decision-making, legal certainty, avoidance of arbitrariness, and procedural and legal transparency.

All these concepts are rather ambiguous. But what is clear is that law is more than "an interpretive concept like courtesy," (Dworkin, 1986, 87) as explained by many scholars, including by one of my most esteemed co-authors, the late law professor Michael H. Davis. (Davis & Neacșu, 2014, 505). To represent a legitimate normative rule, governing our behavior and expecting obedience, law needs legitimacy. That derives from its sources, or what H.L.A. Hart called the "deliberate, datable acts," (Hart, 2012, 44) whether they come from a legislative, judiciary, or executive body.

Furthermore, liberal democracies presuppose constitutional checks and balances between the law-making branches of the government.[3] This principle is fundamental and ensures that power is distributed and limited to prevent authoritarianism and protect citizens' rights.

As a result of this constitutional principle, democratic governments are typically divided into three branches, which ensures their separation of powers and duties. Thus, all such legislative bodies are composed of lawmakers organized in something called either Congress or Parliaments. These bodies alone can pass legislation. Subsequently, legislation is enacted by another branch of the government, called the executive body. Such a body is composed of a president or a prime minister and their cabinet or government ministers. A third branch, called the judiciary, is charged with making sure all legislation, executive orders, or administrative regulations are constitutionally sound. Checks and balances ensure that no single branch becomes too powerful. Consequently, each branch is charged with checking the power of the other and making sure that no branch is usurping the duties of another. Of course,

3 Baron de Montesquieu (Charles-Louis de Secondat) proposed the doctrine of separation of powers in *The Spirit of the Laws* (1748), forming the foundation for modern checks and balances.

parliamentary systems in Europe have less strict separations of powers, i.e., the members of the government are also members of the legislative branch.

The separation of powers in the U.S. Constitution is primarily established in the first three articles, which define the three branches of government and their respective powers. Article I, Section 1 vests legislative power solely in Congress, meaning laws must be made by elected representatives, not the president or courts: "All legislative Powers herein granted shall be vested in a Congress of the United States, which shall consist of a Senate and House of Representatives." Article II, Section 1 vests executive power in the president, meaning only the president can execute and enforce laws: "The executive Power shall be vested in a President of the United States of America." Article III, Section 1 vests judicial power in the courts, meaning only the judiciary can interpret laws and rule on legal disputes: "The judicial Power of the United States shall be vested in one Supreme Court, and in such inferior Courts as the Congress may from time to time ordain and establish."

In addition, other constitutional provisions reinforce this democratic principle. Article I, Section 6, also called the "Incompatibility Clause," states that "Members of Congress cannot simultaneously hold executive or judicial office." Article I, Section 7, also known as the "Presentment Clause," states that "Laws must pass through both Houses of Congress and be signed (or vetoed) by the President, reinforcing separate roles."

The U.S. Constitution adds to this democratic principle of separation of powers provisions about how the three branches of the federal government prevent each other from overreaching through a system of checks and balances. Article I, Section 7 gives the U.S. President the power to veto laws, but then Congress can override the Presidential veto with a two-thirds vote. Furthermore, Congress can impeach and remove the President or federal judges through its impeachment power defined in Article I, Sections 2 and 3. However, the Constitution enumerates the specific powers Congress has in Article I, Section 8, thus preventing overreach into executive or judicial functions. More tenuous from a constitutional perspective is the judicial review check on congressional laws. It is implied in Article III but expressly stated and confirmed in *Marbury v. Madison*, 5 U.S. (1 Cranch 137, 1803). Since 1803, our judiciary has declared laws unconstitutional.

> It is emphatically the province and duty of the Judicial Department to say what the law is. Those who apply the rule to particular cases must, of necessity, expound and interpret that rule. If two laws conflict with each other, the Courts must decide on the operation of each. (1 Cranch 177, 1803)

2 Brief Definition of Soviet Rule of Law in Ersatz Socialism

The Rule of Law thus defines the ruling government and how its goals are translated into normative directions for that state's subjects. Therefore, its basic democratic principles would have to be evident in any legal system. Law is one of the most vivid and real way to express both what is "preached and what is practiced" in any society. As law professor Harold J. Berman explained, (1963, 3) that was true for all countries of the Soviet era, as well (Neacşu, 2025).

All Rule of Law "claims [is] that a legal system is legitimate if its rules are definite and predictable and are applied in a general, impartial, and non-retroactive manner" (Davis & Neacşu, 2001, 733). However, there is an element of normativity missing from this definition: that of the goal. To paraphrase F.A. Hayek, is it slavery or the opposite of slavery (1944, 13) that the Soviet Rule of Law promoted? Or, as captured by Leo Tolstoy's words: "Law? Natural law, state law, civil law, criminal law, catechetical law, law of war, international law, *das Recht, le Droit, parvo*. What does it mean, what is defined by this strange word?"[4]

The Tsarist Rule of Law, to the extent it even existed, was autocratic. After the demise of the Tsarist era, judges and other functionaries charged with preserving order and settling disputes were authorized to use "such laws of the dethroned Tsar as they might think still suitable as guidance."[5] The chaos of the 1919–1920 civil war further made it necessary for the governing forces to restore the previous Rule of Law, sometimes defined with the euphemism "capitalism," (Hazard et al., 1977, 5) which perhaps explains why the citizen's trust in their new legal order was "ambivalent at best" (Heuman, 1990, 3).

After the civil war chaos, nevertheless, the Soviet legal system did not embrace some democratic Rule of Law. To the contrary, it seems to have reverted to its historical tradition: despotism. The path Soviet law took was one of unchecked and unlimited state power, as law professor William E. Butler explained. "The concept of separation of power [had] been emphatically rejected in Soviet constitutional theory and jurisprudence" (Butler, 1988, 41).

Article 2 of the 1936 Constitution stated that "In the U.S.S.R. *all power* belongs to the working people of town and country as represented by the

---

4 Leo Tolstoy, Polnoe sobranie sochinenii, 1st series, vol. 38 (Moscow, 1936) pp. 55–56, as translated in Andrzej Walicki, *Legal Philosophies of Russian Liberalism* (London: Oxford University Press, 1987), pp. 80–81, quoted in Susan Eva Heuman, "Perspectives on Legal Culture in Prerevolutionary Russia", in *Revolution in Law. Contributions to the Development of Soviet Legal Theory, 1917–1938* (Piers Beirne, Ed., M.E. Sharpe, Inc. 1990) p. 3.

5 Decree Number 1 on the Courts, November 27, 1917, referenced in John N. Hazard et al., *The Soviet Legal System* (Oceana Publications, Inc., 1977) p. 5.

Soviets of Working People's Deputies" (emphasis added). By using such all-encompassing terminology, all power as opposed to clearly defined powers separated by each branch of the government, Soviet law clearly rejected liberal democracy. Furthermore, the Constitution separated the working from non-working people. Then, those working were further divided into working class members of various political organizations—such as the Soviets—and the others. Soviets were political councils. Forty years later, people are further distanced away from their government. Power becomes "state power." According to Article 2 on the 1977 Constitution the only power those politicized citizens exercised was "state power" (See Appendix A).[6] No matter how one defines a state, it is a corporate organization. Unless the state is the French King, Louis the XIV, of course. The Soviet corporate state embodied all power.

Certainly, if we were to believe critical legal studies or *crits* jurists,[7] law is political. Only, the *crits* criticize the school of thought which believes that law is a mere normative tool serving at the altar of a non-political Rule of Law, whose aim is social order unsubordinated to a political goal: social liberalism or neoliberalism. The crits' attacks on the legitimacy of the American Rule of Law are on a different level. The Soviet Rule of Law did not ensure the mass representation of the Supreme Soviet of the Soviet Union (Верховный Совет С.С.С.Р., Verkhovny Soviet U.S.S.R.). The Soviet Rule of Law legitimized the mere edicts of power, which represented the volition of the few elite members of the Politburo of the Communist Party of the Soviet Union (CPSU). To use the words of Justice Douglas, the Soviet Rule of Law was whatever the few Politburo members,[8] whose head in 1936 was Stalin, said.

In other words, the problem with the Rule of Law in post-Tsarist Russia was not Lenin's slogan "a law is a political measure, it is politics."[9] The problem was

---

6 See, Article 2. Appendix A.

> "Article 2. All power in the USSR belongs to the people.
>
> *The people exercise state power* through Soviets of People's Deputies, which constitute the political foundation of the USSR. All other state bodies are under the control of, and accountable to, the Soviets of People's Deputies."

Constitution (Fundamental Law) of the Union of Soviet Socialist Republics, Adopted at the Seventh (Special) Session of the Supreme Soviet of the USSR (October 7, 1977), https://www.marxists.org/history/ussr/government/constitution/1977/constitution-ussr-1977.pdf

7 For a history of this jurisprudential school of thought, see, e.g., Dana Neacşu, "CLS Stands for Critical Legal Studies, If Anyone Remembers", 8 *J.L. & Policy* 415, 425 (2000).

8 William O. Douglas. Foreword, vii in *Essays on Jurisprudence form the Columbia Law Review* (1963) ("In other lands 'Law is what the politburo [or church] decrees. [Yet] law is systematized in communist and in church-dominated societies as it is in the Western world.")

9 John N. Hazard et al., *The Soviet Legal System* (Oceana Publications, Inc., 1977) p. 5, paraphrasing V.I. Lenin, concerning a caricature of Marxism and concerning imperialist economism:

that law legitimized despotism—corporate despotism. Soviet politics *was* the law. That was the problem with the Soviet Rule of Law of ersatz socialism.

> With these words V.I. Lenin epitomized in 1916 his thinking on legal systems. The judges and administrators brought to office after the Russian revolution were frequently to cite these words as justification for application of measures dictated by their consciences, even thought they had no support for such action in the document in their hands with is inscription, "law," "decree" or "instruction." (Hazard, 1977, 5)

Soviet law formalized the power of the Politburo, a very small minority of the Soviet population. The law-making institutions of the Soviet regime did not regulate any transition to Marxian communism.

The Soviet power structure was capitalist as shown here. Capitalism means that the vast majority of the members of society work under the direction, "however mediated," of the "owners of the tools they need to provide for themselves, and on terms set by those owners in like with their desire to maximize the rate of increase of their capital" (Streeck, 2016, 2). In the U.S.S.R., the power was so centralized it was a dictatorship, especially under leaders like Stalin.

Evgeny B. Pashukanis published his famous book *The General Theory of Law and Marxism* in 1924, as Lenin's star was waning and Stalin's waxing. His legal analysis was from the perspective of a member of the Soviet intelligentsia. Thus, his legal comprehension offers as insightful a view of the law and the society it regulated as possible. Pashukanis never wavered from his description of Soviet law as bourgeois law. But, as explained here, bourgeois law can encourage social democracy or oligarchy or even dictatorship. Nevertheless, taken in the most generous light, Pashukanis's work only promotes a view of Soviet law as non-socialist. It is outside the scope of socialism.

His argument for the continuation of the previous legal system rests on his analysis of the existing legal institutions as well as on the work Marx and that of Lenin, which Pashukanis quotes often. The logical conclusion of his work is that to the extent that there is no socialist state nor socialist legal system, it is hard to imagine that the society thus governed is socialist. Or, how can one cut an oval-shaped cookie with a square-shaped cookie cutter? Rationally, it is not possible.

Pashukanis is Marxian in his view of the relation of law to society: laws mirror their society governing social behavior in a way that preserves that society's

"Laws are political measures, politics" in 23 *Lenin Collected Works*, (Progress Publishers, Moscow, 1964) p. 48. https://www.marxists.org/archive/lenin/works/1916/carimarx/.

cultural values. For Pashukanis, the Soviet legal system was bourgeois, but the Rule of Law was neither social democracy nor despotic tsarism: "the foundations of the old legal order have collapsed … the old laws, statutes and regulations have been transformed into a heap of waste paper" (Guins, 1954, 42). It was clearly despotic, though: "The system of norms expresses the will of the entire Soviet people, which is led by the working class, *headed by the Communist Party*" (Id., emphasis added). Thus, the laws were not democratic. They did not represent the Russian people. They represented the so-called working class, which was viewed as separate from the peasants, who represented the vast majority of Russians, and even the working class was represented only to the extent it was politicized. The levels of exclusion are remarkable. Or, to continue to use Pashukanis's vocabulary, it was an ever more "narrow horizon of bourgeois right" (Id., 61). Linguistically, Soviet Russia became socialist in 1936. The West went along with this and embraced the Stalinization of the Soviet law under the label of "socialist." In 1954, George C. Guins wrote:

> Socialist law. … is a system of norms established by the *regime of toilers* in the form of legislation for the purpose of protecting, strengthening and developing socialist relations and of building a communist society. (Id.)

As such, the West saw the Soviet Rule of Law as the Rule of Law of the toilers. The West forgot to explain how toilers, who presumably toil for a living, also legislate. More reasonable for our common sense is to accept Lenin's point that whatever the party leaders deemed obeyable was obeyed as law. Such a despotic rule of law could only define ersatz socialism. Taking into consideration that the fundamental law of 1977 defined politics as the province of state corporate power, then it is safe to assume the Soviet Rule of Law was that of the state capital monopoly.

3 Soviet Private (Civil) Law: the Law of Property and Contracts

As Michael Harrington so well summarized in *Socialism* (1989), the apparatchiks (or nomenklatura) and the enlightened workers, the proletariat, were "false brothers." The working class continued to be employed to use those means of production for the benefit of a new class of managers. The Soviet economic forces, as Pashukanis noted in 1930, stopped having "capital entrepreneurs" as their "bearers."[10] Statism or state monopoly was the economic

10 Pashukanis's 1930 Speech on the Soviet State and the Revolution Law, quoted in Robert Conquest, *Justice and the Legal System in the USSR* 16 (1968).

foundation of the Soviet economy, in addition to agricultural collectives. The proletariat used the means of production to create value for the owner, the state, which distributed it to those at the top according to their desires and to those who had produced it according to some qualified need. "The state that possesses those means of production is virtually the private property of a bureaucracy [apparatchiks] that manages them in the name of the people" (Harrington, 1989, 61).

Thus, the Soviet era used legal institutions fit to preserve market production and exchange. The need for private law derived from the existence of private relations.

This book goes beyond the capitalist nature of the Soviet legal system. It identifies a particular type of capitalism with Soviet socialism, or ersatz socialism. While the "vertical system of Soviet law" started with the U.S.S.R. Constitution (Ioffe & Maggs, 1983, 136) it extended to legal norms of local importance. At the horizontal local level, the system contained civil law (private law) and administrative law (public law), which further encompassed penal law. The Soviet state, for instance, was covered by public constitutional and administrative law when acting as the sovereign Russian entity and by private civil law when acting as a property owner, or more accurate yet, as the major property owner (Braginsky, 1988).

That private law, which in Russia and its satellite countries is called "civil law," was derived from continental bourgeois civil law is of a lesser importance (Neacșu, 2025). All aspects of civil law—contracts and property—were published as codifications, not unlike the French Civil Code which codified those rights and duties. Civil law codification was a major achievement of Soviet Russia as well as all ECE countries, as V.S. Pozdnyakov explained, (1982) and here it is used as proof that the type of society—bourgeois—which needed that legislation continued, albeit in a different illiberal and undemocratic manner. But its market economy, also adjusted to state corporate monopoly, continued as well (Zile, 1992, 143).

Lenin's institutional framework, including civil codes, was adapted to the reality of a market economy that built on the Tsarist exchanges between latifundio rural owners and urban, bourgeois areas. With the nationalization of both rural lands and urban factories, the New Economic Policy (NEP) of March 1921 needed new civil legislation, redefining the new market forces: "Market freedom is freedom of trade, and freedom of trade means ... capitalism," (Id., 145) Lenin stated at the Bolshevik Congress of March 15, 1921. What is striking is the property regime in state monopoly capitalism. That state property is a type of corporate property which engaged the marketplace, much like any cartel, trusts, or any vertical monopoly of the size of Amazon or Meta, which still engage the marketplace.

3.1 *Contractual Rights and Obligations*

E. Allan Farnsworth in *Farnsworth on Contracts* (1990), a widely referenced treatise in U.S. contract law, defines contractual rights within the framework of legally enforceable agreements. Contractual rights are expectation interests created through mutual agreement and recognized by law. They oblige parties to perform agreed upon duties or provide remedies if obligations are breached.

Farnsworth studied Soviet law as well. Farnworth and his co-author, Mozolin, started *Contract Law in the USSR and the United States (1987)* by stating that "the concept of contract law in Soviet civil law consists of two elements that are inseparably connected. One of these relates to the legal conception of contract, and the other to its social purposes."[11] Next, the co-authors identified the basic elements of the Soviet contract:

> The components include the agreement between the parties, the means of performance of the contract, and the extent of the responsibilities of the parties for nonperformance or improper performance of their duties.[12]

While I cannot detect any difference between a binding contract in New York and one in the U.S.S.R., Farnsworth found one: "every contract is an agreement, but not every agreement is a contract."[13] It seems circuitous, but what Farnsworth and Mozolin want to say is that only voluntary agreements which satisfy state-endorsed requirements are binding. Again, this is a distinction without difference. In New York, you cannot sell your wife or husband in bondage either. It is against the law of the land.

Nevertheless, Farnsworth and Mozolin presented Soviet contract law as different than what Pashukanis would have called bourgeois contract law. This is because Farnsworth seemed to have drunk the socialist Kool-Aid, so to speak. Farnworth and Mozolin insisted that Soviet contracts represented "the creation of a new contractual relationship in connection with the transition to a socialist organization of the economy, based on *public forms of property and planned supervision of the economy*."[14] That is how Farnsworth incorporated the Soviet propaganda about socialism.

---

11 E. Allan Farnsworth & Mozolin, *Contract Law in the USSR and the United States* (1987), p. 3.
12 Id., p. 4.
13 Id., p. 5.
14 E. Allan Farnsworth and Viktor P. Mozolin, *Contract Law in the USSR and the United States* (1987), p. 47.

> The history of the creation and development of socialism in USSR can be divided into three major stages. These are: first, the stage of the construction of the foundations of socialism (the transitional period), occupying the first two decades of the Great October Socialist Revolution of 1917; second, the stage of the complete and final victory of socialism, from the mid-1930's to the end of the 1950's and early 1960's; and third, the stage of developed socialism. The country is now in the initial stage of developed socialism.[15]

Only four years later, Igor I. Kavass of Vanderbilt University brought to American scholars the view that the Rule of Law under Gorbachev, the last president of the U.S.S.R., slowly promoted transparency, showing the role played by "the Soviet police state."[16] The pretense of socialism was dropped from the legal parlance.

So then why use Farnsworth and Mozolin's faulty analysis? Because it is the commonsense view, and because it is easy to correct. As shown here, there were no socialist stages of development, only stages of police state monopoly. What Farnsworth called "public forms of property" and "planned supervision of the economy" can easily be supplanted by product and geographic market definitions. If our American law was intent on promoting competition and preventing monopolies when it passed antitrust legislation, as the U.S. Supreme Court settled in 1951,[17] a lot has changed since. Or one may say that the economist view of competition has replaced the commonsense, or layperson's, view. It seems rational to assume that the market requires laws which protect competition and thus a variety of contracts.

> When laypersons, including some lawyers, speak of "competition" they think of a market containing numerous firms—the more numerous, the more "competitive" the market. Protecting "competition" may then mean preserving a market structure that permits small firms to enter freely and profit, even if this entails forcing larger firms not to compete too strenuously lest the smaller ones be unable to survive.[18]

---

15 Id.

16 Igor I. Kavass, *Gorbachev's Law* (1991) ix.

17 *Standard Oil Co. v. F.T.C.*, 340 U.S. 231, 249 (1951).

18 Phillip E. Areeda and Herbert Hovenkamp, Vol 1 *Antitrust Law, An Analysis of Antitrust Principles and Their Application*, (Aspen, 2006) p. 3.

In the beginning, as of 1921, the U.S.S.R. encouraged such competitive markets, as when peasants entered in a variety of production and delivery contracts with various state organizations. Farm goods were purchased by the army, the party, and other local organizations. This was a moneyed commodity-exchange marketplace.

Lenin's New Economic Plan promoted the marketplace, although the NEP was explained as "a temporary and restricted rebirth of private property."[19] "*However, as the law shows,* NEP was more far-reaching, because *it placed the entire Soviet economy on a monetary basis* and granted extensive independence to economic organizations"[20] (emphasis added). Even after 1927, when the Fifteenth Party Congress changed the NEP rules, ensuring the economic independence of economic institutions, their legal civil status never changed. The NEP economic trusts morphed into economic organizations. The new economic organizations preserved their ability to negotiate economic contracts: credit, distribution, transportation, etc., only under different parameters.[21] For instance, the individual civil liability of economic enterprises (contractual, quasi contractual and tortious) increased after the 1930–1931 credit reform.[22]

One of the major legal voices in Lenin's Russia, Evgheny Pashukanis, devoted many pages to the formality of civil law, as opposed to public law.[23] He understood that all law, including private law such as the law of contracts, governs a specific slice of reality through abstractions: rights and duties. These concepts are used to distinguish between things which are so often encountered: commodity exchanges, that the concepts defining those activities become clear.

> It is only in the conditions of commodity production that the abstract legal farm is necessary—it is only there that the capacity to have a right in general is distinguished from specific claims and privileges. *It is only the constant transfer of property rights in the market that creates the idea of an immobile bearer of these rights. Indeed, the abstract capacity of everyone to be a bearer of property rights makes it difficult for bourgeois thought*

19 Olympiad S. Ioffe, and Peter B. Maggs, *Soviet Law in Theory and Practice* (Oceana Publications, Inc., 1983), p. 136.
20 Id.
21 Id., p. 138.
22 Id.
23 Evgheny Pashukanis, *The General Theory of Law and Marxism.*

> *to see anything else than subjects of rights*: legal fetishism complements commodity fetishism. (emphasis added)[24]

However, Pashukanis might have engaged in wishful thinking when he thought that identical legal institutions can be used to different, extraordinarily different, ends than their ordinary purpose. Contracts regulate the lack of satisfactory performance: no one signs contracts for their execution but in the advent of a lack of it. Contracts, as a regulated source of individual rights and duties, assume the existence of a market where exchanges take place.

Half a century later, Soviet jurists recognized the role of civil law in the Soviet society.

> Soviet civil law is one of the basic branches of Soviet law. Among the various social relationships, the determinant ones are the economic relationships. *It is the task of civil law to regulate those which are conditioned by commodity-money forms*. Therefore, civil law holds an important place in Soviet society, and its object is a wide range of social relationships. (emphasis added)[25]

The Civil Codes adopted in 1922 and then in 1963–64 were influenced by the Napoleonic Code of 1804.[26] The 1922 Leninist Civil Code recognized "the revolutionary aspect of capitalism: the equal capacity of all citizens to enjoy civil rights, irrespective of their sex, race, nationality, faith, or origin,"[27] Adult women and men could sell their labor for a salary. Civil law legislation governing property relations, personal, and non-property relations focused on the sources of individual and organizational rights and duties, where private persons as well as corporations or other entities acquired contractual, quasi-contractual, or tortious rights and obligations.[28]

Civil contracts, as a legal institution, always existed in the U.S.S.R. "The Soviet Constitution of 1936 fixed the basic socio-economic provisions for civil

---

24 *Evgeny B. Pashukanis, Law and Marxism: A General Theory of Law and Marxism*. 14 (Routledge 2002 [1924]).

25 *Soviet Civil Law* (O.N. Sadikov, Ed., M.E. Sharpe, Inc., 1988), p. 3.

26 *See, Code civil des Français 1804–2024* (under the supervision of Piere-Yves Gautier, Dalloz 2024).

27 Ye. Fleishits, A. Makovsky, *The Civil Codes of the Soviet Republics*, (Progress Publishers, Moscow, 1976) p. 9.

28 See, generally, *Soviet Civil Law* (O.N. Sadikov, Ed., M.E. Sharpe, Inc., 1988).

contracts."[29] Those contractual parties changed, too, as the market became regulated by the "the state national economic plan," formulated in Article 11 of the 1936 Constitution. From the antitrust perspective of the American Bar Association, that only meant that the definition of a market incorporated more of an economist's perspective.[30]

The purpose of a market definition is both to understand the capitalist nature of the Soviet legal system and then its monopolist element. The U.S.S.R.'s economy was defined by the police state ownership—Articles 4, 5 and 6 of the 1936 Constitution—engaged in production and then market contractual exchanges according to the "national economic plan," whose aim was, according to Article 11 of the same constitution, increasing "wealth," as well as "consolidating the [state] independence," and "strengthening" its military. As renowned antitrust scholars Areeda and Hovenkamp explained, such consolidation is the sign of a competitive market, in the capitalist meaning of competition.

> The [capitalist] economist's idea of "competition" is related to performance rather than to mere number of rivals. An economist might say that optimal competition occurs when the firms in a market price their output at marginal cost and costs are minimized by internal efficiency, research and development, and attainment of economies of scale or scope.[31]

If this explanation is not very clear, then Areeda and Hovenkamp further explained that the market is competitive when the most profit is produced. In their words: "a market with three sellers but an output of 100 units per day is more competitive than one with ten sellers but an output of only 80 unites per day."[32] Thus, the heavily planned Soviet market resembles a highly competitive though monopolist market. And this is the goal of this book: to explain the type of capitalist legal system of Soviet Russia and the other ECE countries and debunk the myth of Soviet socialism as ersatz socialism.

---

29 E. Allan Farnsworth and Viktor P. Mozolin, *Contract Law in the USSR and the United States* (1987), p. 72.

30 ABA Section on Antitrust Law. *Market Definition in Antitrust. Theory and Case Studies* (ABA, 2012) p. 1 ("The purpose of market definition is to provide a context within which competitive effects can be analyzed, and it is frequently a critical and extremely fact-intensive element of antirust cases.")

31 Phillip E. Areeda and Herbert Hovenkamp, Vol. 1 *Antitrust Law, An Analysis of Antitrust Principles and Their Application*, (Aspen, 2006) p. 3.

32 Id.

Even Farnsworth and Mozolin had to agree that legislation endorsed both contracts between state organization and those in which the individual participated (Farnsworth & Mozolin, 1987, 74).

> For example, in the field of supply, there was a transition from the system of general and local contracts to one of direct contracts made between producers and consumers of products. In a number of cases, these contracts were made with marketing and supply organizations. This was promoted by such factors as the strengthening of the self-supporting status of productive enterprises, and the transition, in a number of sectors of industry, to the so-called two-tier *system of management* (consisting of the enterprise and the Glavk, of the People's Commissariat) with the abolition of the trust and its intermediate link. (Id., 72)

What transpires from the analysis of scholarship written by American jurists who studied the Soviet legal system is that they did notice the geographical and product consolidation of the Soviet market, but rather than calling it monopolist, they called it whatever their Soviet counterparts chose to call it. The late law professor E. Allan Farnsworth went for "socialist." Nevertheless, their analysis leaves little room for interpretation, conceptual misnomers aside. Defining product (steel or cement) and geographic dimensions of the market (the entire Soviet market dominated by the Soviet police state ownership) helps us identifying market participants and measure market shares and market concentration. Furthermore, that state ownership never deluded any foreign jurists as "property of the people" of the U.S.S.R. is obvious from the very system of management the state property required for the economy to be functional. Contracts were written and entered into by managers. How contractual duties and performances were discharged was the province of managers. The economy might have been planned for "increasing public wealth," but that wealth trickled down from the managerial class to improve "working conditions" of the working class. Certainly, there were contracts whose object was the construction of dams, new factories, new public projects, new schools, and hospitals. The working class worked for these public projects, whose management ensured a hierarchy of profit sharing: the political elite, then the military and paramilitary elite, the professional classes, and, finally, the toilers.

How the state monopoly impacted the regime of property in the Soviet economy further explains the capitalist nature of the Soviet legal system and especially its monopolism. Soviet contract law, as well as the regime of property encouraged in the U.S.S.R. until their demise under Gorbachev, solidified this legal regime.

3.2 *The Soviet Regime of Property: State Monopoly, Collectivist, and Private*

In 1959, Stefan Heym, a German writer of renown, wrote with admiration about the tremendous achievements of Soviet industrialization in four decades. He admired the

> Leningrad Metal Works [which] lie at the Neva where the river turns drab and is no longer fringed by palaces with white columns and pink cornices and golden roofs. It's an old plant, as industry goes, dating back to prerevolutionary times, and it has made electric power history. (Heym, 1959, 38)

That electric power plant was the "state property," which was defined as "the possession of the whole people." Only that was impossible, despite being the letter of the U.S.S.R. 1936 Constitution, Article 5 (See Appendix A). Possession has always meant, in law, physical possession. The Leningrad Metal Works which lied on the Neva River could not possibly be in the physical possession of 100 million Russians. That figure of speech is called, in law, a "legal fiction." Dams are often public property because their product benefits the public. Electricity benefits the public, and as shown in this book in many countries, the state owns all or part of the national electric grid. For instance, in the U.S., the Tennessee Valley Authority (TVA), is a federally owned electric utility serving the Tennessee Valley region. It remains one of the largest public power providers in the U.S. The Bonneville Power Administration (BPA) is a federal agency under the U.S. Department of Energy, which primarily manages hydroelectric dams on the Columbia River and supplies power to utilities in the Pacific Northwest. The Sacramento Municipal Utility District (SMUD) is a publicly owned electric utility serving Sacramento, California. The examples can continue with the EDF (Électricité de France) in France, one of the world's largest electricity companies, which is majority-owned by the French government. There is also the state-owned entity that operates the Three Gorges Dam in China, which is the world's largest hydroelectric power plant.

Thus, state-owned plants whose role is to ensure public wellbeing are the norm. So why was Stefan Heym so impressed with the Leningrad Metal Works? Because there is something hopeful in seeing technological progress in a backward country which suffered enormous destruction during the World War II. But having access to state-produced electricity is not a sign of socializing profit and thus socialism. It is a sign of industrialization, achieved in the United States by cartels and market manipulation by various industry barons through vertical and horizontal market monopolization. It is also a sign of resilience and definitely a sign of great capital investment, which in Soviet Russia was possible only because the market was controlled by state monopoly capitalism.

The economy in Russia was not socialist. It was a hybrid of state, collective, and individual enterprises, as Articles 5–9 of the Constitution reveled. The Soviet state was the main owner despite calling state property "the common possession of the entire Soviet people" (Braginsky, 1988, 5). As shown in this book, names are fundamental, but often they are occluding reality for political gain.

This hybrid regime of property was covered by fundamental pieces of legislation. The 1936 Constitution listed the types of property belonging to the state and to various collectivities. The state was the major property owner (Id.).

> **ARTICLE 6.** The land, its natural deposits, waters, forests, mills, factories, mines, rail, water and air transport, banks, post, telegraph, and telephones, large state organized agricultural enterprises (state farms, machine and tractor stations and the like) as well as municipal enterprises and the bulk of the dwelling houses in the cities and industrial localities, are *state property*, that is, belong to the whole people. (Appendix A, emphasis added)

From a legal perspective, state property could not be in "the possession of the whole people," as claimed by Article 5 of the 1936 Constitution. Indeed, civil legislation stressed the role of the state as the "sole owner of this property" (Appendix A). The common understanding of how legal title—abstract ownership—works is through possession—the de-facto ownership. And here it is really difficult to explain property, if possession, which involves use and enjoyment, is supposed to belong to the holder of legal title. It requires a level of abstraction and mental gymnastics which become dubious to any commoner. "Can I eat the apple?", Eve must have asked the serpent offering it while biting, in a gesture of obvious ownership enjoyment, and thus opening herself to the consequences of her actions. Otherwise, only the serpent would have been responsible.

> Art. 11 also stipulates that state property—the *common possession of the entire Soviet people*—is the principal form of socialist property. The *state possesses* 92 per cent of fixed production assets and this fact highlights its vast importance for the socialist economy. While the *state possesses its own property*, it distributes the greater part of it among state enterprises, associations and other organizations. All of them are *vested with the right to possess, use and dispose of appropriate state property* (the right of operative management of property—according to the terminology of the law giver) and, accordingly they have the possibility of acting on their own behalf as legal persons in civil relations. (emphasis added) (Appendix A)

Title and possession of the object owned are different. Belonging could reference both. Nearly "the entire industrial output and about one-third of farm produce comes from the public sector of the economy," (Braginsky, 1988, 69) and the greater part of the national wealth, land, mineral resources, forests, etc., "*belongs* to the state" (Article 11, Appendix A, emphasis added).

Title and physical possession are separate, especially in corporate law, where personhood is a legal fiction. Such separation enables needed legal flexibility to attain many desired results. For instance, stakeholders have various types of interests, the board of directors, others, and those employed by the corporation, yet a different set of rights and duties. In fact, A.V. Venediktov tried to solve this puzzling issue regarding the state ownership, which is so identical to a corporate monopoly, and he stated that the right to property is different from its three civil law components: use, disposal and possession. His definition is utterly unclear except to say that the right to property is the right to use that property according to the rules in existence.[33] The proletariat did use the means of production according to their employment contracts to fulfill their contractual obligations. The "fruits" of that production were state property (Braginsky, 1988, 71) and were distributed by the various state-owned economic entities according to various contracts, all promoting the status quo of that societal power structure.

Both the 1936 Constitution and the subsequent codification, the Civil Code of 1922, an updated version of the "antiquated draft of the Russian [Tsarist] Civil Code," (Kantorovich, 1922, 782) embraced private property.

At the fourth session of the Ninth Congress of the All-Russian Central Executive Committee of the Soviets, held in October 1922, the Civil Code was passed. It took effect on January 1, 1923. "The very fact of the *adoption of a code* of laws," (Id.) as Jacob Kantorovich noted in 1922, was proof that the Soviet legal regime was amiable to private property. Moreover, Kantorovich identified that codification as more consequential. It was "intended to uphold and regulate *private property relations in Soviet Russia* is a striking indication of the departure of the governing party from the communistic experiment which had been carried on by it during the first three and a half years of its rule" (Id.). In this book, I argue that the soviet Rule of Law was always capitalist, only the property at its heart was not individually owned, but state-owned. Either way, its owners were not the Russian people.

Case on point, Sections 54–57 of the 1922 Code further reference private property. Private property appears in various listings of what is considered "not

---

33 Braginsky, p. 71 (quoting A.V. Venediktov, Socialist State Ownership, 1948, p. 34).

exempt from private business intercourse." That non-exhaustive list contains: "non-municipalized buildings, commercial enterprises, industrial enterprises employing not more than the number of wage earners fixed by special laws, tools and means of production, money, commercial paper and other things of value, including gold and silver coins and foreign currency, articles of domestic and household use, and of personal consumption, merchandise whose sale is not prohibited by law" (Sections 54–57 of the 1922). In addition, "cooperative organizations are granted the privilege, as compared with private individuals, to own industrial enterprises without restriction of the number of workers employed therein" (Id.). The same privilege is likewise granted to those who have received a government concession: "their private property may extend to enterprises wherein the number of hired workers exceeds that fixed by general law, as well as the telegraph and radio-telegraph and other services of public utility" (Id.).

Thus, until the 1936 Constitution, the 1922 Civil Code established a clear private property regime, which was very much like that of any "capitalistic codes."

> The Soviet Code concedes to the proprietor, within limits fixed by law, the right of possession, use, and management of his property and the right to recover the same from persons holding it contrary to law, as well as the right to redress for all violations of his title, even though the same may not involve actual seizure of his property. (Id.)

That Article 10 of the 1936 Constitution (Appendix A) reflected the fact that private property continued to exist indicates that the Rule of Law in Soviet Russia encouraged some form of capitalist property. Private property included income from work, savings, dwellings and houses, household furniture and utensils, articles of personal use and convenience, as well as inherited personal property.

> ARTICLE 10. The right of citizens to personal ownership of their incomes from work and of their savings, of their dwelling houses and subsidiary household economy, their household furniture and utensils and articles of personal use and convenience, as well as the right of inheritance of personal property of citizens, is protected by law. (Appendix A)

Nothing changed with the new Civil Code and U.S.S.R. Constitution. Personal property continued to be protected by Article 13 of the 1977 Constitution (Hecht, 1983, 28) and the 1964 Civil Codes. People owned their earned income and savings, their dwellings and subsidiary home enterprises, including their right to inherit personal property (A.B.A., 1968, 75).[34] The legal system allowed for increased gaps among the haves and the haves-nots.

The basis of personal property stemmed from the labor contract, a basic instrument of any bourgeois society. Labor was still the basis of a worker's wage, even if the market changed its perceived arbitrariness, Pashukanis wrote.[35]

> Not for nothing did Engels call the juridical way of looking at things the classical world view of the bourgeoisie, a kind of "secularisation of the theological" in which "human justice takes the place of dogma and divine right, and the state takes the place of the church". (Engels, 1887)[36]

However, individual private property was never the bulk of Soviet property. State-owned property represented the bulk of property in U.S.S.R. and the ECE countries. Nevertheless, the legal regime that governed both individual and corporate (state) property had many common elements, which support the argument that the Rule of Law was capitalist.

For instance, civil legislation—private law—covered both the regime of personal property—its acquisition and transfer—but also aspects regarding the management of state property. For instance, while the state owned the natural resources and most of the means of production—factories, and land, as well as all schools, hospitals, means of public transportation, etc.—the regime of rights remained influenced by the bourgeois civil codes of the nineteenth century. Thus, "the bulk of state assets were assigned to various state organizations, mainly economic."[37] These subsidiaries exercised corporate "operational management"[38] that delegated "right of possession, use and disposal"[39] according to terms imposed by the parent company, which ultimately directed the subsidiary's operations and decision-making. And the basis of the rights of corporate possession, use, and disposal were those explained in the bourgeois civil codes of nineteenth century.

---

34 The ABA Standing Committee on Education about Communism and Its Contrast with Liberty under Law, *A Contrast between the Legal Systems in the United States and in the Soviet Union* (ABA, 1968), p. 75.

35 *Id.* at 62.

36 Friedrich Engels, Juristensozialismus, in *Neue Zeit* (1887) quoted in *Evgeny B. Pashukanis, Law and Marxism: A General Theory of Law and Marxism*, 33 (Routledge 2002 [1924]).

37 Ye. Fleishits, A. Makovsky, *The Civil Codes of the Soviet Republics*, (Progress Publishers, Moscow, 1976) p. 68.

38 Id.

39 Id.

Despite any fiction to the contrary, the Soviet market continued much as any capitalist market: the democracy or autocracy of the system governing it does not trickle down into the essence of the market transactions—the transfer or rights and duties. Indeed, property became mostly corporate, state monopoly and in a small proportion belonged to kolkhozniks[40] and even less to private individuals. Property needed the "organizing role of contracts" so that the Soviet economy[41] could function. Among those contracts were business contracts.

The Soviet codes regulated all types of business contracts, "contracts of delivery, contracts of capital construction and contracts of delivery,"[42] and also contracts between Soviet banks and the corporate entities and other organizations they served.[43] Finally, those codification covered specific contracts between individuals and state entities, including various letting contracts—the most ordinary being one of letting lodging—and contracts regarding intellectual property, from whose fruits both state organizations and individuals could benefit.[44]

If this ersatz legal theory is not sufficient proof that the difference between the Soviet state as corporate monopolist and the state as "socialist" owner is one without meaning, then perhaps the common agreement between all jurists that the property of "the people" was their income is proof that the Soviet society was one of toilers toiling for the benefit of their rulers. Their income was personal property and did not come from redistributing any industrial output or national wealth. The people's wealth was their income, their salary, their wage, just like all proletarian or salaried employees in any capitalist economy. And like all salaried workers in any capitalist economy, they spent a percentage of it on electricity, water, rented lodging, food, and anything else their salary allowed.

---

40 S. Bratus, E. Fleishits & R. Khalfina eds., *Soviet Civil Legislation and Procedure* 56 (1962). ("Communist construction is based on the principle of material incentives for citizens, enterprises, kolkhozes, and other economic organisations.")

41 Inga S. Markovits, *Civil Law in East Germany-Its Development and Relation to Soviet Legal History and Ideology*, 78 *Yale L.J.* 1, 34 (1968).

42 Ye. Fleishits, A. Makovsky, *The Civil Codes of the Soviet Republics*, (Progress Publishers, Moscow, 1976) p. 145 et al.

43 Id.

44 Id.

4 Soviet Public Law Implemented a Dictatorial Rule of Law

The 1917 Bolshevik Revolution was marred by violence: an international war, World War I, and the internal civil war. Thus, for a few years, the legal order was a hybrid state of emergency normative acts which dealt with real and imagined fears of "counterrevolution, desertion and speculation,"[45] as well as legal rules and principles which ensured "effective functioning of neo-capitalism."[46] But more importantly was that the law of the land was ossifying into an anti-democratic Rule of Law. The new Soviet legal order, despite any pretense of being revolutionary, remained marred in Tsarist principles of legality. Or their lack of it.

After having been deleted from the previous Tsarist criminal code in 1903, the Bolsheviks reintroduced a principle of judging and applying sentences by "analogy" for behavior which appeared criminal to the judge, despite it not being criminalized by the penal code. This political rule of law, judging by analogy, nevertheless seemed to trust the freedom of political conscious of the judges and other magistrates too much. In the words of the People's Commissariat of the Leading Principles of Criminal Law, a primary focus of the new regime of legality became "the struggle against the violators" of the conditions of new life and "the final smashing" of the "overthrown bourgeoisie and intermediate classes."[47] Their menace was terrifying especially because of their lack of basis in reality. The only intermediate classes to overthrow were the military, paramilitary, professional, and managerial classes terrorizing the working class and suspected members of the intermediate classes just listed.

The historic record shows that from the very first days of the Soviet regime, legality was not legitimized by sovereign delegation of power. Legality was whatever the state agencies of terror and intimidation dictated.

> From early days, the Police had openly conducted not only the investigative, but also, in many cases, the "judicial" aspect of political cases. In March, 1920, the Cheka was authorized to sentence people to up to five years in labour camps by administrative decision if the investigation did not "reveal sufficient evidence" for judicial proceedings. We have the Cheka archives from Smolensk covering the period February–April 1921

---

45 Robert Conquest, *Justice and the Legal System in the USSR* 14 (1968).

46 Decree Number 1 on the Courts, November 27, 1917, referenced in John N. Hazard et al., *The Soviet Legal System* (Oceana Publications, Inc., 1977) p. 5.

47 *Id.*

> [and] there is no reference to any law on which decisions are based, the accused are absent, and there is no record of any defense.[48]

Evgeny Pashukanis was a first-rate legal theorist. And his analysis of law, legal norms and the legal system is illuminating yet always contradictory. On one hand, "the characteristic traits of law as a logical category ... as a prescriptive *Ought* is as much an element of ethics, aesthetics, and technology as it is of law."[49] On the other hand, it is a social system which reflects the very society it organizes, being "conditioned by the state of its social productive forces."[50] Pashukanis reconciles these contradictions when he emphasizes that the "legal system" is a "form of social system."[51] But, on the next page, Pashukanis contradicts himself again when he takes back the logical inference that each social system reflects the society which it structures. He states that there no connection between the legal form and the behavior it regulates: the "unconditional subjection to an external norm-setting authority has nothing whatever to do with the legal form."[52] And, as if two sets of contradictions are not enough, Pashukanis then says legal forms are porous, not dogmatic, especially when it comes to the distinction between public and private law, where public law governs the individual's behavior as citizen, and private law governs the egoistic interests of that citizen. Thus, Pashukanis's last word is a plea against his previous denial of the connection between social reality and legal institutions.

The insight from Pashukanis's analysis is that bourgeois legal forms cannot but reflect a bourgeois, capitalist, reality. It did not reflect a liberal capitalism but an illiberal autocratic society whose economic foundation was state capitalism.

Where Marx stopped short of defining the state of the capitalist legal order "bourgeois," Pashukanis relies on Lenin's work, which states that "of course, bourgeois right ... presupposes the existence of a *bourgeois state*" (emphasis added).[53] This is because there cannot be any other state, concludes Pashukanis, further referencing Marx. Until labor remains "a means of life,"[54] then state violence is necessary to implement the legal norms necessary to protect such use of labor, and that state can only be capitalist.

---

48 Robert Conquest, *Justice and the Legal System in the USSR* 8.
49 *Pashukanis, Law and Marxism: A General Theory of Law and Marxism*, 100.
50 *Id.* at 94.
51 *Id.* at 100.
52 *Id.* at 101.
53 *Id.* at 63 (quoting Lenin's State and Revolution).
54 *Id.* at 63 (quoting Marx's Marginal Notes).

If private, contract, and property law, for instance, contain the instruments of the previous legal system which promoted some variety of capitalism in both Tsarist Russia and the various ECE imperial colonies of the Ottoman, Austro-Hungarian, or Tsarist empires, public law, is equally marred in the previous regime.

From 1917 until 1936, the first two decades of transition from a Tsarist rule of law to a Stalinist rule of law, legal scholars did not feel the need to add any other element to the traditional comparatist classification of Western legal systems: common and civil law. Similarly in Russia, the Rule of Law was that of the previous regime.

> It will become possible for the state to wither away completely when society adopts the rule: "From each according to his ability, to each according to his needs," i.e. when people have become so accustomed to observing the fundamental rules of social intercourse and when their labour becomes so productive that they will voluntarily work according to their ability. (Lenin, 1969)[55]

Russia was regarded as a state-capitalist society.[56] The formality of the sources of rights and duties, acknowledging its reductionism, made it clear that legitimately there could only be two in a democracy: the will of the people or the will of judges. But then, in the middle of the 1930s, quite a few illiberal epistemic earthquakes were happening in Europe. Hitler, Mussolini, and Franco were shaking European liberal democracies but not necessarily their capitalist private property foundation. Meanwhile, Stalin was shaking both the liberal democratic structure and its private property ownership, annihilating democracy with a dictatorship and private property with corporate statism.

Once Stalin ascended to power, the Rule of Law solidified its dictatorial nature.

The administration of law produced terror in those applying it and in those who suffered its application. Moreover, the Stalinist state was a ruthless dictatorship. Violence was at its core, as the political purges and the political trials taken place during that era showed. One such trial was the one taken place in

---

55 *Evgeny B. Pashukanis, Law and Marxism: A General Theory of Law and Marxism*. 22 (Routledge 2002 [1924]), quoting *V.I. Lenin, Selected Works*, London 1969, p. 333.

56 *See, e.g., John Hazard, Soviet Legal Philosophy* (1951) (summarizes the evolution of the triumvirate classification). See also *Raya Dunayeveskaya, Russia as State-Capitalist Society* (1973). Similarly, *see, e.g., Ivo Lapenna, State and Law: Soviet and Yugoslav Theory* (1964) (soviet or socialist state was representative of the transition from capitalism to a new society and during that transition the law remained capitalist as its inherited institutions).

absentia, accusing Trotsky of treason because he promoted an internationalist view of socialism while Trotsky was not in Russia. A congressional omission of inquiry into the charges Made against Leon Trotsky in the Moscow Trials, under the leadership of the American philosopher John Dewey, dismantled any pretense of justice in the U.S.S.R. when it concluded: "We therefore find the Moscow Trials to be frame-ups." Trotsky himself remarked at the start of the commission by telephone from Mexico City on February 9th, 1937, that

> The Moscow trials are perpetrated under the banner of socialism. We will not concede this banner to the masters of falsehood! If our generation happens to be too weak to establish Socialism over the earth, we will hand the spotless banner down to our children. The struggle which is in the offing transcends by far the importance of individuals, factions and parties. It is the struggle for the future of all mankind. It will be severe, it will be lengthy. Whoever seeks physical comfort and spiritual calm let him step aside. In time of reaction it is more convenient to lean on the bureaucracy than on the truth. But all those for whom the word 'Socialism' is not a hollow sound but the content of their moral life—forward! Neither threats nor persecutions nor violations can stop us! Be it even over our bleaching bones the truth will triumph! We will blaze the trail for it. It will conquer! Under all the severe blows of fate, I shall be happy as in the best days of my youth! Because, my friends, the highest human happiness is not the exploitation of the present but the preparation of the future.[57]

Nevertheless, the U.S.S.R. Constitution decreed the state as socialist. Philosophically, Stalin made a gross mistake. By continuing the fiction of implementing Marxian theory, Stalin's "on paper" socialism raised the issue of the withering of the very institution which owned and defined the Soviet society and economy, the state. That Stalin saw no incongruence between what he was declaring and his constitutional dictatorship was further demonstrated by the fact that his own decrees violated his own constitutional provisions. For instance, Stalin decreed orally at the constitutional convention that "it is time to put an end to a situation in which not one but a number of bodies legislate." Everyone interpreted Stalin's words to reference the Supreme Soviet as the legislative body Stalin referenced, according to the constitution. They were wrong. Stalin referenced the Presidium, whose supreme leader he was. Thus,

57 Leon Trotsky, "I Stake My Life"—Opening Address to the Dewey Commission, February 9, 1937 (Transcription from a pamphlet issued in Great Britain by the *Workers' International League*, presumably in 1942.) https://www.marxists.org/archive/trotsky/1937/09/life.htm.

at the constitutional convention of 1936, Stalin simplified legal formalism. The Presidium would decree all laws, which the Supreme Soviet would ratify.[58]

To legitimize his power, Stalin redefined the Soviet state and its laws. The Soviet state was as violent as the capitalist state, but its institutions—identical to those of the repressive capitalist state—were nevertheless different, because while there were no classes there still was class struggle. To even imagine abolishing the state, Stalin's mouthpiece, Andrei Vyshinsky, said was "anarchist."[59] Stalin used the very concept of the Rule of Law when he decreed the stability of statutes and had a new constitution drafted.[60] Each republic of the Soviet empire became socialist in 1936, overnight.[61] And the Soviet legal system became socialist too, as shown from a brief analysis of Andrei Vyshinsky's Stalinist jurisprudence.

Somehow, the Western academe went along, and promoted the widely accepted triumvirate of a) common law, b) civil law, and c) socialist law, while making sure that only two of them were the "great legal systems of the world, the civilian and the common law."[62] Unwittingly, perhaps, in the process, those very eminent legal scholars[63] legitimized Stalinism and raised it to the level of an alternate society, competing for the soul of humanity with liberal capitalism. Socialist law replaced the Soviet system with the 1936 Constitution,[64] but the legal system it defined remained as before the 1936 Constitution, when its formal sources of rights and duties were what the Politburo decreed.[65]

---

58 For more see, John N. Hazard, William E. Butler, Peter B. Maggs, *The Soviet Legal System* (Parker School of Foreign and Comparative Law, 1977) 49 et seq.

59 *A.Y. Vyshinsky, Fundamental Tasks of Soviet Law in Soviet Legal Philosophy*, 303, 310 (1951).

60 *See id.*; *Andrei Vyshinsky, The Law of the Soviet State*, (Macmillan, 1948).

61 *Id.*

62 *Editorial Committee, General Introduction to the Series in Soviet Legal Philosophy*, ix (1951). (The members of the Editorial Committee were Jerome Hall, Edmund N. Cahn, Felix, S. Cohen, Lon, L. Fuller, George W. Goble, Edward A. Hogan, Josef L. Kinz, Edwin W. Patterson, Harold G. Reuschlein, and Max Rheinstein). For a more general critique of the disastrous impact of the Old Left on knowledge production, *see, e.g.*, Todd Gitlin, *The Sixties: Years of Hope, Days of Rage* (1987).

63 For an in-depth discussion of the role played by Western jurists in the widespread use of the socialist legal system misnomer see, e.g., Dana Neacşu, Against the Triumvirate of Common, Civil & Soviet/Socialist Law. 34 FJTL __ (2024/25 (forthcoming)).

64 *Andrei Vyshinsky, The Law of the Soviet State*, (Macmillan, 1948).

65 If court-decisions are the main source of rights and duties in common law countries, parliament-voted codifications in civil law countries, and for Soviet Russia and the ECE countries, as noted in passing by Justice Douglas, whatever the politburo decrees. *See.* William O. Douglas, Foreword to *Essays on Jurisprudence from the Columbia Law Review*, at vii (Colum. Univ. Press 1963).

Stalin might not have cared for law as a protector of people's individual rights, but he understood its protective shield of raw power—that legal formalism validates absolute power absent some hereditary or deity legitimation. If legal forms meant the continuation of the strong central state, then the Soviet people shall have legal forms.[66] Stalin's formalism was continued by Brezhnev, who as the supreme leader coalesced both Stalin's title of Chairman of the Presidium of the Supreme Soviet and the title of General Secretary of the Communist Party. More formalism represented more legality for the Soviet autocracy. What is remarkable in the 1977 Constitution is its Article 3, which defines the political system of the U.S.S.R. as "democratic centralism." How more transparent could the members of the Presidium of the Supreme Soviet have been, so the West would call the U.S.S.R. a dictatorship? Their autocracy was democratically exercised.

Prominent legal scholars explained that Soviet law was a direct and at times brutal instrument of policy implementation, though they never stopped to distinguish it from "socialist" law: "Do not forget," Professor Hazard recollected, "that we have in the Soviet Union the dictatorship of the proletariat, and that law must serve the state authority" (Berman, 1957, 1214).

At times it seems that finding a reason for a new legal concept was more worthy than clarifying the confusion or downright fiction of the concept of "socialist law." There is no reason to talk about adding an "extra-legal" lawyer to define a new legal system, as some scholars did. Socialist law was promoted as a political concept, again an ironic move for the legal minds which did not adhere to the Marxian concept that law is politics. Thus, whether through complacency, intellectual collusion, or collaboration with Stalin's view of the authoritative system he was building behind the Iron Curtain, his legal system became sanitized and widely used in comparative jurisprudence under the new label of "socialist law."[67]

Upon reading the final product of The Standing Committee on Education about Communism and Its Contrast with Liberty under Law of the American Bar Association and getting over the ideologized name of the ABA committee, (1968) what remains is an impressive work showcasing first year American law school skills of "compare and contrast". The report avoids any discussion of the meaning of capitalism. It assumes capitalism exists only as liberal democracies. It never intimated the idea of ersatz socialism. The ABA authors assumed its identity as "socialism" at face value, beyond any shadow of a doubt. The ABA

66 *Id.*

67 For a more in-depth analysis see, Dana Neacşu, 'Against the Triumvirate of Common, Civil & Soviet/Socialist Law".

authors skipped the foundational, existential question and delved into four topics: the legislative, the executive, the criminal process, and the judiciary. It won the day while never addressing the type of society Soviet Russia was building. It remained ersatz socialism, an autocratic system whose laws secured its legitimacy internationally and internally for almost the entire twentieth century. Everyone acquiesced perhaps because it made the rest of the world look so humane.

Soviet Russia, like its ECE colonies, quickly learned the value of legal instruments in legitimizing power and managing popular discontent. The constitution contained the legal principles of that society, and what became obvious was that there was no separation of powers or any institutional check and balances. The legislative, executive, and judiciary powers did not really exist in any of the ersatz socialist countries because the state held all the power. Of course, the federal Soviet state delegated some of its powers to the states of the union. Thus, horizontally there was some division but not checks and balances of the power of the centralized group of leaders, the cabinet of trusted counselors to the president-for-life, or more ordinarily, the dictator.

If more proof is necessary to demonstrate that the Soviet public law was indeed dictatorial, in 1956, after the Twentieth Congress of the Soviet Union ruling party denounced Stalin and Stalinism, the Italian socialist leader Pietro Nenni noted that very conclusion. There was no doubt that the Soviet state lacked a "system of juridical guarantees against abuses of power."[68] That was tantamount to declaring the 1936 Constitution a sham.

What happens when a society can point to its fundamental charter, which even when perfectly written, like the Romanian 1967 Constitution drafted by Ted Sorensen, still translates into ersatz socialism because fundamental principles do not fit the principles of socialism? Not much, when the law itself plays such a minor part in a society, as judge Bernhard Schlink pointed out in our brief email exchange about the difference between the West German and the GDR legal system.

Nevertheless, engaging in the ABA exercise of reading the Soviet Constitution, which is never identified as the third Soviet constitution, or Stalin's Constitution of 5 December 1936, and taking it at face value, makes the undemocratic nature of that society became obvious. While the constitution guarantees the right to vote (Article 135) secretly (Article 140) and choose any candidate whose name is written on the ballot, the voting "ballots printed for each district contain only one name" (ABA, 1968, 10). There were no legislative

68 Pietro Nenni, Avanti, October 25, 1964, quoted in Robert Conquest, *Justice and the Legal System in the USSR* 7 (1968).

checks and balances limits imposed on the Supreme Soviet powers other than the powers of the Presidium of the Supreme Soviet, whose decrees became binding as soon as they were passed. There was "no body, tribunal, committee, or council, that [could] pronounce upon the legality of the adopted legislation" (Id., 5). More interestingly, there were not checks and balances to any executive decisions. No governmental act was ever reviewed or reviewable (Id). But the acts of the Presidium took precedence over anything. For instance, according to Article 119 of the 1936 Constitution, the Soviet proletariat—Lenin's dictators, if anyone remembers—received an unprecedented seven-hour workday. However, as in any capitalist institution where profit and productive performance are the crux of their very existence, after four years of falling behind the projected returns, the proletariat was given an extra hour or work, and on June 26, 1940, the "Presidium of the Supreme Soviet decreed an eight-hour working day," (Id., 30) which "went into effect immediately," (Id.) thus amending the Constitution, "without following the procedure prescribed for amending the Constitution" (Id.).

Although a struggle and an obstacle to translating Politburo decision into reality, legality became a principle the Soviet regime learned to care for, perhaps to compensate that after 1936, all power concentrated in the figure of the president-for-life.[69] For instance, Article 119 was ratified seven years later (ABA, 1968, 30).

If constitutions are the fundamental charter which establish the framework of the Rule of Law in each country, much like for the United Nations,[70] and its Charter and *Bill of Rights*[71] subsequently completed by two primary international treaties: *The International Covenant on Economic, Social, and Cultural*

69 But the new constitution and the maintenance of the Romanist codes gave Stalin much that the proposed codes did not have. First, there was the personal motive. Stalin had set himself the task of removing any potential competitors to his rule. [...] Stalin may not have cared much for the law, but above all, the totality of the power of the state had to be maintained. If legal forms meant the continuation of the strong central state, then he would have legal forms. David F. Forte, "Western Law and Communist Dictatorship", 32 *Emory L.J.*, 73, 135 (1983).

70 The United Nations (UN) was officially created on October 24, 1945. This date marks the day when the *UN Charter, June 26, 1945, 59 Stat. 1031, T.S. No. 993*, https://www.un.org/en/about-us/un-charter, signed earlier that year on June 26, 1945, came into effect following its ratification by the five permanent members of the Security Council (China, France, the Soviet Union, the United Kingdom, and the United States) and the majority of other signatory nations.

71 Adopted in 1966, alongside the *Universal Declaration of Human Rights* (UDHR), G.A. Res. 217 (III) A, U.N. Doc. A/810 (Dec. 10, 1948), form the *International Bill of Human Rights.*

Rights (ICESCR)[72] and *The International Covenant on Civil and Political Rights (ICCPR)*[73] it is the constitutional reality people live in which defines a legal system and the society it builds. Whether a legal system provides and ensure basic rights such as the right to work in fair conditions, or the right to society security and adequate living standards, or the right to education is a matter of both the law on the books and the law translated into practice. Only investigating both aspects one can really understand a form of government, its economic and legal system, and thus acquire the wisdom to decide their future at the voting poll. How commonsense knowledge happens is the topic of Part 3 of this book.

---

72 Dec. 16, 1966, 993 U.N.T.S. 3.

73 Dec. 16, 1966, 999 U.N.T.S. 171.

PART 3

Socialism—From Ersatz to Knowledge

CHAPTER 7

The 100-Year-Old Socialist Misnomer and "Dialectical Criticism"

In the realm of the imaginary, capitalism belongs to the brightest constellation. And, like Walter Benjamin's constellations, its structures are also unstable (Krauß, 2011, 439). Moreover, capitalism promotes an imaginary of isolation: the myth of the individual is largely an unresolved myth of simultaneous belonging and non-belonging to a community. Unrestricted individualism is the currency of classical liberal ideology.[1] This liberalism speaks of individuals as "permanently uncommunicative, permanently unknown, in fact, unfound" (Winnicott, 1963, 186–87). They strive for a false sense of autonomy and importance in a competition against nature, themselves, communities, and, unwittingly, against … the future, unwilling to reconsider their value system.

In this book ersatz socialism is state monopoly capitalism. The Soviet and ECE reality of most of the 20th century. Capitalism, a 19th-century French term, emerged on the stage of history as the most progressive system humanity has known (Sonenscher, 2023). Since then, while promoting individual achievements and technological innovation, capitalism risks putting human progress ahead of planet Earth. Scholars must correct the mistaken perception thaf capitalism does not have strong state support, and this book wants to correct that misperception for the public reader. Governments have always enabled capitalist subsidies, only for the benefit of the few charged with owning or managing the capital. While governments might consider limiting concentration of profits in favor of social and environmental justice at the local, national, and planetary levels, if all of use, voters can imagine the many facets of capitalism and learn the difference between state capital monopoly, or ersatz socialism, liberal democratic capitalism, which is now in danger in our country, and socialism, a society where both the production and the profit are socialized in favor of social and environmental justice.

Now, in the 21st century, removed from state capital monopoly, we still hold onto, the myth of unfettered individuality, which has only led to an era of

---

1 The liberal political tradition developed particularly from the views of John Locke and J.S. Mill, who see personal liberty and freedom from interference by others, including the state, as a defining moral and political issue. John Locke, *Second Treatise of Government* (1690); John Stuart Mill, *On Liberty* (1859).

 | DOI:10.1163/9789004747210_009

unleashed capitalism, criticized by economists as the source of unlimited crises (Michie, 2022, 126). Politically, we live in a new era of antidemocratic nationalism and authoritarianism. The slogan of the 2016 U.S. presidential election was "America First," a reminder of the 1930s writings of a fascist sympathizer, American editor William Randolph Hearst (Frank, 2000). In 2024, that slogan won the American presidential elections, again. But dictatorships, such as fascist and Soviet regimes, (Polanyi, 2008) are merely "the most virulent outbreak of the anti-democratic virus ... inherent in early industrial capitalism" (Id., 108). Worldwide, democracy has been weakened by "the pernicious influence of corruption, kleptocracy, and illicit finance" (Michie, 2022, 126) in capitalism (Neacşu, 2004, 213 et seq.).

The proposed solution is not to oppose nationalism to globalization but rather to expand the electorate's commonsense understanding of capitalism, and especially of sustainability. Working with both hard law and soft law rules, from international public entities to companies, legal systems must promote values, policies, and practices that ensure long-term management and sustainability (Michie, 2022, 126).

So, how can we move on and expand our common sense understanding of capitalism? Somewhere else I wrote about how knowledge was the result of meaning-making negotiation between the textual instigator and the textual interpellated.[2] That explanation was limited to scholarship. Commonsense understanding is also the result of negotiating meaning. The tools are different. We are interpellated by observations and information usually instigated by mass media organizations, and we rely on our education, experiences, family, emotions, alienating experiences to define meaning. This book is a textual instigator hoping to raise your curiosity, while bringing gin insight through a slew of textual analyses to expand everyone's common sense understanding of capitalism, and as such of ersatz socialism as a type of illiberal state monopoly capitalism.

By now, the reader has hopefully had their commonsense beliefs about socialist theory and the ersatz socialist reality shaken. Part 1 has reviewed socialist theory with help from experts endorsed by Cambridge University Press, works of indoctrinated journalists during the Bolshevik Revolution, and

2 Knowledge production is a negotiation between those who put forward the foundation of knowledge and those who make use of it. To acknowledge that foundation, one needs to notice it, and then to fit their knowledge needs. Somewhere else I was explaining knowledge production in Althusserian terms of a traffic officer interpellating pedestrians to confine themselves to the sidewalk, for instance. For more, see, Dana Neacşu, *The Bourgeois Charm of Karl Marx and the Ideological Irony of American Jurisprudence*. (Brill, 2020), pp. 113–119.

this author's analysis of socialist theory. Part 2 has introduced the reader to new interpretations of the political, economic and legal regimes scaffolding the post-World War II Russia and its ECE satellites, in hope that the reader connects those non-socialist rules of governing to a non-socialist reality.

Part 3 of this book incorporates Bernard Lonergan's optimism and adapts it to the present corrective epistemic project. While confusion and misunderstanding happen, they evolve if curiosity is encouraged by new evidence or observations. Especially through insight, commonsense understanding can escape error of judgment.

This is not a book of science. This is not a book of political theory. Nor is it a mere book about political economy or law. It is a book about popularizing the joy of understanding life, various explanations, and debunking generalized misunderstandings about socialism as theory and praxis. Its foundation is that socialism was never the intended blueprint for U.S.S.R or any ECE country during the twentieth century. Logically, it was never built. In 1936, Stalin started using the socialist qualifier to legitimize his dictatorship (Neacșu, 2025). The Western intelligentsia accepted Stalinism as socialism and started spreading the news about this new terrorizing society, which is lurking in the dark if the unions and anybody unhappy with the monopolization of capital in the hands of private corporations do not behave. Indeed, for a century, liberal democracy has been able to rein in and slow down the speed of monopolization. During that same century, the Stalinist monopolization of capital in the hands of Stalinist high-end bureaucracy imploded, and it started anew mimicking the political, economic, and legal rules of the West.

Socialism has never been an ECE reality, but the American reality is approaching fast the ECE undemocratic and monopolistic society. This book attempts to correct a misnomer for the sake of praxis. Unchecked greed demands a system sympathetic to unlimited wealth accumulation, which cannot be acceptable in a democracy. But how can one imagine restraining capitalist greed if progressive taxation on the rich will bring in socialism, and socialism is Stalinism and the Gulag archipelago?

Our reelected president, Donald Trump, used to say, "Listen to your gut, no matter how good something sounds on paper" (Zhang, 2019). Another variant on the theme was "I have a gut, and my gut tells me more sometimes than anybody else's brain can ever tell me" (Le Miere, 2018). Interestingly, during his first attempt at derailing democracy, Trump relied on his instinct, under the guise of his "gut." He is not the first American president to find "gut instincts" reliable. They do have the benefit of being one approach to decision-making, and, given how scared we all are of both the present and especially our future, we tend to rally behind people who can make decisions. Who can forget our decider-in-chief, Bush-fils, or George Walker Bush, 43rd president of the United States? (*The New York Times*, 2016).

If we all like deciders, it is because we trust them, irrespective of how they reach their decisions: from the gut or from commonsense. It is a relief to notice that our reelected president has moved away from gut to "common sense." However, he still uses common sense in the meaning of "gut" when he blamed DEI for an aviation accident instead of waiting to hear for the accident investigation.

Trump's use of common sense might be seen as obstacle unforeseen only weeks ago. His approach to commonsense understanding is unlike the one used here: fueled by curiosity and based on empirical data, insight, and reasoning.

> President Trump blamed diversity requirements at the Federal Aviation Administration and his two Democratic predecessors for the midair collision over the Potomac River on Wednesday night, saying that standards for air traffic controllers had been too lax. ... Mr. Trump cited no evidence, and even admitted when pressed that the investigation had only just begun. When asked how he could say that diversity hiring was to blame for the crash even though basic facts about the midair collision were still being sought by investigators, he said, "*Because I have common sense*". (Sanger, 2025)

Common sense is not a quality we have or do not have, like it is a particular skin or hair color. It is based on a state of mind, on curiosity. Therefore, when our president says that he has common sense he confuses it with curiosity, which is the beginning of common-sense knowledge, or with the end result of common sense, which is knowledge incorporating some empirical data or insight. If the president poses curiosity, there is no evidence to support that. If the president states that he knows because he knows, then that is not common sense either. It is perhaps magical, or maybe our reelected president is thinking about instinct, as in a dog knows where his food is instinctively. I will try to reflect upon this here in order to avoid confusing commonsense knowledge with instinct. Thus, given our new set of circumstances, my approach to commonsense knowledge seems necessary.

In this book, the main reason for engaging in various textual analyses is that unquestioned commonsense knowledge can produce confusion and misunderstanding. Some of us only eat meat because our commonsense knowledge tells us that the cavemen must have been both lean and athletic. Eating meat—raw or cooked—was part of the reason for the caveman body shape. Similarly, for almost 100 years, we have used the concept "socialism" to define an atrocious form of state capitalism, "Soviet socialism." Here, I have tried to offer the necessary insight to create curiosity as the first step in changing one's commonsense understanding of socialism. I used socialist theory analysis, combined with literary analysis of texts from witnesses to the Bolshevik Revolution and from those who visited Soviet Russia, in addition to analysis of legal, political, and economic theory as evidence that the tenets of socialism, a fair society for all, were never part of the Soviet equation. There was no democratic government—only an oligarchy facetiously called "the dictatorship of the proletariat." There was no property owned, used, or enjoyed by the people, or at least managed for the good of the people, only a corporate state monopoly run for the benefit of the managers. There was no planned economy of the benefit of the people. The planification was of the type that any cartel engages in to manipulate prices and drive out competition.

While using this type of "dialectical criticism" to uncover the otherwise occluded reality of Soviet capitalism, Russian and ECE, a technique made popular by Frederic Jameson and so well explained by Bejamin Kunkel and *The Art of Criticism, No.5,* (Kunkel, 2024, 31) another tool became available to my commonsensical approach to understanding. The literary insight of my analysis is matched by mere lived observations. The evidence produced by my textual analysis matches more and more our lived experiences under Trump.

Common sense is practical. It rests on observations obtained from reading and reasoning or exploring reality and living it. It seeks knowledge not necessarily for the sake of pleasure of contemplation but as a necessity of living in a human-made environment with other humans. It is common sense to support tax cuts because taxes take away the salary I am owed and I rightfully own. Because in this country private property matters, not like in those socialist countries where, look at them, they either all fled their poverty-stricken countries or died trying. This type of thinking makes sense. People of the Eastern bloc tried to flee their poverty-stricken countries, and many did die trying. Taxes tax income—they do not add to individual income—but they add to the collective income, if used to fund schools and means of transportation and hospitals. Call me a cockeyed optimist, but by adding information about dictatorships as being individual and not collective, inquiry will flow. We will understand the incongruity of a society of millions of dictators. All we need is to think about what a dictator is. A dictator is a leisure class of one. The proletariat toiling in 8-hour shifts dressed up in singularly badly tailored overalls, unwashed with bad teeth, are not members of that leisure class. The proletariat in any country is the mass of toilers. So, when taxes are discussed, imposing or raising them progressively to match income, that is not socialism akin to some deplorable Russian experiment. It is macroeconomics. There was no socialism in Russia. It was monopolist capitalism, economically speaking, and the government was a dictatorship. But don't believe me—inquire and gain insight. Compare the lives of dictators like Argentina's Juan and Eva Perón with those of Romania's Nicolae and Elena Ceaușescu. Disregard differences in hair color or singing ability, and determine if you can find any fundamental distinctions between the two couples.

Only trough inquiry and expanded insight, what is common sense about socialism might change. If my narrative is sufficiently comprehensible, I have a chance at offering new insight into that social, economic, political, and legal experiment. I merely encourage changing misunderstanding to understanding. I am relying on common sense as being both pragmatic and dynamic, like life. Thus, each one of us can correct their own incongruities of representations and the order of things imposed by a soon-to-be outdated common sense.

Common sense is intellectual, Lonergan asserts convincingly (vol. 3, p. 196). In the previous chapter, I adapted Lonergan's empirical method to ways in which common sense can unfold methodically. Furthermore, Lonergan elaborates that just as there is spontaneous inquiry, there is spontaneous process of learning though the accumulation of insight, "in which each successive act complements the accuracy and covers over the deficiency of those that went before" (Lonergan, 1992, 197). Once on this path, humans developed a drive for inquiry and understanding. In the process, each self-corrects themselves when sharing those understandings. Of course, the problem is when what is shared is the same misunderstanding promoted through the media coverage of events, institutional schooling, and pretty much everything around. I am referencing the divergent situation of a concept which induces collaboration and hope, socialism, with the 100-year reality of mass oppression for the benefit of those at the very top of that social and political ladder.

It is the aim of this book to create a break into that ossified misunderstanding of socialism as Stalinism or the ECE social experiment. It aims to open a creek from which a gentle rivulet of spontaneous inquiry will start. Common sense as an intellectual development springs, according to Lonergan, from "spontaneous inquiry, the spontaneous accumulation of related insights, and the spontaneous collaboration of communication" (Id., 198). Because its nature is a specialization of intelligence in the particular and the concrete, I find it very useful for this book's project—unfolding misconceptions in a very well-defined area.

Common sense is supposed to validate a particular insight in a particular situation. Often it is inarticulate, and often it can constitute an obstacle to the very process of unfolding misunderstanding. But to open an avenue of understanding, common sense is needed. Short of obtaining graduate degrees in history, economics, politics, and law, the way to promote generalized understanding is the intellectual development of common sense. To advance common sense, this book has to successfully appear as relevant and offer answers to immediately palpable questions in a digestible yet not silly manner. The beauty of common sense is that it remains highly practical and specialized. And this is the only way to unpack highfalutin theories built on sand. The only way through is by unraveling the current common-sense understanding.

For instance, the gulags, a creation which preceded Stalin but which he brought to perfection, were perceived as an inevitability of building socialism. By reading this book you are already inquiring into established knowledge about socialism. You wonder whether all this talk about socialism is really accurate. Or some might say that all this talk is just fearmongering about socialism, especially when recalling that Stalin was one of the most ruthless dictators. This epistemic connection makes socialism undesirable. But is Stalinism synonymous with socialism?

Having received the seed of doubt, you will do some digging about Stalin, and see that he was a dictator interested in his power. What is hard to understand is that, indeed, powerful dictators have an interest in creating a powerful country over which they rule. No dictator dreams of ruling a banana republic! Thus, dictators will engage in two seemingly contradictory sets of rules. One set of rules will strengthen their country's economy, and the other set of rules will strengthen their hold on the politics by eliminating all people who oppose their rule. Elimination can happen in multiple ways. Building on the Tsarist labor camps and prison system, Stalin further developed that solid foundation of mass control. Stalin's German homologue, Hitler, also was fond of labor camps, especially extermination camps. No one accuses Hitler of socialism, though Hitler's regime did incorporate that terminology. Hitler's concentration camps used physical appearance as an entry ticket: color of the skin, of the eyes, or hair, the last name, or the religion, or sexuality, or political party membership. The deportations to Siberia were neither whimsical, nor based on evidence. They were a brutal means of eliminating millions of people Stalin imagined as a threat to his regime. One might say that their cumulative large number was the only qualifier for Stalin's enemies.

Sarcasm and irony are not conducive to commonsense knowledge. Commonsense knowledge is nevertheless deeply personal.

Unlike commonsense, scientific knowledge is to a certain degree objective, for Lonergan, because it focuses on the relations between the object of the various type of scientific inquiry. Indeed, a piece of wood has an objective existence, independent of my observing it. But my understanding of that piece of wood is highly subjective. It is subjective because as humans engaged in thinking we cannot be devoid of our public and private subjectivity, whether we instigate knowledge production, as I am doing here by writing this book, or whether we are interpellated by knowledge products, as I am also engaged in each time I edit this text.

Understanding is highly subjective, and the generalized misinformation about 100 years of political, economic, and legal experiments in Eastern Europe suggests a highly subjective knowledge production process though propaganda and disinformation, collaboratively produced by the West and the East to control their populations, I believe it is more suitable. Now, this is not a conspiracy book. It is a book about a generalized socialist misnomer. It is not a journalistic investigation into how lack of ethical inquiry, opportunism, fame, recognition, professional advancement, and a place at the big table of world intelligentsia has caused it. Most likely.

This book is an exercise in epistemic optimism, building on Lonergan's theory of knowledge (Id., 242 et seq.). Sometimes commonsense insight is so generalized that it is accepted, and no inquiry happens for decades. Case in point is the lack of knowledge about Soviet Russia, or U.S.S.R., which has generalized into commonsense insight. It is assumed. But life is dynamic and so is common knowledge based on common sense. The amalgam of contradictions and false assumptions raised to the bubble of history will erode the crust of established socialist nonsense, especially in times of crises of consciousness or, absent such crises, in times of abuse of power. Bickering, insinuations, and recriminations foment inquisitiveness. And I become hopeful and start writing about the dialectic nature of life and especially knowledge, a conscious reflection of life, and everything in it, of things.

Dialectics has been with us since human inquisitiveness became an object of introspection. Plato used this qualifier. As did Aristotle to denote knowledge production based on reviewing and scrutinizing the existing knowledge, including the contradictory constructs.

This is especially relevant in times of prolonged crises, like the one in which we live. Since 2016 our representative democracy has reached new levels of malfunctioning for the benefit of those represented. We have not had a president representing a clear majority of the voting-age population for almost a decade. We have had majorities of those exercising their right to vote. That is perhaps due in part to the commonsense understanding of the role of the government: permissive and irresponsible. The levels of political participation are dwindling.

For instance, in the 2008 U.S. presidential election, according to electproject.org, Barack Obama received 69,50 million votes, accounting for 52.9% of the total votes cast, which represented approximately 32.6% of the voting-eligible population (VEP). In the 2016 U.S. presidential election, according to The American Presidency Project, Voter Turnout Data, Donald Trump received approximately 62.98 million votes, which was about 46.1% of the total votes cast, and represented approximately 27.3% of VEP. In the 2020 U.S. presidential election, according to The American Presidency Project, Joe Biden received approximately 81.3 million votes, accounting for about 51.3% of the total votes cast, which was about 34.0% of VEP. In the 2024 U.S. presidential election, former President Donald Trump garnered approximately 74.65 million votes, or about 49.8% of the total votes cast, which is estimated to be 31–33% of VEP (See Figure 11).

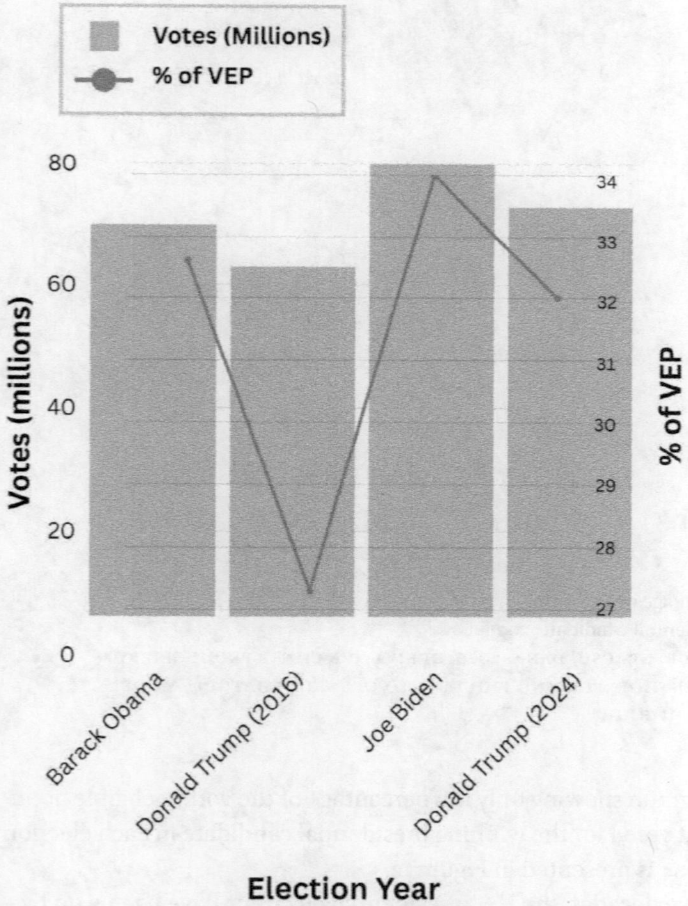

FIGURE 11 Presidential votes and voting-eligible population (VEP) share by candidate, 2008–2024
SOURCE: NEACȘU, DANA. 2025. ORIGINAL BAR CHART PRODUCED BY THE AUTHOR USING MICROSOFT EXCEL AND DATA FROM THE AMERICAN PRESIDENCY PROJECT, "GENERAL ELECTION RESULTS." UNIVERSITY OF CALIFORNIA, SANTA BARBARA. ACCESSED MAY 16, 2025. HTTPS://WWW.PRESIDENCY.UCSB.EDU/STATISTICS/ELECTIONS, AND REFINED USING OPENAI'S CHATGPT (MODEL O4-MINI-HIGH)

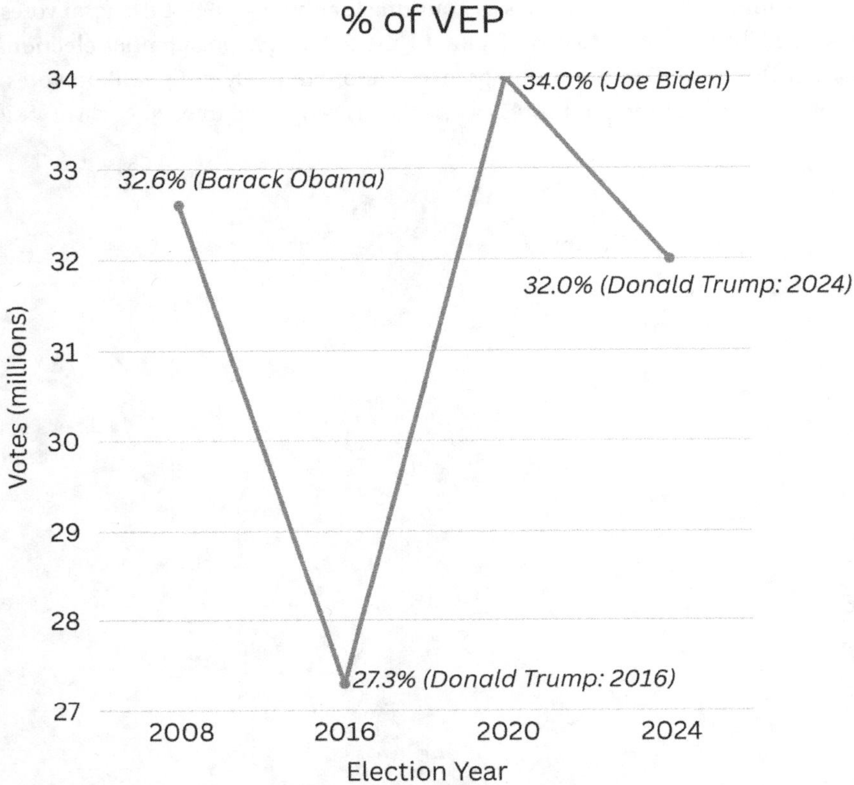

FIGURE 12 Percentage of the voting-eligible population (VEP) voting for the winning presidential candidate, 2008–2024
SOURCE: NEACŞU, DANA. 2025. DERIVATIVE CHART PRODUCED BY THE AUTHOR, FEEDING FIGURE 11 TO OPENAI'S CHATGPT (MODEL O4-MINI-HIGH)

Or a cleaner graph showing only the percentage of the voting-eligible population (VEP) that voted for the winning presidential candidate in each election from 2008 to 2024 is presented in Figure 12.

For almost two decades, the U.S. presidential elections have been won by a minority of eligible voters, which is already a significantly lower number than the U.S. population. That is why, if people inquire about alternative forms of government, the discovery will astound them, encouraging a reevaluation of their assumption and commonsense understanding.

The ECE governments for most of the twentieth century were as irresponsible as the recent American government. Until recently, they were less permissive, because they were perceived as being paternalistic. But, once we start inquiring, we discover that assumptions we have held were wrong because we did not have access to information from a variety of sources holding a variety of biases. To be able to build insight promoting understanding we need a variety of biased stories so we can sense the difference or the contradictions and be able to make up our mind, through the canons of empirical observation mentioned above. Through multiple inquiries and assessments built on a multitude of observations, new insight expands. In the process, it becomes apparent how commonsense understanding incorporates concrete, dynamic, and contradictory information. Through private or public ruminations, inquiry continues, and ambiguity shifts within a frame of clarity, and common sense itself upends.

CHAPTER 8

Things, Concepts, and Judgment Calls as the Building Block of Common Knowledge

This book is a celebration of commonsense understanding. The thing or concept at the heart of this book is rather abstract. It is socialism. It is a thing, a concept. And like the moon, another thing, socialism occupies our understanding both like an abstraction made up of many abstract insights about its appearance, size, light, etc., but also concrete insights. The moon has craters. The society we generally refer to as socialism, abounded in rationed food, lack of electricity, and especially the lack of privacy.

If we are curious and inquire, we discover attributes about the things we are interested in and then develop logical relations between attributes from various areas of specialized knowledge. Aristotle wrote about the moon, for instance. He developed syllogisms where he put an intelligible order into the attributes of the thing—the moon. It is interesting to note that understanding requires both detailed attributes and an intelligible order so we can create a unity, or a unit of understanding to use when we need to reference *it*, the thing. Once that unity of understanding, the abstraction, is formed, it tends not to change, unless challenged by another unit of understanding. Constantly we adjust our expanded understanding with new pieces of information, even if the basic common sense we use to engage with the world seems stabilized.

If things are hard to grasp, then we tend to form correlations between things, so we define them contextually. The easiest such correlation is judgment calls. A is unknown. B is equally unknown. But somehow the common knowledge is that A is better than B, therefore let's choose the lesser evil. Judgment calls are subjective. Therefore, they express our biases. Often, they mirror our emotions. Then, they are unfounded, and opinionated. Everyone has them and brags about having them. "Capitalism is preferable to socialism," is a generalized judgment call. From a relative opinion statement about two abstract things rarely engaged with it has become the mantra of common sense.

Luckily, as Bernard Lonergan reminds us, "knowing is a dynamic structure" (Lonergan, 1992, 302) and each judgment represents one contribution to the larger picture. Therefore, the effort undertaken by this book to create a small tear in the canvas of knowledge about 100 years of solitude behind the Iron Curtain and since its fall, within the fog of misunderstanding. As Lonergan explains, even comprehensive judgements, like the one mentioned above,

 | DOI:10.1163/9789004747210_010

which "bear witness to the depth and breadth of our perspectives" (Id., 303) are open to replacement in the face of new insight. The more comprehensive and all-inclusive our judgment is the less concrete it is, and we cannot hold off a judgement which wants itself both comprehensive and concrete for long. It is incongruous, and it begs for new insight to fix what it feels discordant.

> All we know is somehow with us; it is present and operative within our knowing; but it lurks behind the scenes, and it reveals itself only in the exactitude with which each minor increment to our knowing is effected. The business of the human mind in this life seems to be, not contemplation of what we know, but relentless devotion to the task of adding increments to a merely habitual knowledge. (Id.)

This continuous process of knowing questions and seeking answers to those inquiries is born of as much a desire as a habit to understand. When Archimedes shouted "Eureka!" he acknowledged the satisfaction of making sense. Suddenly his insight made sense within his larger intellectual quest. In everyday life we shout "Eureka!"

Those of us who love literature and old classic movies may be able to say without blinking that U.S.S.R., whose political regime Yuri Zhivago described spectacularly in Pasternak's masterpiece, *Doctor Zhivago* (1957), belonged to a special class of political regimes: socialist. That quick assessment comes with our dislike of what we read or see in David Lean's *Dr. Zhivago*, the movie—obviously not Omar Sharif who plays the doctor's character. Quickly we think that if Marxism brought that awful socialism to Russia, then indeed, Trump is correct to ask us to distance ourselves from Marxism and especially from their manifestation, from socialists. This book uses insight provided by works which already populate the public imagination to induce a desire to reconsider their tale and then recalibrate what is commonsense understanding.

David Lean's *Dr. Zhivago*, still playing in airport lounges, may be a piece of evidence sufficient to supports a prospective judgment in a direct, unconditioned manner. We see something tragic, and we conclude it is not the society we want to live in. Boris Pasternak's novel is extraordinary, and Pasternak is correct in his assessment of history, and why misconceptions about it stay around for centuries. The power transition from the tsar to the Bolsheviks took place through organized events led by "one-track minds":

> No single man makes history. History cannot be seen, just as one cannot see grass growing. Wars and revolutions, kings and Robespierres, are history's organic agents, its yeast. But revolutions are made by fanatical

men of action with one-track minds, geniuses in their ability to confine themselves to a limited field.

History remembers Lenin and Trotsky. Each one played their role in overthrowing the old Tsarist movement. But it is very hard to create a clear image of the ordinary folks' lives because the overall flavor of it, like a popular song's humming, is what people use as common knowledge.

> They overturn the old order in a few hours or days, the whole upheaval takes a few weeks or at most years, but the fanatical spirit that inspired the upheavals is worshiped for decades thereafter, for centuries. (Pasternak, 1958, 454)

Doctor Zhivago, Pasternak's epic novel, centers on a narrow segment of the Russian population: the professional elite, embodied most vividly by the doctor at its heart. Under the Tsarist regime, his life—while far from idyllic—retained a certain stability and privilege. That security rapidly disintegrates with the Bolshevik Revolution, as the sweeping changes of the new regime impose a far harsher reality on individuals like him.

To fully grasp the novel's underlying commentary, one must first understand the bleakness of pre-Soviet life for the broader Russian population. Against that backdrop, it becomes clearer how radical policies like collectivization found traction in the collective imagination—they offered, at least in theory, a break from centuries of inequality and desperation. The famine exacerbated by World War I, the devastating foreign interventions following the revolution, and the acute scarcity of food and resources laid the groundwork for extreme state interventions. Within this context, even the horrors of the forced labor camps and the Siberian Gulag can be seen not as anomalies, but as continuations of a brutal logic set in motion by war, deprivation, and ideological zeal.

Life in the U.S.S.R. during the first half of the twentieth century was, for many, unimaginably harsh. Yet, labeling that experience as "socialism" allowed the West to dismiss the Soviet project wholesale—reducing it to a dystopian cautionary tale and thereby neutralizing any ideological challenge it might have posed. This reductionist labeling came with sweeping judgments, often made without full access to the inner workings or lived realities of Soviet society.

Doctor Zhivago, though a deeply personal and poetic account, was also a political act. It could not be published in the Soviet Union upon completion. Instead, it first appeared in Italy in 1957, at a time when the U.S.S.R. had ossified into a mediocracy—a rigid, bureaucratic structure focused less on the ideals of socialism and more on preserving the power and privileges of its newly formed elite. In this sense, Pasternak's novel is both a love story and a quiet indictment of a regime that promised transformation but delivered repression.

Reading *Doctor Zhivago* through this lens reveals more than a critique of a failed revolution or a betrayed professional class—it exposes the hollowness of the ideological framework imposed on Soviet society. The novel does not indict Marxism as a set of ideas, but rather the bureaucratic mediocrity that masqueraded as revolutionary leadership. This distinction matters. To avoid the kind of sweeping judgments that reduce complex histories to slogans, we must resist conflating the lived experience of Soviet citizens with the theoretical architecture of socialism. Instead, we need access to multiple perspectives, each filtered through its own biases, to piece together a more honest picture.

Commonsense knowledge begins not with certainty, but with the impulse to question: What is really socialism or for that matter, Marxism? Who defines it, who benefits from its definition, and who is silenced by it? Just as the Bible has been interpreted and reinterpreted through centuries to serve divergent ends, so too has "Marxism" become a vessel for agendas far removed from anything Marx himself wrote, and socialism a catalyst for mindless despotism. *Doctor Zhivago* suggests that ideology, when stripped of moral imagination and hijacked by opportunists, becomes little more than a hollow label—one that allows the powerful to rule unchallenged while claiming revolutionary legitimacy.

This book seeks to ignite that impulse toward inquiry—to reconsider what we think we know about socialism, particularly in societies where the word became a state mantra divorced from its ethical roots. If understanding requires judgment, let us first ensure that our judgments rest on method, not myth.

CHAPTER 9

The Dynamic Nature of Insight and Commonsense Knowledge

For Descartes, mastery of science or of philosophy, as Lonergan reminds us, rests on "slow and steady accumulation of little insights" (Lonergan, 1992, 27). Marx, too, vetted that approach in his theory of capitalist accumulation.

Insight rests on an assumption of intellectual curiosity, often the opposite of the impetus behind most everything written about what has become to be called the twentieth-century Russian and Eastern European socialism or communism. Think about inquisitiveness—what keeps one up at night and sends people on dangerous expeditions. Insight comes suddenly and unexpectedly as a result of strenuous intellectual drive. It may come in a flash.

The example of Archimedes and his "Eureka!" moment showcases the belief that while we acquire insights through observation, we "see" them, or become aware of our insights in moments of relaxation. When taking a bath, Archimedes "visualized" the principles of hydrostatics. Noticing his own body displaced water and was subject to the forces of gravity, Archimedes suggested that his king's crown could be easily weighed in water to test the metal used for its manufacture: gold or something of a lesser gravity.

Archimedes' insight suggests that insight is highly subjective. It follows both the textual instigator, this text, and anyone engaging with this text, but it "makes sense" or "comes to light" only if understood and especially when needed.

For instance, no understanding can come from one insight. Archimedes' "Eureka!" rested on a foundation of hydrostatic principles. Insight rests on an inquisitive mind and an education which supports intellectual journey with a multitude of insights. Insights support each other and promote growth of understanding but also openness to substitute images, symbolism, as well as a search for empirical data. What is fundamental is that half answers do not become full answers. Answers are deciphered before they become knowledge or substitute knowledge and ossify into misunderstanding.

For anyone who has not obsessively wondered about the nature of that egregious form of state monopolism developed in that undemocratic, dictatorial society, it is hard to imagine how to begin to inquire or even how to distinguish between the known and unknown.

The unknown, in my estimate, very early on became miss-known. How did that happen? Through symbolism. "Socialism" and "communism" were used

 | DOI:10.1163/9789004747210_011

by Western theoreticians to supplant any explanations. Mathematicians name unknowns and write down in equations their symbolic properties, and when they reach a particular number of equations, for instance, without even reaching a solution, mathematicians declare that the solution is automatic. Given the heuristic value of symbolism, everyone behaves as if all has been deciphered when in fact nothing has.

Furthermore, symbolism rests on clues, on hints, on suggestions. We use symbolism without any expectations of understanding what it is meant to be. With something like the organization of the human societies behind the symbolism of The Socialist Republic of Romania, for instance, it is very hard, if not impossible, to grasp its complexity without a hint of possibility. And that possibility did not come from having experienced life there, heard stories about it, or watched movies about it. Because while all those exercises may contain a possibility of insight into understanding what is going on, they are also replete with risks. They require guidance, which was usually offered in ideologically unchallenged ways (Hayek, 1944). But that guidance was contained in the title so clearly that it gave me no reason to waste my time reading it in its entirety until now, for this book.

For over 100 years, socialism and communism have remained misnomers, symbols for a societal riddle, a dictatorship using state repression to ensure state monopolism for the benefit of the 1 percent. Writing this book, the epistemic question becomes: How can one turn the unknown into genuine insight and understanding, rather than using it for academic self-aggrandizement?

Guesswork is a refreshing start. In science, as Lonergan reminds us, the unknowns are what one grasps by insight through conceptions and suppositions. Understanding can be reached through empirical inquiry, methodical research, and insight into all that effort, while aware that generalizations, which are often the end result of understanding, can be half-answers. At this junction, correlations and classifications become essential.

As Lonergan alerts us, there are similarities among things as they appear to us and similarities among those things irrespective of our perception of them. Think about how we describe property, for instance. We look at the object of said property and describe it as belonging to one of us or to no one. When it belongs to one of us, we think about our agency over that object. I can eat an apple. I can sell that apple. That apple belongs to me. If in the Boston Common there is an apple tree, and that park belongs to no one, anyone can take that apple and eat it or sell it. But we cannot envisage property between those two apples. To even imagine property over anything, one needs to imagine agency over that thing. And only thinking hard about that expression of agency over things can one even have an insight into whether ownership is a mere statement of ownership or whether ownership is connected with the physical use or disposition of an object. Imagine the kerfuffle if everyone who says it is theirs shows up at the same time to take control over a thing! Because ownership includes the ability to use your property whenever and with whomever you want and refuse to share it with those you want to exclude.

Those who have lived in the spaces described here as Eastern and Central Europe or U.S.S.R., or read about them, might say that what I described is private property and that legal institution—because it is an institution governed by soft and hard legal norms—was not applied in the so-called socialist and communist countries. Property belonged to the state in the name of the people. Each factory and each weaving machine in each factory, no matter how remote, belonged to the state in the name of everyone, child or adult. I could see how an NFT, a cryptographic token that is recorded on a blockchain and cannot be replicated, might belong to everyone, if the entire Romanian population so decides, because we could look at it, enjoy it, and then put our minds together and sell it or destroy it. Being digital, and having no other functionality but visual gratification, lends itself to a multitude of owners. It makes sense, and it is intelligible. But, short of intangible objects, shared property among millions of people for one weaving machine, now that becomes unintelligible if property remains property and includes use, enjoyment, and any other form of agency displayed over that object.

In the same vein, if we were to discuss dictatorship as a form of government, almost everyone would have some understanding of it: one person is in charge, and no law applies to or in any way shapes their behavior. The state is the personification of the dictator, who is one individual. Now, to hear that all the adults working in factories are dictators of each of those countries behind the Iron Curtain, one must chuckle or dismiss the concept as an aberration, especially if they also know that all those so-called dictators work in 8-hour factory shifts.

That is why Lonergan's insight is so fundamental to all understanding. Insight rests on a methodical genesis. Scientists achieve understanding, but they do so only at the end of an inquiry. Their inquiry is methodical, and method consists in ordering means to achieve an end. But how can means be ordered to an end when the end is knowledge and the knowledge is not yet acquired? Furthermore, how can we do that if knowledge depends on having lived and consciously thought about that society, how it was governed, legally organized, and performed economically.

In this chapter, I tried to settle on a methodical beginning into studying something foreign, like the taste of dust on Mars, without having the chance of actually handling that dust. I suggest that when what we attempt to know is filled with contradictory or unintelligible concepts or even empirical data, we need to note that unintelligibility. If connections between the dictatorship of the proletariat, which in one ECE country, such as Romania, represented millions of adults, does not make sense with preexisting knowledge about dictatorships, that very lack of fitting is relevant to understanding. Two pieces of puzzles which do not fit next to each other may still belong to one image. But even some piece of information which seems incidental, irrelevant, or negligible, which might possess no intelligibility on its own, I encourage you to keep it handy. It will offer some explanation of why I am certain by the end of this book you, too, will reach the same meaning, the same understanding, as the one I am arguing: no matter what the concept used to describe a society where 99 percent of the population toils for the benefit of 1 percent, that concept cannot denote a socialist or a communist society. A socialist or communist society seems to require something more than prison-like exploitation while living in terror.

But rather than formulating answers, this book offers a way forward challenging what has been assumed for a century and encouraging inquisitiveness and knowing. Human intelligence, inquisitiveness, and the search for answers are reflected in our ability to live with ambiguity. Lonergan calls it the "essential dynamism of human intelligence" (Lonergan, 1992, 57). Others have noticed that thinking is a process whose pathway is difficult, because while it brings about a result, understanding, or knowing that makes sense and thus it is closest to us, it relies on a much vaster horizon, whose depth is often uncharted.

Our facility to socialize and live communally is the result of our intelligence, our ability to create and follow directives that serve to guide us to a sought-after result. Knowing symbolically becomes a set of insights that unify our empirical, intellectual, and rational acts of positioning ourselves in the surrounding environment and making sense of it. Below, I will explore the method which Lonergan believes exists in the most basic commonsense process of knowing and thus understanding, though he does not focus his generalized method of inquiry and its implications on common sense. Nevertheless, he articulates a persuasive theory of the role of common sense in human knowing, which I find persuasive and thus the foundation of this book intent in correcting 100-year-old generalized misconceptions produced by the professional intelligentsia. Lonergan limits his study of common sense because of "the difficulty of distinguishing experience, understanding, and judgment in common sense" (Lonergan, 1990, 304). More precisely, he is unsettled by the mixture of empirical use of data, experience, which also includes observations and understanding:

> If one wants to speak of a commonsense insight, one starts from where so-and-so is; but to give an adequate description of how much he already understands, and how much and what is to be added to that, is to give a biography. (Id.)

Lonergan then tries to separate understanding from judgments, but he finds his attempt unsatisfactory. He uses a simple account of commonsense judgment. It assumes that a person is familiar with a certain routine and understands it perfectly, but a change will occur:

> He comes home from work and finds the windows smashed, water on the floor, smoke in the air, and the smell of fire. And he makes a judgment. He doesn't say. "There's been a fire." He says, "Something happened." (Id.)

This inability of accounting for each component of the knowledge process makes Lonergan not focus on common sense but on philosophical and scientific inquiry. However, this book does not need to separate inquiry from explanation and judgement as it reaches an insight. It only needs to show that knowing is dynamic, and even the most generally accepted beliefs are open to maturation and change. Being is knowing, as Lonergan would say, and thus dynamic and open to change, ergo, this project on righting misconceptions about things.

Knowing is about symbolic reality, sometimes called heuristics. It is hard to imagine commonsense understanding being conceptual. But it is. Even in the example with understanding a fire accident, the man faced with the aftermath of the fire had to use symbols—cinder—in lieu of the fire, for instance, to bring the unknown—what really happened without him witnessing it—into the realm of the known.

The easiest way to manage the abyss of the unknown or understandable is to use a limited number of symbols and move them along the path of thinking, much like chess pieces on a chess board, until the result is reached. Lonergan defines this as classic heuristics because it anticipates connections, like the moves in a game of chess, and the results are also anticipated, even if that is in the type of their nature. Galileo anticipated a particular structure of the solar system which included planetary movement. He did not know from the beginning that the Earth moves around the Sun, but he anticipated it. He had insight into it. Similarly, Newton, did not know how gravity worked, but he anticipated a result of that nature.

Classical heuristics anticipate the possibility of an insight that grasps relations or methodical inquiry of anticipated insights. What classical heuristics offers is the possibility of a unitary view. While gaining insight into the organization of human society for almost 100 years might seem daunting, this book limits that inquiry into three areas: economics, politics, and law. While unsure about what one may discover, if the insights gained show an economic organization akin to highly monopolistic capitalist society, even if the monopolies are not owned by multinational corporations but by the state organized as a corporation, if the result is the same, the beneficiaries are not the workers but a well identified limited group, akin to corporate stakeholders, then it becomes easier to understand the economic organization of that society, despite such unknown as economic planification. Of course, those annual reports exist for all corporations.

The U.S. Securities and Exchange Commission, the SEC, is full of corporate filings, and Edgar is the technology—database—used to make those filings public. Corporate filings for Amazon and Walmart, for instance, currently employ about a third of today's Romanian (once an ECE country) workforce of about 9 million, according to data from LSO. However, in the 1960s–1970s when the Romanian Communist Party created its first five-year and annual economic reports, the Romanian workforce was around 6 million. The Romanian workforce has always been divided among three sectors, industry, agriculture, and services, where the military, paramilitary, and security services were considered services. So, we could safely say that almost the entire factory workforce was equal to the employees used by Amazon and Walmart today. Now, those corporations monopolize their fields as much as the Romanian industry was monopolized by the Romanian state. Like the Romanian Communist Party, which annually produced reports about estimated costs and profits and offered prediction for future economic performance, those corporations file corporate reports with the SEC. In those reports, the salaries received by Romanian workers were as much a cost of doing business as the salaries paid by those corporations to their employees. There was no rent paid for the space used by those Romanian factories, but there were many examples where corporations own their spaces and do not pay rent.

The analogies can continue ad infinitum. What I would like you to retain is their nature and similarities. If Walmart does not belong to its employees, who physically work in those places, why would anyone believe that they belonged to their workers or, even more absurdly, that the Romanian people who did not even work in those factories owned those factories? Returning to learning from insight, once we can dynamically connect understanding we possess, to unknown entities of similar nature, we can build insights that might be verifiable, by using methodical understanding.

Commonsense incorporates insights, which represent a sliver of the observations we make each day. To know, we select. We limit the field of data collection. Insight always provides an angle of reality. That is why it is so important to access as many insights as possible. Imagine all the possible thoughts in connection to what the world refers to as the socialist or communist era of the twentieth century. To be able to peruse through all the available data and formulate hypotheses to promote understanding, it would help to formulate a definition of socialism and communism and find the rules of intellectual engagement.

Bernard Lonergan talks about selection of sensible data. But what is sensible data? Empirical data is provided by all our senses, for instance. That is way too much, and even more insidious and troubling is that data is incorporated not on a cognitive vacuum. The moment we acquire data, we analyze them according to our own interests and abilities in a context of preexisting understanding or a lack of it.

Because the common misunderstanding is that socialism and communism are fascist states which started from a utopia, I will offer a summary of Karl Marx's thought on these societies, as well as Lenin's and Stalin's. One of Marx's clearest articulations of socialism can be found in his work *Critique of the Gotha Program* (1875). In this text, he critiques the German Workers' Party's platform and provides insight into his vision for a socialist society. He describes a society where individuals would be compensated based on their contribution ("from each according to his ability, to each according to his work"[1]) but argues that true equality and freedom could only be realized fully under communism, where class distinctions have entirely disappeared.

However, as Lenin easily observed by reading one work by Marx, thus making it easy for everyone else, Marx did not spend time thinking about a recipe for the future. Thus, he had no theory about socialism, and he had no theory about communism. Marx criticized capitalism as he could observe it.

Marx deduced, Lenin noticed in *The State and Revolution* (1917), from studying history that the state was bound to disappear, and that the transitional form of its disappearance (the transition from state to non-state) would be the "proletariat organized as the ruling class" (Id., 381 et seq.).

> Marx, however, did not set out to discover the political forms of this future stage. He limited himself to carefully observing French history, to analyzing it, and to drawing the conclusion to which the year 1851 had led, namely, that matters were moving towards destruction of the bourgeois state machine. And when the mass revolutionary movement of the

1 Karl Marx, *Critique of the Gothic Program* (1875), in In *Marx/Engels Selected Works*, Volume 3, 13–30. Moscow: Progress Publishers, 1970. https://www.marxists.org/archive/marx/works/1875/gotha/.

> proletariat burst forth, Marx, in spite of its failure, in spite of its short life and patent weakness, began to study the forms it had discovered. The Commune is the form "at last discovered" by the proletarian revolution, under which the economic emancipation of labor can take place. (Id.)

Lenin viewed socialism as a transitional society between capitalism and communism. In his work *The State and Revolution* (1917), he argued that socialism would entail a "dictatorship of the proletariat," where the working class controls the state. During this phase, the means of production (factories, land, resources) would be transferred to state control on behalf of the people. This period would still see remnants of capitalist society, such as the need for a state apparatus to enforce socialist policies and prevent counterrevolution.

> Socialism means the abolition of classes. To achieve socialism, the proletariat must carry out a ruthless suppression of the resistance of the exploiting class, develop the discipline and solidarity of the working class, and create the conditions that will ultimately lead to the disappearance of classes. Socialism is nothing but the state-capitalist monopoly turned in the interests of the whole people and, therefore, has ceased to be a capitalist monopoly. (Id.)

Stalin produced a new definition of socialism. First, he believed that socialism could be fully realized within a single country, a significant departure from Marx and Lenin's emphasis on international revolution. In 1936, Stalin, as a true dictator, devised a society and gave it a name: socialism. His 1936 constitution declared that the Soviet Union had achieved "socialism in one country." From an economic and legal point of view, Stalin held the state as the center of economic power, which owned it on behalf of the people. Class exploitation was said to have largely ended. He argued that socialism entailed the centralization of economic planning under state control, industrialization, and collectivized agriculture, all guided by the Communist Party. In his view, socialism would feature a powerful state apparatus to enforce collectivist principles and suppress opposition. What Stalin succeeded in was having himself at the helm of a very powerful state which kept him in power. Now, all dictators stay in power in the absence of popular revolt. A strong state apparatus suppressing everything other than complete obedience tends to protect the dictator.

That is socialism according to Marx, Lenin, and Stalin. It seems pretty bleak, and it has nothing to do with the people. In terms of redistributive justice, the data available about reels of movies, books, and testimonials all show that only the 1 percent of the higher echelons of the Communist Party, military, paramilitary, and security forces had a luxurious living standard, while the working classes had a modest or very modest living standard. So, we cannot believe that those toilers owned anything or that they were in the mind of anyone. True, electrification produced electric outlets in every home, but electricity was scarce.

But, if we use Lenin's and Stalin's definitions of socialism, indeed a vile and violent oppressive state took control of all aspects of the public life of its citizens and terrorized them so well that their private life was equally alienated.

If a fascist police state is socialism, then it is vile, and we know everything about it. But then, that is as capitalist as anything else, because of the political and social hierarchy in the society. Thus, by using one canon of empirical method, we discover that there is no difference between socialism and capitalism, except sometimes capitalism does not displace a democratic form of government, as the Western history of the second half of the twentieth century showed, and sometimes it does, as most of the twentieth-century history of the Soviet Union and its satellite members of the Warsaw Pact[2] (the other NATO pact) illustrates.

Applying selection, socialism is a form of government which is supposed to be a less exploitative form of capitalism, according to Marx who was interested in redistributive justice. According to Marx, communism was going to be akin to the Paris Commune, which unfortunately was chaotic and anarchic. According to Lenin, socialism is a dictatorship, whose only redeeming quality is its temporality. The state engages in capitalist monopoly and in the ruthless oppression of anyone who is opposed to the new power structure. Stalin shared that view fully. For Lenin, communism was the final stage of societal development, achievable only after socialism had succeeded in eradicating class distinctions. In a true communist society, the state would "wither away," as he put it, because it would no longer be needed once class conflicts ceased to exist.

Thus, if we want to use socialism and communism in a historic way, then we need qualifiers. Otherwise, if we were to use socialism and communism in a poetic, lose meaning as a less individualistic, more collaborative, and resilient society, then we need to state that these forms of government have no apostle yet and that the field is empty. One thing is clear: socialism was never attempted nor realized, except in a Stalinist definition. And this is how

---

2 For a brief history of the Warsaw Pact and NATO, see Dana Neacșu, "Romania, Bulgaria, The United States and the European Union: The Rules of Empowerment at the Outskirts of Europe", 30 *Brooklyn Journal of International Law* 185 (2005) at https://doi.org/10.7916/D8W09GF4.

selection as an empirical canon streamlines both empirical data and the consequences of using it. A definition, observations, and examining the connection between observations and the definition give us an insight that something is not as it should be. This suggests a cognitive disconnect or, worse, a very successful manipulation of knowledge production and its dissemination. Meaning-making is not possible if there is no knowledge to use as an intellectual building block. Understanding is not supported but obstructed, and everyone who used "socialism" and "communism" as epistemic shortcuts to something that did not exist played a role in it.

By being selective with our observations and trying to fit the reality of labor camps and the Stalinist purges with Marx's redistributive dream and a common-sense idea of social wellbeing for all, we raise questions about any rational engineering of a society for the masses. Most likely it was an exploitative creation to keep the new power structure in power. It needed some founding father figures, and by the mere virtue that they were men, Marx, Engels, Lenin, and Stalin fit that bill.

Commonsense incorporates insights, which represent a sliver of the observations we make each day. To know, we limit the field of data collection according to our own subjectivity. We acquire knowledge positioning each insight with our personal experience. The resulting understanding is as complex and thus representative of the reality as possible, according to our own ability to incorporate it in our daily lives.

Lonergan explains operations as a principle of analysis though accuracy testing the accumulation of observations. For instance, at one point during our schooling, each one of us has verified the laws of gravity. We used a stone and a feather, and we explained the difference in time taken to reach the ground with the laws for friction. We did not simply memorize these laws; we attempted to understand them. The same principle should be applied when one discusses socialism and communism, and whether there was any attempt to build such hefty societies in a rational manner, similar to creating the government of the U.S., for example, where state representatives really thought about the political power structure—a federation of independent states—and the form of government—presidential republic—and the economy those rich men wanted to promote—a capitalist economy whose most profitable form of ownership was the property of people of African origin and land. The main preoccupation of the American Founding Fathers was the power structure. The masses were not trusted and the people in power already wanted to remain in power.

Similarly, in the Eastern bloc, like in Russia, their founding fathers wanted to ensure that they held the power yielded to them by the war circumstances.

World War I produced a vacuum of power in Tsarist Russia and a band of like-minded intellectuals with military help ignited popular support to promote change. The people in power were replaced by other people in power. As a percentage, probably the number of people in power remain similar. What changed was the barons: local and national. New dynasties were established using old methods of force, bloodshed, intimidation. The tsar was a dictator. The new system changed the name of the dictator but not his role.

Using operations as a principle of validating our insights, I encourage everyone to see the historical realities, available on any number of media platforms, and connect them using common sense to analyze and validate the result of our individual analysis.

Both selection and operations might be regarded to analyze whether what we observe makes sense according to our inquiry. Going a step further, relevance limits those efforts and their results to what is of immediate interest to our intellectual journey. It aims for the insight that arises immediately from the data collected to answer the specific inquiry. Galileo formulated his law in response to these observations about falling bodies, for instance, because his inquiry was whether there was such a law.

Similarly, if we want to understand the type of property the socialist state in Soviet Russia promoted, we need to use observations about who had agency over the object of property, who used it, and for what end—or better yet who benefitted from it.

Some have excused their classification of the Soviet regime as socialist because they identified soviet property with the sovereignty of the people, stating that it was not the people in their collective individuality, as themselves who were the owners, but the people in their abstract sovereign peoplehood. Now, that explanation is removed from commonsense. When we talk about property we think in terms of Who possesses? Who uses? Who disposes? And Professor Berman never really answered those questions when he told us that the Soviet state owned most of the property (Berman, 1948, 325). He might have added that the Soviet state did all the possession, use, and disposition, as any good corporate owner does it. Not the people. If we were to think about a Soviet factory in terms of a mere bike. Whoever owns the bike has to use it. Can that bike belong to everyone living on our street? What about to everyone in our neighborhood? Can it belong to everyone in the city? In the state? In the country? How could my bike be the property of everyone in the entire country? Would it be enough if I post that statement on a social media platform, but I continue to ride it as I please, paint it, or even abandon it? So, the answer depends on who possess it, who uses it, and who can dispose of it. Whoever repairs the bike, or maintains it, or paints it is not the owner. Even if its last name is Joe Owner.

Now, returning to the U.S.S.R. and its satellite countries, commonsense knowledge can only comprise a limited version of that reality. But nevertheless, it can bring some insight to understanding that state capitalism, like monopolies or dictatorships or property as the legal institution for ownership, is a concept with a clear reality. While ambiguous, it can be unfolded by insight and common sense to a satisfactory explanation.

Certainly, the problem with our investigation is that usually when a scientist overlooks some data or their insights are incomplete, the work of another scientist would be used to fill in the gaps. However, this book appeared because my belief that, for reasons unclear—or for many reasons, including lack of perseverance or pure inertia—Western intellectuals went along with the intimidated intellectuals of the Eastern bloc and redefined observation, common sense, and insight to produce unintelligible conclusion, intellectual aberrations which have all but muddied the waters of alternative ways of governing society.

And all this depends on one's desire to understand. This book can only whet that appetite. The work is with each one of you, depending on where you are on that journey.

Conclusion

This book demystifies capitalism as a political, economic, and legal system that is far more flexible—and adaptable—than is commonly accepted. Through a layered analysis and close readings of key texts, it exposes the intellectual incongruities surrounding a geopolitical past often mislabeled as socialism. The society of the former U.S.S.R. and its satellites did not eliminate class exploitation; it merely rebranded it. The ruling elite replaced the bourgeoisie, and the class struggle was maintained through state monopolism, backed by dictatorship and enforced through surveillance and repression. To describe such a system as "socialist"—without the qualifier fascist—is at best inaccurate, and at worst, a historical distortion.

Nazism (German fascism) and fascism (Italian and Spanish variants) were occasionally labeled "socialist" due to the state's control over economic life, but this control was wielded in service of nationalist, authoritarian, and anti-egalitarian goals. During World War II, even the United States implemented extensive economic controls—rationing, price fixing, and centralized planning—yet no one credibly called that socialism. If mere state control equates to socialism, then the term becomes so broad it collapses under its own weight.

If, however, socialism is understood as a system marked by centralized corporate monopolization of major economic sectors under the guise of public good, then we must reconsider what is unfolding in America today. The current Trump administration's consolidation of power among state-backed corporate actors bears a troubling resemblance to the Soviet model—not in ideology, but in structure and method. Ironically, those most loudly proclaiming opposition to socialism may, in practice, be reproducing its most coercive features.

This book argues that the fundamental distinction between capitalism and socialism lies in the distribution of wealth. Socialism, by definition, requires both social and economic equality. This work challenges the commonsense belief that capitalism is inevitable or eternal—what Fredric Jameson and Slavoj Žižek, as cited by Mark Fisher (2009, 2), have described as the difficulty of imagining the end of capitalism, even more so than the end of the world.

Unlike my previous work (Neacșu, 2020) which focused on the process of scholarly understanding, this book turns to commonsense understanding, a form of knowledge born not from academic inquiry but from insight, shaped by experience, observation, and accessible information. Where I once emphasized meaning-making as a negotiation between the scholarly author and the

 | DOI:10.1163/9789004747210_012

scholar interpellated by the text, I now shift the focus to how everyday knowledge is acquired, absorbed, and evolves over time.

In this approach, knowledge production begins with a desire to cognitively interpret our environment by distinguishing between its different elements. Some are tangible objects—factories, bicycles, computers, telephones. Others are intangible entities—the Internet, cryptocurrencies, NFTs. Still others are conceptual representations—capitalism, socialism, dictatorship, representative democracy, property rights.

This book proceeds from the premise that to be human is to inquire, to seek insight, and to use common sense as a cognitive guide for what is believable and thus worth incorporating into our daily lives. By exploring how concepts like capitalism and socialism are experienced, understood, and reinterpreted through this commonsense lens, the book opens space for reimagining both our present and our possible futures.

Bernard Lonergan's cognitive theory about insight is the theoretical foundation of this argument. His optimistic views are mine, too, so that while we tend to regard ourselves as "knowing" with little empirical data and much judgment, knowing is not a static quality. Like being alive, it changes. Each day we are alive we are unlike how we were only a day before. We are more or less tired, for instance, and are able to hear things differently or see them in a different light and then reflect about their meaning in a disparate or even divergent way. With these changes, we can then accept a new insight to challenge our commonsense understanding about things, including such a thing as socialism.

This book is an invitation to be conscious—that is, to be alert, to dwell knowingly in the world. It summons us to express the desire to know, to understand. We understand something when we access information about it and make sense of it. Commonsense knowing may not be professional or scientific, but it originates from the same inquisitive impulse—a drive to be "in the know."

Unlike wishful thinking, which is explicitly shaped by personal desire and emotion, understanding—though it may be emotionally motivated—strives to be grounded in observation, experience, and analysis. Commonsense knowing often follows the canons of empirical inquiry, relying on observation and subsequent reflection or judgment. Even when cursory or emotionally charged, it contains a critical, analytical thread that makes it dynamic and malleable. It allows for the possibility of revision: when new or divergent insights emerge that contradict existing beliefs, commonsense understanding is capable of transformation.

In this sense, commonsense knowing reflects intelligence by default—the result of inquiry and reflection that generates meaning. It is "being in knowing," and this process of understanding is what gives rise to reflective, even transformative, judgment.

This book offers a clear distinction between socialism and capitalism, not in ideological abstraction but in terms of wealth distribution and ownership structures. In socialism, wealth is distributed with the goal of promoting the general welfare of society. In capitalism, by contrast, the logic of profit maximization tends to reduce the number of people who benefit from wealth, even as the rate of profit increases. Sustaining those profits often requires narrowing ownership, consolidating power, and marginalizing more and more of the population.

This book challenges the misnomer of "Soviet socialism," pointing instead to the nature of property regimes as the real dividing line. Personal property refers to what individuals own. State property, however, is not automatically the people's property. Rather, it often functions as corporate property—even when financed with public money. Its public financing does not guarantee public benefit.

Consider the Bayh-Dole Act,[1] which allows government-funded research to be transformed into privately held intellectual property, often controlled by corporations and patented for profit.[2] This example illustrates how even

---

1 Patent and Trademark Law Amendments Act, Pub. L. No. 96–517, 94 Stat. 3015 (1980) (codified as amended at 35 U.S.C. §§ 200–212).

2 Peter S. Arno and Michael H. Davis have critically examined the Bayh-Dole Act's impact on drug pricing through both a scholarly article and an op-ed piece. In their 2001 article, Arno and Davis discuss the Bayh-Dole Act's mechanisms and legislative history. They highlight that, since its enactment in 1980, the Act includes a price-control clause mandating that inventions resulting from federally funded research be sold at reasonable prices. The authors argue that enforcing this clause could address high drug prices without requiring new legislation. See, Peter S. Arno and Michael H. Davis, "Why Don't We Enforce Existing Drug Price Controls? The Unrecognized and Unenforced Reasonable Pricing Requirements Imposed upon Patents Deriving in Whole or in Part from Federally Funded Research", 75 *Tul. L. Rev.* 631 (2001) published in the *Tulane Law Review*. In their Op-Ed Piece, Arno and Davis contend that the Bayh-Dole Act allows the government to ensure that drugs developed with federal funding are available to the public at reasonable prices. They argue that despite the public's significant investment in pharmaceutical research, the government has not enforced provisions that would prevent excessive drug pricing.

These works have sparked ongoing debate about the government's role in regulating drug prices for medications developed with public funds. See, Peter S. Arno, and Michael H. Davis. "Paying Twice for the Same Drugs." *The Washington Post*, March 27, 2002, p. A21. Two decades later, Arno continues to explain the value of the Bayh-Dole amendment in regulating the public access to drugs developed using public money. See, Arno, Peter S., and Dana Neacşu. 2021. Comment on "Rights to Federally Funded Inventions and Licensing of Government Owned Inventions." Docket No. 201207-0327, ID NIST-2021-0001-648. Submitted to the National Institute of Standards and Technology (NIST), U.S. Department of

publicly funded innovation can become privatized—monetized not for public use but for private gain. Whether corporate property is owned by private firms, the state, or a hybrid of the two, its dominance reflects the continued capitalist character of the United States.

In the United States, corporations, whether private, public or hybrid, drive the economy—both in terms of employment and revenue generation. According to data from the U.S. Bureau of Labor Statistics (January 2025), the national unemployment rate stood at approximately 4 percent, representing about 6.8 million people. This places the total workforce (employed and those actively seeking work) at around 170 million individuals. As of early 2025, about 32 million small businesses—defined as companies with fewer than 500 employees—formed the bulk of U.S. enterprises. These included retail shops, restaurants, construction firms, mom-and-pop stores, and professional service offices like those of doctors and lawyers. Collectively, small businesses accounted for roughly 46 to 50 percent of the private-sector workforce. The remainder of the private workforce was employed by large multinational corporations, many of which have global operations and staff counts in the hundreds of thousands or even millions. These private corporate employers, often intersect with the federal government, whose employment, on paper, makes up only 15 percent of the total workforce, on paper only counts for 15% of the work force, through contracts, public-private partnerships, and institutional procurement.[3]

Thus, what it might change under the second Trump administration, is the paper-role of the federal government as a major employer. It might, because despite mass firings initiated by the Department of Government Efficiency (DOGE) (Kirkpatrick, 2025), the largest employer, the United States Department of Defense (DoD)—which includes both military and civilian personnel—followed by the United States Postal Service (USPS) and the

---

Commerce. https://www.regulations.gov/comment/NIST-2021-0001-6485. In this comment the co-authors specifically focus on the implications of the proposed rule 37 C.F.R. § 401.6(e). Arno and Neacșu express concern that this amendment would eliminate the existing requirement for inventions developed with federal funding—particularly pharmaceuticals—to be made reasonably available to the public. They argue that removing this obligation could lead to increased financial burdens on Americans, exacerbate health disparities, harm public health, and enhance the power of unchecked monopolies in the pharmaceutical industry. Their comment underscores the importance of maintaining provisions that ensure public access to affordable medications developed through taxpayer-funded research.

3 For more data on current population survey and employment statistics, go to the U.S. Bureau of Labor Statistics (BLS), at https://www.bls.gov/cps/.

Department of Homeland Security (DHS),[4] seem unlikely to lose employees, given the administration's politics. But the major change will happen in the role of the government in promoting so-called private employment by increasing corporate subsidies to already heavily government-sponsored monopolies.

This type of factual data, analyzed through multi-layered context and contingency, permeates this book. These observations offer insights meant to spark curiosity and invite deeper inquiry into the assumptions we hold about our form of government, politics, economic system, and Rule of Law. In this example, the analysis underscores that the type of employer—whether private or public—is not what defines a capitalist or socialist society. The true dividing line lies in the distribution of wealth. If the financial power of most workers or employees is declining while that of their employers is skyrocketing—and if those employees collectively possess less wealth than a single employer—then commonsense reasoning makes it clear: America is not becoming socialist. It remains firmly capitalist.

In a recent work on sustainable capitalism, (Scott, 2024) all the contributors seemed to have agreed with Milton Friedman's definition of capitalism in *Capitalism and Freedom* (1962) that capitalism is a nebulous concept. "Capitalism is often referenced without a generally accepted definition. When authors describe it, their explanations are highly politicized, even when focused on its economic aspect" (Neacșu, 2024, 21). However, everyone seems to agree that capitalism is not socialism. But not everyone agrees with what socialism is, especially in light of the 100-year-old misnomer of Soviet socialism. The commonsense knowledge behind socialism remained limited to its misnomer, to ersatz socialism, the reality developed in post-Tsarist Russia and the ECE countries in the twentieth century, one of the most inhuman corporate state capitalist societies imaginable.

Milton Friedman emphasized private enterprise in his definition of capitalism, describing it as the system in which the "bulk of the economic activity"

---

4 For specific data, go to United States Department of Defense (DoD): https://www.defense.gov/; United States Postal Service (USPS): https://www.usps.com/, and Department of Homeland Security (DHS): https://www.dhs.gov/. For detailed information on federal employment statistics, you can refer to the U.S. Office of Personnel Management's reports: Federal Civilian Employment: https://www.opm.gov/policy-data-oversight/data-analysis-documentation/federal-employment-reports/reports-publications/federal-civilian-employment/.

U.S. Office of Personnel Management; the U.S. Government Manual provides insights into various federal agencies:

U.S. Government Manual; Department of Defense Overview: https://www.usgovernmentmanual.gov/Agency?EType=jY3M4CTKVHY%3D&EntityId=tv4LVSeIL00%3D&ParentEId=+klubNxgV00%3D.

is conducted by private actors. I would argue, however, that corporatism is a more accurate descriptor. The very purpose of the corporation is to insulate those who benefit from its revenues—from shareholders to executives—from liability, unlike those earning wages or salaries. If Friedman considers the control of property and profit by private hands essential to defining capitalism, then we are, in principle, in agreement.

In ersatz socialism, the beneficiaries were the managerial class whose members doubled as elite affiliates of the sole political party, the military, militia, and the paramilitary organizations keeping the population obediently terrorized. Moreover, even when Friedman—one of the most influential American economists—defined capitalism as "the organization of the bulk of economic activity through private enterprise operating in a free market ... a society dedicated to freedom and relying primarily on the market to organize economic activity," (Friedman, 1962, 4) his definition could just as easily apply to ersatz socialism. The Soviet regime in Russia, as well as regimes in Eastern and Central Europe, relied on their national and regional markets to organize economic activity. These markets were legally regulated, and goods of all kinds—arms, electronics, natural resources, textiles, food—were exchanged within them.

Thus, Friedman's definitions are of limited utility if our aim is to draw a clear distinction between ersatz socialism and capitalism. In fact, the relationship is better understood in terms of genus and species: capitalism is the genus, and ersatz socialism is one of its species—distorted, coercive, and state-driven, but structurally and economically similar.

Such close reading and layered analysis of a variety of sources abounds though this book, because its aim is to provide compelling reasons to reassess common misunderstanding about socialism. This book is not a political theory of capitalism, though it does include Soviet socialism, or ersatz socialism, among the many types of capitalism. It does, however, merge theories of politics, economics, and law to produce new insight into the horrors of state capitalism, a variety of monopoly capitalism. Even the most astute theoreticians seem so taken by the fiction of socialism, or worse "the collapse of Communism in 1990" (Streeck, 2024, 18).

This book is structured in three parts. Part 1 offers a critical survey of socialist theories, juxtaposed with a layered analysis of testimonials about the creation of the U.S.S.R. by philosophers (e.g., Bertrand Russell), journalists (e.g., John Reed), and fiction writers (e.g., Boris Pasternak). This analysis aims to demystify the persistent belief that socialism inevitably devolves into dictatorship. Given the wide range of socialist theory available to the founding fathers of the U.S.S.R. and a review of their actual decisions, it becomes clear that the sole objective of the October Revolution was not the establishment of socialism, but rather the replacement of the Tsarist regime with a Bolshevik one. Socialism was not the goal—consolidating power was. The structure of the U.S.S.R. was designed not for a classless society, but to maintain authoritarian control under a new elite.

Part 2 continues the book's challenge to the prevailing commonsense (mis)understanding of socialism—both as concept and praxis. Conceptually, socialism is a theory about building a just society for all. In practice, however, Soviet Russia and the Eastern and Central European (ECE) countries justified their political and military coups as socialist revolutions. In doing so, they enacted a form of state capitalist accumulation, skipping over intermediary capitalist stages and adopting the final form of capitalism—corporate monopoly—under state control. Part 2 applies political, economic, and legal theory to demonstrate that Soviet praxis amounted to one of the most inhumane dictatorships in modern history: a regime built on mass exploitation, legally sanctioned under a perverse Rule of Law that promoted the socialization of labor and the private distribution of wealth to political loyalists.

Part 3 completes this exposé of ersatz socialism by offering a theory of knowledge grounded in commonsense and insight. It is an argument that demystifying socialism—and thus capitalism—is essential for any honest conversation about political and economic justice.

This project was made possible by the transformation of our political reality, which has rendered capitalism's ambiguous nature increasingly transparent. It is now clearer that capitalism, not socialism, was the reality that surrounded us in the United States, in Europe, and in all former ECE countries—including Russia. There remains much confusion about what capitalism is, but as this book shows, capitalism has never been inherently opposed to dictatorship. Today, across the globe, we are witnessing a march toward illiberal democracy, where human rights—especially those of immigrants and their children—are under threat. These vulnerable "other Persons," to borrow the phrase from Article I, Section 2, Clause 3 of the U.S. Constitution,[5] are the canaries in the coal mine.

To demystify socialism is also to demystify capitalism. It is a matter of first-order importance, so that no one may continue to say, "Socialism was tried

---

5 Representatives and direct Taxes shall be apportioned among the several States which may be included within this Union, according to their respective Numbers, which shall be determined by adding to the whole Number of free Persons, including those bound to Service for a Term of Years, and excluding Indians not taxed, three fifths of all *other Persons*. (emphasis added)

https://constitution.congress.gov/browse/article-1/section-2/clause-3/.

and it failed"—when in fact, what was tried was a monstrosity falsely labeled as socialism. True socialism, as envisioned by FDR's Second Bill of Rights, was never implemented on a societal scale. In that vision, there remains hope.

This book is, ultimately, an ode to knowledge and understanding—a declaration that commonsense insight is the bedrock of human decency. And like democracy and decency, it too is dynamic.

APPENDIX A

J.V. Stalin: Constitution (Fundamental Law) of the Union of Soviet Socialist Republics

With Amendments and Additions adopted by the First, Second, Third, Sixth, Seventh and Eighth Sessions of the Supreme Soviet of the U.S.S.R.

Kremlin, Moscow, December 5, 1936
https://www.marxists.org/reference/archive/stalin/works/1936/12/05.htm

Chapter I: The Organization of Society

ARTICLE 1. The Union of Soviet Socialist Republics is a socialist state of workers and peasants.

ARTICLE 2. The Soviets of Working People's Deputies, which grew and attained strength as a result of the overthrow of the landlords and capitalists and the achievement of the dictatorship of the proletariat, constitute the political foundation of the U.S.S.R.

ARTICLE 3. In the U.S.S.R. all power belongs to the working people of town and country as represented by the Soviets of Working People's Deputies.

ARTICLE 4. The socialist system of economy and the socialist ownership of the means and instruments of production, firmly established as a result of the abolition of the capitalist system of economy, the abrogation of private ownership of the means and instruments of production and the abolition of the exploitation of man by man, constitute the economic foundation of the U.S.S.R.

ARTICLE 5. Socialist property in the U.S.S.R. exists either in the form of state property (the possession of the whole people), or in the form of cooperative and collective-farm property (property of a collective farm or property of a cooperative association).

ARTICLE 6. The land, its natural deposits, waters, forests, mills, factories, mines, rail, water and air transport, banks, post, telegraph, and telephones, large state organized agricultural enterprises (state farms, machine and tractor stations and the like) as well

 | DOI:10.1163/9789004747210_013

as municipal enterprises and the bulk of the dwelling houses in the cities and industrial localities, are state property, that is, belong to the whole people.

ARTICLE 7. Public enterprises in collective farms and cooperative organizations, with their livestock and implements, the products of the collective farms and cooperative organizations, as well as their common buildings, constitute the common, socialist property of the collective farms and cooperative organizations.

In addition to its basic income from the public, collective-farm enterprise, every household in a collective farm has for its personal use a small plot of land attached to the dwelling and, as its personal property, a subsidiary establishment on the plot, a dwelling house, livestock, poultry and minor agricultural implements—in accordance with the statutes of the agricultural artel.

ARTICLE 8. The land occupied by collective farms is secured to them for their use free of charge and for an unlimited time, that is, in perpetuity.

ARTICLE 9. Alongside the socialist system of economy, which is the predominant form of economy in the U.S.S.R., the law permits the small private economy of individual peasants and handicraftsmen based on their personal labour and precluding the exploitation of the labour of others.

ARTICLE 10. The right of citizens to personal ownership of their incomes from work and of their savings, of their dwelling houses and subsidiary household economy, their household furniture and utensils and articles of personal use and convenience, as well as the right of inheritance of personal property of citizens, is protected by law.

ARTICLE 11. The economic life of the U.S.S.R. is determined and directed by the state national economic plan with the aim of increasing the public wealth, of steadily improving the material conditions of the working people and raising their cultural level, of consolidating the independence of the U.S.S.R. and strengthening its defensive capacity.

ARTICLE 12. In the U.S.S.R. work is a duty and a matter of honour for every able-bodied citizen, in accordance with the principle: "He who does not work, neither shall he eat."

The principle applied in the U.S.S.R. is that of socialism: "From each according to his ability, to each according to his work."

Chapter II: The Organization of the State

ARTICLE 13. The Union of Soviet Socialist Republics is a federal state, formed on the basis of the voluntary association of Soviet Socialist Republics having equal rights, namely:

The Russian Soviet Federative Socialist Republic
The Ukrainian Soviet Socialist Republic
The Byelorussian Soviet Socialist Republic
The Azerbaijan Soviet Socialist Republic
The Georgian Soviet Socialist Republic
The Armenian Soviet Socialist Republic
The Turkmen Soviet Socialist Republic
The Uzbek Soviet Socialist Republic
The Tajik Soviet Socialist Republic
The Kazakh Soviet Socialist Republic
The Kirghiz Soviet Socialist Republic
The Karelo-Finnish Soviet Socialist Republic
The Moldavian Soviet Socialist Republic
The Lithuanian Soviet Socialist Republic
The Latvian Soviet Socialist Republic
The Estonian Soviet Socialist Republic

ARTICLE 14. The jurisdiction of the Union of Soviet Socialist Republics, as represented by its highest organs of state authority and organs of government, covers:

a) Representation of the Union in international relations, conclusion and ratification of treaties with other states;
b) Questions of war and peace;
c) Admission of new republics into the U.S.S.R.;
d) Control over the observance of the Constitution of the U.S.S.R. and ensuring conformity of the Constitutions of the Union Republics with the Constitution of the U.S.S.R.;
e) Confirmation of alterations of boundaries between Union Republics;
f) Confirmation of the formation of new Territories and Regions and also of new Autonomous Republics within Union Republics;
g) Organization of the defence of the U.S.S.R. and direction of all the armed forces of the U.S.S.R.;
h) Foreign trade on the basis of state monopoly;
i) Safeguarding the security of the state;
j) Establishment of the national economic plans of the U.S.S.R.;

k) Approval of the single state budget of the U.S.S.R. as well as of the taxes and revenues which go to the all-Union, Republican and local budgets;
l) Administration of the banks, industrial and agricultural establishments and enterprises and trading enterprises of all-Union importance;
m) Administration of transport and communications;
n) Direction of the monetary and credit system;
o) Organization of state insurance;
p) Raising and granting of loans;
q) Establishment of the basic principles for the use of land as well as for the use of natural deposits, forests and waters;
r) Establishment of the basic principles in the spheres of education and public health;
s) Organization of a uniform system of national economic statistics;
t) Establishment of the principles of labour legislation;
u) Legislation on the judicial system and judicial procedure; criminal and civil codes;
v) Laws on citizenship of the Union; laws on the rights of foreigners;
w) Issuing of all-Union acts of amnesty.

ARTICLE 15. The sovereignty of the Union Republics is limited only within the provisions set forth in Article 14 of the Constitution of the U.S.S.R.

Outside of these provisions, each Union Republic exercises state authority independently. The U.S.S.R. protects the sovereign rights of the Union Republics.

ARTICLE 16. Each Union Republic has its own Constitution, which takes account of the specific features of the Republic and is drawn up in full conformity with the Constitution of the U.S.S.R.

ARTICLE 17. To every Union Republic is reserved the right freely to secede from the U.S.S.R.

ARTICLE 18. The territory of a Union Republic may not be altered without its consent.

ARTICLE 19. The laws of the U.S.S.R. have the same force within the territory of every Union Republic.

ARTICLE 20. In the event of a discrepancy between a law of a Union Republic and an all-Union law, the all-Union law prevails.

ARTICLE 21. A single Union citizenship is established for all citizens of the U.S.S.R.

Every citizen of a Union Republic is a citizen of the U.S.S.R.

ARTICLE 22. The Russian Soviet Federative Socialist Republic consists of the Altai, Krasnodar, Krasnoyarsk, Orjonikidze, Primorye and Khabarovsk Territories; the Archangel, Vologda, Voronezh, Gorky, Ivanovo, Irkutsk, Kalinin, Kirov, Kuibyshev, Kursk, Leningrad, Molotov, Moscow, Murmansk, Novosibirsk, Omsk, Orel, Penza, Rostov, Ryazan, Saratov, Sverdlovsk, Smolensk, Stalingrad, Tambov, Tula, Chelyabinsk, Chita, Chjkalov and Yaroslavl Regions; the Tatar, Bashkir, Daghestan, Buryat-Mongolian, Kabardino- Balkarian, Kalmyk, Komi, Crimean, Mari, Mordovian, Volga German, North Ossetian, Udmurt, Chechen- Ingush, Chuvash and Yakut Autonomous Soviet Socialist Republics; and the Adygei, Jewish, Karachai, Oirot, Khakass ans Cherkess Autonomous Regions.

ARTICLE 23. The Ukrainian Soviet Socialist Republic consists of the Vinnitsa, Volhynia, Voroshilovgrad, Dniepropetrovsk, Drohobych, Zhitomir, Zaporozhye, Izmail, Kamenets-Podolsk, Kiev, Kirovograd, Lvov, Nikolayev, Odessa, Poltova, Rovno, Stalino, Stanislav, Sumi, Tarnapol; Kharkov, Chernigov and Chernovitsi Regions.

ARTICLE 24. The Azerbaijan Soviet Socialist Republic includes the Nakhichevan Autonomous Soviet Socialist Republic and the Nagarno-Karabakh Autonomous Region.

ARTICLE 25. The Georgian Soviet Socialist Republic includes the Abkhazian Autonomous Soviet Socialist Republic, the Adjar Autonomous Soviet Socialist Republic and the South Ossetian Autonomous Region.

ARTICLE 26. The Uzbek Soviet Socialist Republic consists of the Bukhara, Samarkand, Tashkent, Ferghana and Khorezm Regions, and the Kara-Kalpak Autonomous Soviet Socialist Republic.

ARTICLE 27. The Tajik Soviet Socialist Republic consists of the Garm, Kulyab, Leninabad and Stalinabad Regions, and the Gorno-Badakhshan Autonomous Region.

ARTICLE 28. The Kazakh Soviet Socialist Republic consists of the Akmolinsk, Aktyubinsk, Alma-Ata East Kazakhstan, Guriev, Jambul, West Kazakhstan, Karaganda, Kzyl-Orda, Kustanai, Pavlodar, North Kazakhstan, Semipalatinsk and South Kazakhstan Regions.

ARTICLE 29. The Byelorussian Soviet Socialist Republic consists of the Baranovichi, Byelostok, Brest, Vileyka, Vitebsk, Gomel, Minsk, Moghilev, Pinsk and Polessye Regions.

ARTICLE 29-a. The Turkmen Soviet Socialist Republic consists of the Ashkhabad, Krasnovodsk, Mari, Tashauz and Charjow Regions.

ARTICLE 29-b. The Kirghiz Soviet Socialist Republic consists of the Dzhalal-Abad, Issyk-Kul, Osh, Tien-Shan and Frunze Regions.

Chapter III: The Highest Organs of State Authority of the Union of Soviet Socialist Republics

ARTICLE 30. The highest organ of state authority of the U.S.S.R. is the Supreme Soviet of the U.S.S.R.

ARTICLE 31. The Supreme Soviet of the U.S.S.R. exercises all rights vested in the Union of Soviet Socialist Republics in accordance with Article 14 of the Constitution, in so far as they do not, by virtue of the Constitution, come within the jurisdiction of organs of the U.S.S.R. that are accountable to the Supreme Soviet of the U.S.S.R., that is, the Presidium of the Supreme Soviet of the U.S.S.R., the Council of People's Commissars of the U.S.S.R. and the People's Commissariats of the U.S.S.R.

ARTICLE 32. The legislative power of the U.S.S.R. is exercised exclusively by the Supreme Soviet of the U.S.S.R.

ARTICLE 33. The Supreme Soviet of the U.S.S.R. consists of two chambers: the Soviet of the Union and the Soviet of Nationalities.

ARTICLE 34. The Soviet of the Union is elected by the citizens of the U.S.S.R. according to electoral areas on the basis of one deputy for every 300,000 of the population.

ARTICLE 35. The Soviet of Nationalities is elected by the citizens of the U.S.S.R. according to Union and Autonomous Republics, Autonomous Regions and national areas on the basis of twenty-five deputies from each Union Republic, eleven deputies from each Autonomous Republic, five deputies from each Autonomous Region and one deputy from each national area.

ARTICLE 36. The Supreme Soviet of the U.S.S.R. is elected for a term of four years.

ARTICLE 37. Both Chambers of the Supreme Soviet of the U.S.S.R., the Soviet of the Union and the Soviet of Nationalities, have equal rights.

ARTICLE 38. The Soviet of the Union and the Soviet of Nationalities have an equal right to initiate legislation.

ARTICLE 39. A law is considered adopted if passed by both Chambers of the Supreme Soviet of the U.S.S.R. by a simple majority vote in each.

ARTICLE 40. Laws passed by the Supreme Soviet of the U.S.S.R. are published in the languages of the Union Republics over the signatures of the President and Secretary of the Presidium of the Supreme Soviet of the U.S.S.R.

ARTICLE 41. Sessions of the Soviet of the Union and the Soviet of Nationalities begin and terminate simultaneously.

ARTICLE 42. The Soviet of the Union elects a Chairman of the Soviet of the Union and two Vice- Chairmen.

ARTICLE 43. The Soviet of Nationalities elects a Chairman of the Soviet of Nationalities and two Vice-Chairmen.

ARTICLE 44. The Chairmen of the Soviet of the Union and the Soviet of Nationalities preside over the sittings of the respective Chambers and direct the procedure of these bodies.

ARTICLE 45. Joint sittings of both Chambers of the Supreme Soviet of the U.S.S.R. are presided over alternately by the Chairman of the Soviet of the Union and the Chairman of the Soviet of Nationalities.

ARTICLE 46. Sessions of the Supreme Soviet of the U.S.S.R. are convened by the Presidium of the Supreme Soviet of the U.S.S.R. twice a year.

Special sessions are convened by the Presidium of the Supreme Soviet of the U.S.S.R. at its discretion or on the demand of one of the Union Republics.

ARTICLE 47. In the event of a disagreement between the Soviet of the Union and the Soviet of Nationalities, the question is referred for settlement to a conciliation commission formed on a parity basis. If the conciliation commission fails to arrive at an agreement, or if its decision fails to satisfy one of the Chambers, the question is considered for a second time by the Chambers. Failing agreement between the two Chambers, the Presidium of the Supreme Soviet of the U.S.S.R. dissolves the Supreme Soviet of the U.S.S.R. and orders new elections.

ARTICLE 48. The Supreme Soviet of the U.S.S.R. at a joint sitting of both Chambers elects the Presidium of the Supreme Soviet of the U.S.S.R., consisting of a President of the Presidium of the Supreme Soviet of the U.S.S.R., sixteen Vice- Presidents, a Secretary of the Presidium and twenty-four members of the Presidium.

The Presidium of the Supreme Soviet of the U.S.S.R. is accountable to the Supreme Soviet of the U.S.S.R. for all its activities.

ARTICLE 49. The Presidium of the Supreme Soviet of the U.S.S.R.:

a) Convenes the sessions of the Supreme Soviet of the U.S.S.R.;
b) Interprets laws of the U.S.S.R. in operation, issues decrees;
c) Dissolves the Supreme Soviet of the U.S.S.R.in conformity with Article 47 of the Constitution of the U.S.S.R. and orders new elections;
d) Conducts referendums on its own initiative or on the demand of one of the Union Republics;
e) Annuls decisions and orders of the Council of People's Commissars of the U.S.S.R. and of the Council of People's Commissars of the Union Republics in case they do not conform to law;
f) In the intervals between sessions of the Supreme Soviet of the U.S.S.R., relieves of their posts and appoints People's Commissars of the U.S.S.R. on the recommendation of the Chairman of the Council of People's Commissars of the U.S.S.R., subject to subsequent confirmation by the Supreme Soviet of the U.S.S.R.;
g) Awards with decorations and confers titles of honour of the U.S.S.R.;
h) Exercises the right of pardon;
i) Appoints and removes the higher commands of the armed forces of the U.S.S.R.;
j) In the intervals between sessions of the Supreme Soviet of the U.S.S.R., proclaims a state of war in the event of armed attack on the U.S.S.R., or whenever necessary to fulfil international treaty obligations concerning mutual defence against aggression;
k) Orders general or partial mobilization;
l) Ratifies international treaties;
m) Appoints and recalls plenipotentiary representatives of the U.S.S.R. to foreign states;
n) Receives the credentials and letters of recall of diplomatic representatives accredited to it by foreign states;
o) Proclaims martial law in separate localities or throughout the U.S.S.R. in the interests of the defence of the U.S.S.R. or for the purpose of ensuring public order and state security.

ARTICLE 50. The Soviet of the Union and the Soviet of Nationalities elect Credentials Commissions which verify the credentials of the members of the respective Chambers.

On there commendation of the Credentials Commissions, the Chambers decide either to endorse the credentials or to annul the election of the deputies concerned.

ARTICLE 51. The Supreme Soviet of the U.S.S.R. when it deems necessary, appoints commissions of enquiry and investigation on any matter.

It is the duty of all institutions and public servants to comply with the demands of these commissions and to submit to them the necessary materials and documents.

ARTICLE 52. A member of the Supreme Soviet of the U.S.S.R. may not be prosecuted or arrested without the consent of the Supreme Soviet of the U.S.S.R., and during the period when the Supreme Soviet of the U.S.S.R. is not in session, without the consent of the Presidium of the Supreme Soviet of the U.S.S.R.

ARTICLE 53. On the expiration of the term of office of the Supreme Soviet of the U.S.S.R., or after the dissolution of the Supreme Soviet prior to the expiration of its term of office, the Presidium of the Supreme Soviet of the U.S.S.R. retains its powers until the formation of a new Presidium of the Supreme Soviet of the U.S.S.R. by the newly-elected Supreme Soviet of the U.S.S.R.

ARTICLE 54. On the expiration of the term of office of the Supreme Soviet of the U.S.S.R., or in the event of its dissolution prior to the expiration of its term of office, the Presidium of the Supreme Soviet of the U.S.S.R. orders new elections to be held within a period not exceeding two months from the date of expiration of the term of office or dissolution of the Supreme Soviet of the U.S.S.R.

ARTICLE 55. The newly-elected Supreme Soviet of the U.S.S.R. is convened by the outgoing Presidium of the Supreme Soviet of the U.S.S.R. not later than one month after the elections.

ARTICLE 56. The Supreme Soviet of the U.S.S.R. at a joint sitting of both Chambers, appoints the Government of the U.S.S.R., namely, the Council of People's Commissars of the U.S.S.R.

Chapter IV: The Highest Organs of State Authority of the Union Republics

ARTICLE 57. The highest organ of state authority of a Union Republic is the Supreme Soviet of the Union Republic.

ARTICLE 58. The Supreme Soviet of a Union Republic is elected by the citizens of the Republic for a term of four years.

The basis of representation is established by the Constitution of the Union Republic.

ARTICLE 59. The Supreme Soviet of a Union Republic is the sole legislative organ of the Republic.

ARTICLE 60. The Supreme Soviet of a Union Republic:
a) Adopts the Constitution of the Republic and amends it in conformity with Article 16 of the Constitution of the U.S.S.R.;
b) Confirms the Constitutions of the Autonomous Republics forming part of it and defines the boundaries of their territories;
c) Approves the national economic plan and also the budget of the Republic;
d) Exercises the right of amnesty and pardon of citizens sentenced by the judicial organs of the Union Republic.

ARTICLE 61. The Supreme Soviet of a Union Republic elects the Presidium of the Supreme Soviet of the Union Republic, consisting of a Chairman of the Presidium of the Supreme Soviet of the Union Republic, Vice-Chairmen, a Secretary of the Presidium and members of the Presidium of the Supreme Soviet of the Union Republic.

The powers of the Presidium of the Supreme Soviet of a Union Republic are defined by the Constitution of the Union Republic.

ARTICLE 62. The Supreme Soviet of a Union Republic elects a Chairman and a Vice-Chairman to conduct its sittings.

ARTICLE 63. The Supreme Soviet of a Union Republic appoints the Government of the Union Republic, namely, the Council of People's Commissars of the Union Republic.

Chapter V: The Organs of Government of the Union of Soviet Socialist Republics

ARTICLE 64. The highest executive and administrative organ of state authority of the Union of Soviet Socialist Republics is the Council of People's Commissars of the U.S.S.R.

ARTICLE 65. The Council of People's Commissars of the U.S.S.R. is responsible to the Supreme Soviet of the U.S.S.R. and accountable to it; and in the intervals between sessions of the Supreme Soviet it is responsible and accountable to the Presidium of the Supreme Soviet of the U.S.S.R.

ARTICLE 66. The Council of People's Commissars of the U.S.S.R. issues decisions and orders on the basis and in pursuance of the laws in operation, and supervises their execution.

ARTICLE 67. Decisions and orders of the Council of People's Commissars of the U.S.S.R. are binding throughout the territory of the U.S.S.R.

ARTICLE 68. The Council of People's Commissars of the U.S.S.R.:

a) Coordinates and directs the work of the All- Union and Union-Republican People's Commissariats of the U.S.S.R. and of other institutions, economic and cultural, under its administration;
b) Adopts measures to carry out the national economic plan and the state budget, and to strengthen the credit and monetary system;
c) Adopts measures for the maintenance of public order, for the protection of the interests of the state, and for the safeguarding of the rights of citizens;
d) Exercises general guidance in respect of relations with foreign states;
e) Fixes the annual contingent of citizens to be called up for military service and directs the general organization and development of the armed forces of the country;
f) Sets up, whenever necessary, special Committees and Central Administrations under the Council of People's Commissars of the U.S.S.R. for matters concerning economic, cultural and defence organization and development.

ARTICLE 69. The Council of People's Commissars of the U.S.S.R. has the right, in respect of those branches of administration and economy which come within the jurisdiction of the U.S.S.R., to suspend decisions and orders of the Councils of People's Commissars of the Union Republics and to annul orders and instructions of People's Commissars of the U.S.S.R.

ARTICLE 70. The Council of People's Commissars of the U.S.S.R. is appointed by the Supreme Soviet of the U.S.S.R. and consists of:

The Chairman of the Council of People's Commissars of the U.S.S.R.;
The Vice-Chairmen of the Council of People's Commissars of the U.S.S.R.;
The Chairman of the State Planning Commission of the U.S.S.R.;
The Chairman of the Soviet Control Commission;
The People's Commissars of the U.S.S.R.;
The Chairman of the Committee on Arts;
The Chairman of the Committee on Higher Education;
The Chairman of the Board of the State Bank.

ARTICLE 71. The Government of the U.S.S.R. or a People's Commissar of the U.S.S.R. to whom a question of a member of the Supreme Soviet of the U.S.S.R. is addressed must give a verbal or written reply in the respective Chamber within a period not exceeding three days.

ARTICLE 72. The People's Commissars of the U.S.S.R. direct the branches of state administration which come within the jurisdiction of the U.S.S.R.

ARTICLE 73. The People's Commissars of the U.S.S.R. issue, within the limits of the jurisdiction of the respective People's Commissariats, orders and instructions on the basis and in pursuance of the laws in operation, and also of decisions and orders of the Council of People's Commissars of the U.S.S.R., and supervise their execution.

ARTICLE 74. The People's Commissariats of the U.S.S.R. are either All-Union or Union-Republican Commissariats.

ARTICLE 75. The All-Union People's Commissariats direct the branches of state administration entrusted to them throughout the territory of the U.S.S.R. either directly or through bodies appointed by them.

ARTICLE 76. The Union-Republican People's Commissariats, as a rule, direct the branches of state administration entrusted to them through the corresponding People's Commissariats of the Union Republics; they administer directly only a definite and limited number of enterprises according to a list confirmed by the Presidium of the Supreme Soviet of the U.S.S.R.

ARTICLE 77. The following People's Commissariats are All-Union People's Commissariats:

Defence
Foreign Affairs
Foreign Trade
Railways
Post, Telegraph and Telephones
Maritime Fleet
River Fleet
Coal-Mining Industry
Oil Industry
Electric Power Stations
Electrical Engineering Industry

Iron and Steel Industry
Non-Ferrous Metals Industry
Chemical Industry
Aircraft Industry
Shipbuilding Industry
Munitions Industry
Armaments Industry
Heavy Machine-Building Industry
Medium Machine-Building Industry
General Machine-Building Industry
Navy
Agricultural Stocks
Civil Engineering Industry
Cellulose and Paper Industry.

ARTICLE 78. The following People's Commissariats are Union-Republican People's Commissariats:

Food Industry
Fishing Industry
Meat and Dairy Produce Industry
Light Industry
Textile Industry
Timber Industry
Agriculture State Grain and Livestock Farms
Finance
Trade
Internal Affairs
State Security
Justice
Public Health
Building Materials Industry
State Control.

Chapter VI: The Organs of Government of the Union Republics

ARTICLE 79. The highest executive and administrative organ of state authority of a Union Republic is the Council of People's Commissars of the Union Republic.

ARTICLE 80. The Council of People's Commissars of a Union Republic is responsible to the Supreme Soviet of the Union Republic and accountable to it; and in the intervals between sessions of the Supreme Soviet of the Union Republic it is responsible and accountable to the Presidium of the Supreme Soviet of the respective Union Republic.

ARTICLE 81. The Council of People's Commissars of a Union Republic issues decisions and orders on the basis and in pursuance of the laws in operation of the U.S.S.R. and of the Union Republic, and of the decisions and orders of the Council of People's Commissars of the U.S.S.R., and supervises their execution.

ARTICLE 82. The Council of People's Commissars of a Union Republic has the right to suspend decisions and orders of Councils of People's Commissars of Autonomous Republics, and to annul decisions and orders of Executive Committees of Soviets of Working People's Deputies of Territories, Regions and Autonomous Regions.

ARTICLE 83. The Council of People's Commissars of a Union Republic is appointed by the Supreme Soviet of the Union Republic and consists of:

The Chairman of the Council of People's Commissars of the Union Republic;
The Vice-Chairmen;
The Chairman of the State Planning Commission;
The People's Commissars of:
Food Industry
Fishing Industry
Meat and Dairy Produce Industry
Light Industry
Textile Industry
Timber Industry
Building Materials Industry
Agriculture
State Grain and Livestock Farms
Finance
Trade
Internal Affairs
State Security
Justice
Public Health
State Control
Education

Local Industry
Municipal Economy
Social Maintenance
Motor Transport
The Chief of the Arts Administration;
The Representatives of the All-Union People's Commissariats.

ARTICLE 84. The People's Commissars of a Union Republic direct the branches of state administration which come within the jurisdiction of the Union Republic.

ARTICLE 85. The People's Commissars of a Union Republic issue, within the limits of the jurisdiction of their respective People's Commissariats, orders and instructions on the basis and in pursuance of the laws of the U.S.S.R. and of the Union Republic, of the decisions and orders of the Council of People's Commissars of the U.S.S.R. and that of the Union Republic, and of the orders and instructions of the Union-Republican People's Commissariats of the U.S.S.R.

ARTICLE 86. The People's Commissariats of a Union Republic are either Union-Republican or Republican Commissariats.

ARTICLE 87. The Union-Republican People's Commissariats direct the branches of state administration entrusted to them, and are subordinate both to the Council of People's Commissars of the Union Republic and to the corresponding Union-Republican People's Commissariats of the U.S.S.R.

ARTICLE 88. The Republican People's Commissariats direct the branches of state administration entrusted to them and are directly subordinate to the Council of People's Commissars of the Union Republic.

Chapter VII: The Highest Organs of State Authority of the Autonomous Soviet Socialist Republics

ARTICLE 89. The highest organ of state authority of an Autonomous Republic is the Supreme Soviet of the Autonomous Soviet Socialist Republic.

ARTICLE 90. The Supreme Soviet of an Autonomous Republic is elected by the citizens of the Republic for a term of four years on the basis of representation established by the Constitution of the Autonomous Republic.

ARTICLE 91. The Supreme Soviet of an Autonomous Republic is the sole legislative organ of the Autonomous Soviet Socialist Republic.

ARTICLE 92. Each Autonomous Republic has its own Constitution, which takes account of the specific features of the Autonomous Republic and is drawn up in full conformity with the Constitution of the Union Republic.

ARTICLE 93. The Supreme Soviet of an Autonomous Republic elects the Presidium of the Supreme Soviet of the Autonomous Republic and appoints the Council of People's Commissars of the Autonomous Republic, in accordance with its Constitution.

Chapter VIII: The Local Organs of State Authority

ARTICLE 94. The organs of state authority in territories, regions, autonomous regions, areas, districts, cities and rural localities (stanitsas, villages, hamlets, kishlaks, auls) are the Soviets of Working People's Deputies.

ARTICLE 95. The Soviets of Working People's Deputies of territories, regions, autonomous regions, areas, districts, cities and rural localities (stanitsas, villages, hamlets, kishlaks, auls) are elected by the working people of the respective territories, regions, autonomous regions, areas, districts, cities or rural localities for a term of two years.

ARTICLE 96. The basis of representation for Soviets of Working People's Deputies is defined by the Constitutions of the Union Republics.

ARTICLE 97. The Soviets of Working People's Deputies direct the work of the organs of administration subordinate to them, ensure the maintenance of public order, the observance of the laws and the protection of the rights of citizens, direct local economic and cultural organization and development and draw up the local budgets.

ARTICLE 98. The Soviets of Working People's Deputies adopt decisions and issue orders within the limits of the powers vested in them by the laws of the U.S.S.R. and of the Union Republic.

ARTICLE 99. The executive and administrative organs of the Soviets of Working People's Deputies of territories, regions, autonomous regions, areas, districts, cities and rural localities are the Executive Committees elected by them, consisting of a Chairman, Vice-Chairmen, a Secretary and members.

ARTICLE 100. The executive and administrative organ of rural Soviets of Working People's Deputies in small localities, in accordance with the Constitutions of the Union Republics, is the Chairman, the Vice-Chairman and the Secretary elected by them.

ARTICLE 101. The executive organs of the Soviet s of Working People's Deputies are directly accountable both to the Soviets of Working People's Deputies which elected them and to the executive organ of the superior Soviet of Working People's Deputies.

Chapter IX: The Courts and Procurator's Office

ARTICLE 102. In the U.S.S.R. justice is administered by the Supreme Court of the U.S.S.R., the Supreme Courts of the Union Republics, the Territorial and the Regional courts, the courts of the Autonomous Republics and the Autonomous Regions, the Area courts, the special courts of the U.S.S.R. established by decision of the Supreme Soviet of the U.S.S.R., and the People's Courts.

ARTICLE 103. In all courts cases are tried with the participation of people's assessors, except in cases specially provided for by law.

ARTICLE 104. The Supreme Court of the U.S.S.R. is the highest judicial organ. The Supreme Court of the U.S.S.R. is charged with the supervision of the judicial activities of all the judicial organs of the U.S.S.R. and of the Union Republics.

ARTICLE 105. The Supreme Court of the U.S.S.R. and the special courts of the U.S.S.R. are elected by the Supreme Soviet of the U.S.S.R. for a term of five years.

ARTICLE 106. The Supreme Courts of the Union Republics are elected by the Supreme Soviets of the Union Republics for a term of five years.

ARTICLE 107. The Supreme Courts of the Autonomous Republics are elected by the Supreme Soviets of the Autonomous Republics for a term of five years.

ARTICLE 108. The Territorial and the Regional courts, the courts of the Autonomous Regions and the Area courts are elected by the Territorial, Regional or Area Soviets of Working People's Deputies of the Autonomous Regions for a term of five years.

ARTICLE 109. People's Courts are elected by the citizens of the district on the basis of universal, direct and equal suffrage by secret ballot for a term of three years.

ARTICLE 110. Judicial proceedings are conducted in the language of the Union Republic, Autonomous Republic or Autonomous Region, persons not knowing this language being guaranteed every opportunity of fully acquainting themselves with the material of the case through an interpreter and likewise the right to use their own language in court.

ARTICLE 111. In all courts of the U.S.S.R. cases are heard in public, unless otherwise provided for by law, and the accused is guaranteed the right to be defended by Counsel.

ARTICLE 112. Judges are independent and subject only to the law.

ARTICLE 113. Supreme supervisory power over the strict execution of the laws by all People's Commissariats and institutions subordinated to them, as well as by public servants and citizens of the U.S.S.R. is vested in the Procurator of the U.S.S.R.

ARTICLE 114. The Procurator of the U.S.S.R. is appointed by the Supreme Soviet of the U.S.S.R. for a term of seven years.

ARTICLE 115. Procurators of Republics, Territories and Regions, as well as Procurators of Autonomous Republics and Autonomous Regions are appointed by the Procurator of the U.S.S.R. for a term of five years.

ARTICLE 116. Area, district and city procurators are appointed for a term of five years by the Procurators of the Union Republics, subject to the approval of the Procurator of the U.S.S.R.

ARTICLE 117. The organs of the Procurator's Office perform their functions independently of any local organs whatsoever, being subordinate solely to the Procurator of the U.S.S.R.

Chapter X: Fundamental Rights and Duties of Citizens

ARTICLE 118. Citizens of the U.S.S.R. have the right to work, that is, are guaranteed the right to employment and payment for their work in accordance with its quantity and quality.

The right to work is ensured by the socialist organization of the national economy, the steady growth of the productive forces of Soviet society, the elimination of the possibility of economic crises, and the abolition of unemployment.

ARTICLE 119. Citizens of the U.S.S.R. have the right to rest and leisure.

The right to rest and leisure is ensured by the reduction of the working day to seven hours for the overwhelming majority of the workers, the institution of annual vacations with full pay for workers and employees and the provision of a wide network of sanatoria, rest homes and clubs for the accommodation of the working people.

ARTICLE 120. Citizens of the U.S.S.R. have the right to maintenance in old age and also in the case of sickness or loss of capacity to work.

This right is ensured by the extensive development of social insurance of workers and employees at state expense, free medical service for the working people and the provision of a wide network of health resorts for the use of the working people.

ARTICLE 121. Citizens of the U.S.S.R. have the right to education.

This right is ensured by universal, compulsory elementary education; by education, including higher education, being free of charge; by the system of state stipends for the overwhelming majority of students in the universities and colleges; by instruction in schools being conducted in the native language, and by the organization in the factories, state farms, machine and tractor stations and collective farms of free vocational, technical and agronomic training for the working people.

ARTICLE 122. Women in the U.S.S.R. are accorded equal rights with men in all spheres of economic, state, cultural, social and political life.

The possibility of exercising these rights is ensured to women by granting them an equal right with men to work, payment for work, rest and leisure, social insurance and education, and by state protection of the interests of mother and child, pre-maternity and maternity leave with full pay, and the provision of a wide network of maternity homes, nurseries and kindergartens.

ARTICLE 123. Equality of rights of citizens of the U.S.S.R., irrespective of their nationality or race, in all spheres of economic, state, cultural, social and political life, is an indefeasible law.

Any direct or indirect restriction of the rights of, or, conversely, any establishment of direct or indirect privileges for, citizens on account of their race or nationality, as well as any advocacy of racial or national exclusiveness or hatred and contempt, is punishable by law.

ARTICLE 124. In order to ensure to citizens freedom of conscience, the church in the U.S.S.R. is separated from the state, and the school from the church. Freedom of religious worship and freedom of anti-religious propaganda is recognized for all citizens.

ARTICLE 125. In conformity with the interests of the working people, and in order to strengthen the socialist system, the citizens of the U.S.S.R. are guaranteed by law:

a) freedom of speech;
b) freedom of the press;
c) freedom of assembly, including the holding of mass meetings;
d) freedom of street processions and demonstrations; These civil rights are ensured by placing at the disposal of the working people and their organizations printing presses, stocks of paper, public buildings, the streets, communications facilities and other material requisites for the exercise of these rights.

ARTICLE 126. In conformity with the interests of the working people, and in order to develop the organizational initiative and political activity of the masses of the people, citizens of the U.S.S.R. are ensured the right to unite in public organizations—trade unions, cooperative associations, youth organizations, sport and defence organizations, cultural, technical and scientific societies; and the most active and politically most conscious citizens in the ranks of the working class and other sections of the working people unite in the Communist Party of the Soviet Union (Bolsheviks), which is the vanguard of the working people in their struggle to strengthen and develop the socialist system and is the leading core of all organizations of the working people, both public and state.

ARTICLE 127. Citizens of the U.S.S.R. are guaranteed inviolability of the person. No person may be placed under arrest except by decision of a court or with the sanction of a procurator.

ARTICLE 128. The inviolability of the homes of citizens and privacy of correspondence are protected by law.

ARTICLE 129. The U.S.S.R. affords the right of asylum to foreign citizens persecuted for defending the interests of the working people, or for their scientific activities, or for their struggle for national liberation.

ARTICLE 130. It is the duty of every citizen of the U.S.S.R. to abide by the Constitution of the Union of Soviet Socialist Republics, to observe the laws, to maintain labour discipline, honestly to perform public duties, and to respect the rules of socialist intercourse.

ARTICLE 131. It is the duty of every citizen of the U.S.S.R. to safeguard and strengthen public, socialist property as the sacred and inviolable foundation of the Soviet system, as the source of the wealth and might of the country, as the source of the prosperous and cultured life of all the working people.

Persons committing offences against public, socialist property are enemies of the people.

ARTICLE 132. Universal military service is law.

Military service in the Workers' and Peasants' Red Army is an honourable duty of the citizens of the U.S.S.R.

ARTICLE 133. To defend the fatherland is the sacred duty of every citizen of the U.S.S.R. Treason to the country—violation of the oath of allegiance, desertion to the enemy, impairing the military power of the state, espionage—is punishable with all the severity of the law as the most heinous of crimes.

Chapter XI: The Electoral System

ARTICLE 134. Member s of all Soviets of Working People's Deputies—of the Supreme Soviet of the U.S.S.R., the Supreme Soviets of the Union Republics, the Soviets of Working People's Deputies of the Territories and Regions, the Supreme Soviets of the Autonomous Republics, the Soviets of Working People's Deputies of Autonomous Regions, area, district, city and rural (stanitsa, village, hamlet, kishlak, aul) Soviets of Working People's Deputies—are chosen by the electors on the basis of universal, direct and equal suffrage by secret ballot.

ARTICLE 135. Elections of deputies are universal: all citizens of the U.S.S.R. who have reached the age of eighteen, irrespective of race or nationality, religion, educational and residential qualifications, social origin, property status or past activities, have the right to vote in the election of deputies and to be elected, with the exception of insane persons and persons who have been convicted by a court of law and whose sentences include deprivation of electoral rights.

ARTICLE 136. Elections of deputies are equal: each citizen has one vote; all citizens participate in elections on an equal footing.

ARTICLE 137. Women have the right to elect and be elected on equal terms with men.

ARTICLE 138. Citizens serving in the Red Army have the right to elect and be elected on equal terms with all other citizens.

ARTICLE 139. Elections of deputies are direct: all Soviets of Working People's Deputies from rural and city Soviets of Working People's Deputies to the Supreme Soviet of the U.S.S.R., inclusive, are elected by the citizens by direct vote.

ARTICLE 140. Voting at elections of deputies is secret.

ARTICLE 141. Candidates for election are nominated according to electoral areas.

The right to nominate candidates is secured to public organizations and societies of the working people: Communist Party organizations, trade unions, cooperatives, youth organizations and cultural societies.

ARTICLE 142. It is the duty of every deputy to report to his electors on his work and on the work of the Soviet of Working People's Deputies, and he is liable to be recalled at any time in the manner established by law upon decision of a majority of the electors.

Chapter XII: Arms, Flag, Capital

ARTICLE 143. The arms of the Union of Soviet Socialist Republics consists of a sickle and hammer against a globe depicted in the rays of the sun and surrounded by ears of grain with the inscription "Workers of All Countries, Unite!" in the languages of the Union Republics. At the top of the arms is a five-pointed star.

ARTICLE 144. The state flag of the Union of Soviet Socialist Republics is of red cloth with the sickle and hammer depicted in gold in the upper corner near the staff and above them a five-pointed star bordered in gold. The ratio of the width to the length is 1:2.

ARTICLE 145. The capital of the Union of Soviet Socialist Republics is the City of Moscow.

Chapter XIII: Procedure for Amending the Constitution

ARTICLE 146. The Constitution of the U.S.S.R. may be amended only by decision of the Supreme Soviet of the U.S.S.R. adopted by a majority of not less than two-thirds of the votes cast in each of its Chambers.

Appendices: Laws Adopted by the Tenth Session of the Supreme Soviet of the U.S.S.R.

APPENDIX I

LAW

On Creating Troop Formations of the Union Republics and on Reorganizing the People's Commissariat of Defence in Connection therewith from an All-Union into a Union Republican People's Commissariat

With the object of strengthening the defence capacity of the Union of Soviet Socialist Republics, the Supreme Soviet of the Union of Soviet Socialist Republics decrees:

1. To establish that the Union Republics shall organize troop formations of their respective Republics.
2. To introduce into the Constitution of the U.S.S.R. the following amendments:
   a) to insert in ARTICLE 14g of the Constitution of the U.S.S.R. after the words "Organization of the defence of the U.S.S.R. and direction of all the armed forces of the U.S.S.R.," the words—"establishment of the guiding principles of organization of the troop formations of the Union Republics," thus formulating this point as follows:

      "g) Organization of the defence of the U.S.S.R., direction of all the armed forces of the U.S.S.R., establishment of the guiding principles of organization of the troop formations of the Union Republics."

   b) To add to the Constitution of the U.S.S.R.

      ARTICLE 18-b, as follows:

      "ARTICLE 18-b Each Union Republic has its own Republican troop formations."

   c) To add to ARTICLE 60 of the Constitution of of the U.S.S.R. sec. f, as follows:

      "f) Establishes the system of organization of the Republican troop formations."

3) To reorganize the People's Commissariat of Defence from an All-Union into a Union-Republican People's Commissariat.

M. KALININ
President of the Presidium of the Supreme Soviet of the U.S.S.R.

A. GORKIN
Secretary of the Presidium of the Supreme Soviet of the U.S.S.R.

APPENDIX II
LAW

On Granting the Union Republics Plenipotentiary Powers in the Sphere of Foreign Relations and on Reorganizing the People's Commissariat of Foreign Affairs in Connection Therewith from an All-Union into a Union Republican People's Commissariat

With the object of extending international connections and strengthening the collaboration of the Union of Soviet Socialist Republics with other states and taking into consideration the growing requirements of the Union Republics in the matter of establishing direct relations with foreign states, the Supreme Soviet of the Union of Soviet Socialist Republics decrees:

1) To establish that the Union Republics may enter into direct relations with foreign states and conclude agreements with them.
2) To introduce into the Constitution of the U.S.S.R. the following amendments:
    a) To insert in ARTICLE 14a of the Constitution of the U.S.S.R., after the words "Representation of the Union in international relations, conclusion and ratification of treaties with other states," the words—"establishment of a uniform system in the relations between the Union Republics and foreign states," thus formulating this point as follows:

    "a) Representation of the Union in international relations, conclusion and ratification of treaties with other states, establishment of a uniform system in the relations between the Union Republics and foreign states."

    b) To add to the Constitution of the U.S.S.R.

    ARTICLE 18-a, as follows:

    "ARTICLE 18-a Each Union Republic has the right to enter into direct relations with foreign states, conclude agreements with them and exchange diplomatic and consular representatives."

c) To add to ARTICLE 60 of the Constitution of the U.S.S.R. sec. e, as follows:

"e) Establishes representation of the Union Republic in international relations."

3) To reorganize the People's Commissariat of Foreign Affairs from an All-Union into a Union- Republican People's Commissariat.

M. KALININ
President of the Presidium of the Supreme Soviet of the U.S.S.R.

A. GORKIN
Secretary of the Presidium of the Supreme Soviet of the U.S.S.R.

Moscow, The Kremlin
February 1, 1944.

APPENDIX B

U.S. Constitution. 1787. https://constitution.congress.gov/constitution/

Legislative Branch; Executive Branch; and Judicial Branch: Article I, II, and III.

Article I (Legislative Branch)

Section 1

All legislative Powers herein granted shall be vested in a Congress of the United States, which shall consist of a Senate and House of Representatives.

Section 2

The House of Representatives shall be composed of Members chosen every second Year by the People of the several States, and the Electors in each State shall have the Qualifications requisite for Electors of the most numerous Branch of the State Legislature.

No Person shall be a Representative who shall not have attained to the Age of twenty five Years, and been seven Years a Citizen of the United States, and who shall not, when elected, be an Inhabitant of that State in which he shall be chosen.

Representatives and direct Taxes shall be apportioned among the several States which may be included within this Union, according to their respective Numbers, which shall be determined by adding to the whole Number of free Persons, including those bound to Service for a Term of Years, and excluding Indians not taxed, three fifths of all other Persons. The actual Enumeration shall be made within three Years after the first Meeting of the Congress of the United States, and within every subsequent Term of ten Years, in such Manner as they shall by Law direct. The Number of Representatives shall not exceed one for every thirty Thousand, but each State shall have at Least one Representative; and until such enumeration shall be made, the State of New Hampshire shall be entitled to chuse three, Massachusetts eight, Rhode Island and Providence Plantations one, Connecticut five, New-York six, New Jersey four, Pennsylvania eight, Delaware one, Maryland six, Virginia ten, North Carolina five, South Carolina five, and Georgia three.

 | DOI:10.1163/9789004747210_014

When vacancies happen in the Representation from any State, the Executive Authority thereof shall issue Writs of Election to fill such Vacancies.

The House of Representatives shall chuse their Speaker and other Officers; and shall have the sole Power of Impeachment.

Section 3

The Senate of the United States shall be composed of two Senators from each State, chosen by the Legislature thereof, for six Years; and each Senator shall have one Vote.

Immediately after they shall be assembled in Consequence of the first Election, they shall be divided as equally as may be into three Classes. The Seats of the Senators of the first Class shall be vacated at the Expiration of the second Year, of the second Class at the Expiration of the fourth Year, and of the third Class at the Expiration of the sixth Year, so that one third may be chosen every second Year; and if Vacancies happen by Resignation, or otherwise, during the Recess of the Legislature of any State, the Executive thereof may make temporary Appointments until the next Meeting of the Legislature, which shall then fill such Vacancies.

No Person shall be a Senator who shall not have attained to the Age of thirty Years, and been nine Years a Citizen of the United States, and who shall not, when elected, be an Inhabitant of that State for which he shall be chosen.

The Vice President of the United States shall be President of the Senate, but shall have no Vote, unless they be equally divided.

The Senate shall chuse their other Officers, and also a President pro tempore, in the Absence of the Vice President, or when he shall exercise the Office of President of the United States.

The Senate shall have the sole Power to try all Impeachments. When sitting for that Purpose, they shall be on Oath or Affirmation. When the President of the United States is tried, the Chief Justice shall preside: And no Person shall be convicted without the Concurrence of two thirds of the Members present.

Judgment in Cases of Impeachment shall not extend further than to removal from Office, and disqualification to hold and enjoy any Office of honor, Trust or Profit under the United States: but the Party convicted shall nevertheless be liable and subject to Indictment, Trial, Judgment and Punishment, according to Law.

Section 4

The Times, Places and Manner of holding Elections for Senators and Representatives, shall be prescribed in each State by the Legislature thereof; but the Congress may at any time by Law make or alter such Regulations, except as to the Places of chusing Senators.

The Congress shall assemble at least once in every Year, and such Meeting shall be on the first Monday in December, unless they shall by Law appoint a different Day.

Section 5

Each House shall be the Judge of the Elections, Returns and Qualifications of its own Members, and a Majority of each shall constitute a Quorum to do Business; but a smaller Number may adjourn from day to day, and may be authorized to compel the Attendance of absent Members, in such Manner, and under such Penalties as each House may provide.

Each House may determine the Rules of its Proceedings, punish its Members for disorderly Behaviour, and, with the Concurrence of two thirds, expel a Member.

Each House shall keep a Journal of its Proceedings, and from time to time publish the same, excepting such Parts as may in their Judgment require Secrecy; and the Yeas and Nays of the Members of either House on any question shall, at the Desire of one fifth of those Present, be entered on the Journal.

Neither House, during the Session of Congress, shall, without the Consent of the other, adjourn for more than three days, nor to any other Place than that in which the two Houses shall be sitting.

Section 6

The Senators and Representatives shall receive a Compensation for their Services, to be ascertained by Law, and paid out of the Treasury of the United States. They shall in all Cases, except Treason, Felony and Breach of the Peace, be privileged from Arrest during their Attendance at the Session of their respective Houses, and in going to and returning from the same; and for any Speech or Debate in either House, they shall not be questioned in any other Place.

No Senator or Representative shall, during the Time for which he was elected, be appointed to any civil Office under the Authority of the United States, which shall have been created, or the Emoluments whereof shall have been encreased during such time; and no Person holding any Office under the United States, shall be a Member of either House during his Continuance in Office.

Section 7

All Bills for raising Revenue shall originate in the House of Representatives; but the Senate may propose or concur with Amendments as on other Bills.

Every Bill which shall have passed the House of Representatives and the Senate, shall, before it become a Law, be presented to the President of the United States; If he approve he shall sign it, but if not he shall return it, with his Objections to that House in which it shall have originated, who shall enter the Objections at large on their Journal, and proceed to reconsider it. If after such Reconsideration two thirds of that House shall agree to pass the Bill, it shall be sent, together with the Objections, to the other House, by which it shall likewise be reconsidered, and if approved by two thirds of that House, it shall become a Law. But in all such Cases the Votes of both Houses shall be determined by yeas and Nays, and the Names of the Persons voting for and against the Bill shall be entered on the Journal of each House respectively. If any Bill shall not be returned by the President within ten Days (Sundays excepted) after it shall have been presented to him, the Same shall be a Law, in like Manner as if he had signed it, unless the Congress by their Adjournment prevent its Return, in which Case it shall not be a Law.

Every Order, Resolution, or Vote to which the Concurrence of the Senate and House of Representatives may be necessary (except on a question of Adjournment) shall be presented to the President of the United States; and before the Same shall take Effect, shall be approved by him, or being disapproved by him, shall be repassed by two thirds of the Senate and House of Representatives, according to the Rules and Limitations prescribed in the Case of a Bill.

Section 8

The Congress shall have Power To lay and collect Taxes, Duties, Imposts and Excises, to pay the Debts and provide for the common Defence and general Welfare of the United States; but all Duties, Imposts and Excises shall be uniform throughout the United States;

To borrow Money on the credit of the United States;

To regulate Commerce with foreign Nations, and among the several States, and with the Indian Tribes;

To establish an uniform Rule of Naturalization, and uniform Laws on the subject of Bankruptcies throughout the United States;

To coin Money, regulate the Value thereof, and of foreign Coin, and fix the Standard of Weights and Measures;

To provide for the Punishment of counterfeiting the Securities and current Coin of the United States;

To establish Post Offices and post Roads;

To promote the Progress of Science and useful Arts, by securing for limited Times to Authors and Inventors the exclusive Right to their respective Writings and Discoveries;

To constitute Tribunals inferior to the supreme Court;

To define and punish Piracies and Felonies committed on the high Seas, and Offences against the Law of Nations;

To declare War, grant Letters of Marque and Reprisal, and make Rules concerning Captures on Land and Water;

To raise and support Armies, but no Appropriation of Money to that Use shall be for a longer Term than two Years;

To provide and maintain a Navy;

To make Rules for the Government and Regulation of the land and naval Forces;

To provide for calling forth the Militia to execute the Laws of the Union, suppress Insurrections and repel Invasions;

To provide for organizing, arming, and disciplining, the Militia, and for governing such Part of them as may be employed in the Service of the United States, reserving to the States respectively, the Appointment of the Officers, and the Authority of training the Militia according to the discipline prescribed by Congress;

To exercise exclusive Legislation in all Cases whatsoever, over such District (not exceeding ten Miles square) as may, by Cession of particular States, and the Acceptance of Congress, become the Seat of Government of the United States, and to exercise like Authority over all Places purchased by the Consent of the Legislature of the State in which the Same shall be, for the Erection of Forts, Magazines, Arsenals, dock-Yards, and other needful Buildings;–And

To make all Laws which shall be necessary and proper for carrying into Execution the foregoing Powers, and all other Powers vested by this Constitution in the Government of the United States, or in any Department or Officer thereof.

Section 9

The Migration or Importation of such Persons as any of the States now existing shall think proper to admit, shall not be prohibited by the Congress prior to the Year one thousand eight hundred and eight, but a Tax or duty may be imposed on such Importation, not exceeding ten dollars for each Person.

The Privilege of the Writ of Habeas Corpus shall not be suspended, unless when in Cases of Rebellion or Invasion the public Safety may require it.

No Bill of Attainder or ex post facto Law shall be passed.

No Capitation, or other direct, Tax shall be laid, unless in Proportion to the Census or enumeration herein before directed to be taken.

No Tax or Duty shall be laid on Articles exported from any State.

No Preference shall be given by any Regulation of Commerce or Revenue to the Ports of one State over those of another: nor shall Vessels bound to, or from, one State, be obliged to enter, clear, or pay Duties in another.

No Money shall be drawn from the Treasury, but in Consequence of Appropriations made by Law; and a regular Statement and Account of the Receipts and Expenditures of all public Money shall be published from time to time.

No Title of Nobility shall be granted by the United States: And no Person holding any Office of Profit or Trust under them, shall, without the Consent of the Congress, accept of any present, Emolument, Office, or Title, of any kind whatever, from any King, Prince, or foreign State.

Section 10

No State shall enter into any Treaty, Alliance, or Confederation; grant Letters of Marque and Reprisal; coin Money; emit Bills of Credit; make any Thing but gold and silver Coin a Tender in Payment of Debts; pass any Bill of Attainder, ex post facto Law, or Law impairing the Obligation of Contracts, or grant any Title of Nobility.

No State shall, without the Consent of the Congress, lay any Imposts or Duties on Imports or Exports, except what may be absolutely necessary for executing it's inspection Laws: and the net Produce of all Duties and Imposts, laid by any State on Imports or Exports, shall be for the Use of the Treasury of the United States; and all such Laws shall be subject to the Revision and Controul of the Congress.

No State shall, without the Consent of Congress, lay any Duty of Tonnage, keep Troops, or Ships of War in time of Peace, enter into any Agreement or Compact with another State, or with a foreign Power, or engage in War, unless actually invaded, or in such imminent Danger as will not admit of delay.

Article II (Executive Branch)

Section 1

The executive Power shall be vested in a President of the United States of America. He shall hold his Office during the Term of four Years, and, together with the Vice President, chosen for the same Term, be elected, as follows

Each State shall appoint, in such Manner as the Legislature thereof may direct, a Number of Electors, equal to the whole Number of Senators and Representatives to which the State may be entitled in the Congress: but no Senator or Representative, or Person holding an Office of Trust or Profit under the United States, shall be appointed an Elector.

The Electors shall meet in their respective States, and vote by Ballot for two Persons, of whom one at least shall not be an Inhabitant of the same State with themselves. And they shall make a List of all the Persons voted for, and of the Number of Votes for each; which List they shall sign and certify, and transmit sealed to the Seat of the Government of the United States, directed to the President of the Senate. The President of the Senate shall, in the Presence of the Senate and House of Representatives, open all the Certificates, and the Votes shall then be counted. The Person having the greatest Number of Votes shall be the President, if such Number be a Majority of the whole

Number of Electors appointed; and if there be more than one who have such Majority, and have an equal Number of Votes, then the House of Representatives shall immediately chuse by Ballot one of them for President; and if no Person have a Majority, then from the five highest on the List the said House shall in like Manner chuse the President. But in chusing the President, the Votes shall be taken by States, the Representation from each State having one Vote; A quorum for this Purpose shall consist of a Member or Members from two thirds of the States, and a Majority of all the States shall be necessary to a Choice. In every Case, after the Choice of the President, the Person having the greatest Number of Votes of the Electors shall be the Vice President. But if there should remain two or more who have equal Votes, the Senate shall chuse from them by Ballot the Vice President.

The Congress may determine the Time of chusing the Electors, and the Day on which they shall give their Votes; which Day shall be the same throughout the United States.

No Person except a natural born Citizen, or a Citizen of the United States, at the time of the Adoption of this Constitution, shall be eligible to the Office of President; neither shall any Person be eligible to that Office who shall not have attained to the Age of thirty five Years, and been fourteen Years a Resident within the United States.

In Case of the Removal of the President from Office, or of his Death, Resignation, or Inability to discharge the Powers and Duties of the said Office, the Same shall devolve on the Vice President, and the Congress may by law provide for the Case of Removal, Death, Resignation or Inability, both of the President and Vice President, declaring what Officer shall then act as President, and such Officer shall act accordingly, until the Disability be removed, or a President shall be elected.

The President shall, at stated Times, receive for his Services, a Compensation, which shall neither be encreased nor diminished during the Period for which he shall have been elected, and he shall not receive within that Period any other Emolument from the United States, or any of them.

Before he enter on the Execution of his Office, he shall take the following Oath or Affirmation:—I do solemnly swear (or affirm) that I will faithfully execute the Office of President of the United States, and will to the best of my Ability, preserve, protect and defend the Constitution of the United States.

Section 2

The President shall be Commander in Chief of the Army and Navy of the United States, and of the Militia of the several States, when called into the actual Service of the United States; he may require the Opinion, in writing, of the principal Officer in each of the executive Departments, upon any Subject relating to the Duties of their respective Offices, and he shall have Power to grant Reprieves and Pardons for Offences against the United States, except in Cases of Impeachment.

He shall have Power, by and with the Advice and Consent of the Senate, to make Treaties, provided two thirds of the Senators present concur; and he shall nominate, and by and with the Advice and Consent of the Senate, shall appoint Ambassadors, other public Ministers and Consuls, Judges of the supreme Court, and all other Officers of the United States, whose Appointments are not herein otherwise provided for, and which shall be established by Law: but the Congress may by Law vest the Appointment of such inferior Officers, as they think proper, in the President alone, in the Courts of Law, or in the Heads of Departments.

The President shall have Power to fill up all Vacancies that may happen during the Recess of the Senate, by granting Commissions which shall expire at the End of their next Session.

Section 3

He shall from time to time give to the Congress Information of the State of the Union, and recommend to their Consideration such Measures as he shall judge necessary and expedient; he may, on extraordinary Occasions, convene both Houses, or either of them, and in Case of Disagreement between them, with Respect to the Time of Adjournment, he may adjourn them to such Time as he shall think proper; he shall receive Ambassadors and other public Ministers; he shall take Care that the Laws be faithfully executed, and shall Commission all the Officers of the United States.

Section 4

The President, Vice President and all civil Officers of the United States, shall be removed from Office on Impeachment for, and Conviction of, Treason, Bribery, or other high Crimes and Misdemeanors.

Article III (Judicial Branch)

Section 1

The judicial Power of the United States, shall be vested in one supreme Court, and in such inferior Courts as the Congress may from time to time ordain and establish. The

Judges, both of the supreme and inferior Courts, shall hold their Offices during good Behaviour, and shall, at stated Times, receive for their Services, a Compensation, which shall not be diminished during their Continuance in Office.

Section 2

The judicial Power shall extend to all Cases, in Law and Equity, arising under this Constitution, the Laws of the United States, and Treaties made, or which shall be made, under their Authority;—to all Cases affecting Ambassadors, other public Ministers and Consuls;—to all Cases of admiralty and maritime Jurisdiction;—to Controversies to which the United States shall be a Party;—to Controversies between two or more States;—between a State and Citizens of another State,—between Citizens of different States,—between Citizens of the same State claiming Lands under Grants of different States, and between a State, or the Citizens thereof, and foreign States, Citizens or Subjects.

In all Cases affecting Ambassadors, other public Ministers and Consuls, and those in which a State shall be Party, the supreme Court shall have original Jurisdiction. In all the other Cases before mentioned, the supreme Court shall have appellate Jurisdiction, both as to Law and Fact, with such Exceptions, and under such Regulations as the Congress shall make.

The Trial of all Crimes, except in Cases of Impeachment, shall be by Jury; and such Trial shall be held in the State where the said Crimes shall have been committed; but when not committed within any State, the Trial shall be at such Place or Places as the Congress may by Law have directed.

Section 3

Treason against the United States, shall consist only in levying War against them, or in adhering to their Enemies, giving them Aid and Comfort. No Person shall be convicted of Treason unless on the Testimony of two Witnesses to the same overt Act, or on Confession in open Court.

The Congress shall have Power to declare the Punishment of Treason, but no Attainder of Treason shall work Corruption of Blood, or Forfeiture except during the Life of the Person attainted.

References

Althusser, Louis. 1976. *Positions (1964–1975)*. Paris: Les Éditions sociales.

American Bar Association, Section on Antitrust Law. 2012. *Market Definition in Antitrust: Theory and Case Studies*. Chicago: American Bar Association.

American Bar Association, Standing Committee on Education about Communism and Its Contrast with Liberty under Law. 1968. *A Contrast Between the Legal Systems in the United States and in the Soviet Union*. Chicago: American Bar Association.

Acemoglu, Daron. 2008. "Oligarchic versus Democratic Societies." *Journal of the European Economic Association* 6(1): 1–44.

Applebaum, Anne. 2003. *Gulag: A History*. New York: Doubleday.

Areeda, Phillip E., and Herbert Hovenkamp. 2006. *Antitrust Law, An Analysis of Antitrust Principles and Their Application*. Vol. 1. Aspen.

Arestis, Philip, and Malcolm Sawyer, eds. 2022. *Economic Policies for Sustainability and Resilience*. Cheltenham, UK: Edward Elgar Publishing.

Arestis, Philip, and Malcolm Sawyer. 2022. "Macro-Economic and Financial Policies for Sustainability and Resilience." In *Economic Policies for Sustainability and Resilience*, edited by Philip Arestis and Malcolm Sawyer. Cheltenham, UK: Edward Elgar Publishing.

Aristotle. [ca. 350 BCE] 1885. *Politics*, Book 4. Translated by Benjamin Jowett. Oxford: Clarendon Press. https://classics.mit.edu/Aristotle/politics.4.four.html.

Aristotle. [ca. 340–330 BCE] 1941. *Metaphysics*. In *The Basic Works of Aristotle*, edited by Richard McKeon and translated by W.D. Ross, 681–926. New York: Random House.

Aristotle. 1998. "Aristotle's Political Theory." *Stanford Encyclopedia of Philosophy*. First published July 1, 1998; substantive revision July 1, 2022. https://plato.stanford.edu/entries/aristotle-politics/.

Arno, Peter S., and Michael H. Davis. 2001. "Why Don't We Enforce Existing Drug Price Controls? The Unrecognized and Unenforced Reasonable Pricing Requirements Imposed upon Patents Deriving in Whole or in Part from Federally Funded Research." *Tulane Law Review* 75, no. 3: 631–693.

Arno, Peter S., and Michael H. Davis. "Paying Twice for the Same Drugs." *The Washington Post*, March 27, 2002, p. A21.

Arno, Peter S., and Dana Neacșu. 2021. Comment on "Rights to Federally Funded Inventions and Licensing of Government Owned Inventions." Docket No. 201207-0327, ID NIST-2021-0001-648. Submitted to the National Institute of Standards and Technology (NIST), U.S. Department of Commerce. https://www.regulations.gov/comment/NIST-2021-0001-6485.

Bakunin, Mikhail. [1873] 2023. *Statism and Anarchy*. In Wolfgang Eckhardt, "Mikhail Bakunin and Social Anarchism," in *The Cambridge History of Socialism*, vol. 1, edited by Marcel van der Linden, 321. Cambridge: Cambridge University Press.

Benes Vaclav et al., 1969. *Eastern European Government and Politics.* Harper & Row.

Benjamin, Walter. 1999. *The Arcades Project.* Translated by Howard Eiland and Kevin McLaughlin. Cambridge, MA: Belknap Press of Harvard University Press.

Bentham, Jeremy. [1809] 1817. *Plan of Parliamentary Reform: In the Form of a Catechism, with Reasons for Each Article.* London: R. Hunter.

Berger, Chloe. 2024. "Jeff Bezos Revealed His Secret to Amazon's Success 25 Years Ago." *Fortune,* May 15, 2024. https://fortune.com/2024/05/15/jeff-bezos-revealed-secret-drenched-terrified-sweat/.

Bergson, Henri. 1946. *The Creative Mind.* Translated by Mabelle L. Andison. New York: Philosophical Library.

Berman, Harold J. 1963. *Justice in the USSR.* Harvard University Press.

Berman, Harold J. 1957. "Soviet Law Reform—Dateline Moscow 1957." *Yale Law Journal* 66: 1191–1214.

Berman, Harold J. 1948. "Soviet Property in Law and in Plan." *University of Pennsylvania Law Review* 96, no. 3 (1948): 324–366.

Berstein, Serge, and Pierre Milza. n.d. *Histoire du 20e siècle.* Paris: Hatier.

Bezos, Jeff. 1999. Letter to Amazon Shareholders. In *Invent and Wander: The Collected Writings of Jeff Bezos,* edited by Walter Isaacson. Seattle: Amazon Publishing. https://media.corporate-ir.net/media_files/irol/97/97664/reports/Shareholderletter98.pdf.

Biden, Joseph R. 2025. "Farewell Address." January 15.

Blanc, Louis. 1845. *Le Socialisme; Droit au Travail.* Paris: Pagnerre. http://books.google.com/books?id=fJMSAAAAIAAJ.

Blanc, Louis. 1849. *Le Socialisme; Droit au Travail.* Paris: Pagnerre.

Blanc, Louis. 1839. *L'Organisation du Travail.* Paris: Pagnerre.

Bottomore, T. 1981. Introduction to the First English Translation of *Finance Capital.* In Rudolf Hilferding, *Finance Capital: A Study of the Latest Phase of Capitalist Development,* 16–17. London: Routledge & Kegan Paul.

Braginsky, Mikhail. 1988. *The Soviet State and a Subject of Civil Law.* Progress Publishers.

Bulgakov, Mikhail. 1967. *The Master and Margarita.* Translated by Michael Glenny. London: Harvill Press.

Butler, William E. 1988. *Soviet Law.* 2nd ed. London: Butterworths.

Cambridge History of Socialism, The. 2022–23. Edited by Marcel Van Der Linden and Magaly Rodríguez García. 2 vols. Cambridge: Cambridge University Press.

Cancryn, Adam. 2025. "Biden Warns of Rising Democracy-threatening 'Oligarchy' in Grim Farewell Speech." *Politico,* January 15. https://www.politico.com/news/2025/01/15/biden-oligarchy-farewell-speech-00198565.

Cannon, James P. 1943. *Socialism on Trial: The Official Court Record of James P. Cannon's Testimony in the Minneapolis Sedition Trial.* New York: Pioneer Publishers.

Churchill, Winston. 1947. Speech to the House of Commons, November 11. In *Hansard Parliamentary Debates.*

Claeys, Gregory. 2022. "Robert Owen and Owenism." In *The Cambridge History of Socialism*, vol. 1, edited by Marcel van der Linden, 151. Cambridge: Cambridge University Press.

Code civil des Français 1804–2024. 2024. Under the supervision of Pierre-Yves Gautier. Dalloz.

Commission of Inquiry into the Charges Made Against Leon Trotsky in the Moscow Trials. 1938. *Not Guilty*. Edited by Albert Goldman and John Dewey. New York: Harper & Brothers.

Conquest, Robert. 1968. *Justice and the Legal System in the USSR*. New York: Macmillan.

Conquest, Robert. 1968. *Justice and the Legal System in the USSR*. Macmillan.

Dahl, Robert A. 2020. *On Democracy*. New Haven, CT: Yale University Press.

Dahl, Robert A. 1971. *Polyarchy: Participation and Opposition*. New Haven, CT: Yale University Press.

Davis, Michael, and Dana Neacșu. 2014. "The Many Texts of the Law." *British Journal of American Legal Studies* 3: 481.

Davis, Michael, and Dana Neacșu. 2001. "Legitimacy, Globally: The Incoherence of Free Trade Practice, Global Economics and Their Governing Principles of Political Economy." *UMKC Law Review* 69: 733.

Dennett, Daniel C. 1996. *Kinds of Minds: Toward an Understanding of Consciousness*. New York: Basic Books.

Dennett, Daniel C. 1991. *Consciousness Explained*. Boston: Little, Brown and Company.

De Tocqueville, Alexis. 1835–40. *Democracy in America*. 2 vols. Translated by Henry Reeve. New York: Saunders and Otley.

Dewey, John. [1888] 2024. *Leibniz's New Essays Concerning the Human Understanding: A Critical Exposition*. Lettel Books.

Dewey, John. 1927. *The Public and Its Problems*. New York: Henry Holt and Company.

Dickens, Charles. 1859. *A Tale of Two Cities*. London: Chapman and Hall.

Douglas, William O. 1963. Foreword to *Essays on Jurisprudence from the Columbia Law Review*, vii. Columbia University Press.

Dunayevskaya, Raya. 1973. *Russia as State-Capitalist Society*. Detroit: News & Letters.

Dunn, William Newlin. 1969. *Yugoslavia: National Communist Ideology and Political Integration*. PhD diss., Claremont Graduate School.

Durkheim, Émile. 1928. *Le socialisme: Sa définition. Ses débuts. La doctrine saint-simonienne*. Paris: Félix Alcan. http://www.uqac.uquebec.ca/zone30/Classiques_des_sciences_sociales/index.html.

Dworkin, Ronald. 1986. *Law's Empire*. Harvard University Press.

Eastman, Max. 1940. *Stalin's Russia and the Crisis of Socialism*. New York: Duell, Sloan and Pearce.

Eco, Umberto. 1968. *La Struttura Assente*. Milan: Bompiani.

Eco, Umberto. 1984. *Semiotics and the Philosophy of Language*. Bloomington: Indiana University Press.

Editors of Encyclopaedia Britannica, The. 2024. "Dictator." *Britannica*. Last modified December 15. https://www.britannica.com/topic/dictator-ruler.

Editors of Encyclopaedia Britannica, The. n.d. "Politburo." *Britannica*. https://www.britannica.com/topic/Politburo.

Engels, Friedrich. 1891. "Introduction to Karl Marx's *The Civil War in France*." In *Marx-Engels Collected Works*, vol. 27, 191. Moscow: Progress Publishers. Quoted in Lucia Pradella, "Karl Marx, Friedrich Engels, and the Early Workers' Movement," in *The Cambridge History of Socialism*, vol. 1, edited by Marcel van der Linden, 283. Cambridge: Cambridge University Press, 2023.

Engels, Friedrich. 1887. "Juristensozialismus." In *Neue Zeit*.

Engels, Friedrich. 1935. *Socialism: Utopian and Scientific*. Reprint, New York: International Publishers.

Erikson, Robert S., and Kent L. Tedin. 2011. *American Public Opinion: Its Origins, Content and Impact*. 7th ed. New York: Longman.

Farnsworth, E. Allan, and Viktor P. Mozolin. 1987. *Contract Law in the USSR and the United States*. Oceana Publications.

Fisher, Mark. 2009. *Capitalist Realism: Is There No Alternative?* London: Zero Books.

Fleishits, Ye., and A. Makovsky. 1976. *The Civil Codes of the Soviet Republics*. Progress Publishers.

Forte, David F. 1983. "Western Law and Communist Dictatorship." *Emory Law Journal* 32: 73–135.

Foucault, Michel. 1977. *Discipline and Punish: The Birth of the Prison*. Translated by Alan Sheridan. New York: Vintage.

Fourier, Charles. 1808. *Théorie des Quatre Mouvements et des Destinées Générales*. Lyon: L'Imprimerie de Ballanche.

Frank, Dana. 2000. "The Devil and Mr. Hearst." *The Nation*, June 22. https://www.thenation.com/article/archive/devil-and-mr-hearst/.

Friedman, Milton. 1962. *Capitalism and Freedom*. Chicago: University of Chicago Press.

Geertz, Clifford. 1973. *The Interpretation of Cultures: Selected Essays*. New York: Basic Books.

George, Henry. 1879. *Progress and Poverty*. San Francisco: W.M. Hinton & Co.

Georgescu-Roegen, Nicholas. 1971. *The Entropy Law and the Economic Process*. Cambridge, MA: Harvard University Press.

Gerhardt, C.I., ed. 1875–90. *Die philosophischen Schriften von G.W. Leibniz*. 7 vols. Berlin: Weidmann.

Gitlin, Todd. 1987. *The Sixties: Years of Hope, Days of Rage*. Bantam.

Givens, Terri E. 2022. *Radical Empathy: Finding a Path to Bridging Racial Divides*. Bristol, UK: Bristol University Press.

Graetz, Michael J. 2024. *The Power to Destroy: How the Antitax Movement Hijacked America*. Cambridge, MA: Harvard University Press.

Gray, John. 1831. *The Social System: A Treatise on the Principle of Exchange*. Edinburgh: William Tait.

Greene, Doug. 2022. *A Failure of Vision: Michael Harrington and the Limits of Democratic Socialism*. London: Zero Books.

Gregory, Paul R. 2019. "How Socialist Is Bernie Sanders? The Democratic Candidate Owes America Some Answers." *Hoover Institution*, May 2. https://www.hoover.org/research/how-socialist-bernie-sanders.

Griffith, Saul. 2022. "Scientists May Have Already Discovered a 'Miracle' Fix for Climate Change." *Inverse*, October 1. https://www.inverse.com/science/fix-for-climate-change.

Guins, George C. 1954. *Soviet Law and Soviet Society*. Martinus Nijhoff.

Hanke, Edith. 2024. "What about Democracy? Approaches to Max Weber's Political Sociology." In *Max Weber at 100: Legacies and Prospects*, edited by Joshua Derman and Peter E. Gordon. New York: Oxford Academic. https://doi.org/10.1093/9780197604953.003.0013.

Harcourt, Bernard. 2020. *Critique & Praxis*. New York: Columbia University Press.

Harrington, Michael. 1989. *Socialism: Past and Future*. New York: Arcade Publishing.

Hart, H.L.A. 2012. *The Concept of Law*. 3rd ed. Oxford University Press.

Hayek, Friedrich A. 1944. *The Road to Serfdom*. Chicago: University of Chicago Press.

Hazard, John N. 1951. *Soviet Legal Philosophy*. Harvard University Press.

Hazard, John N., William E. Butler, and Peter B. Maggs. 1977. *The Soviet Legal System*. Oceana Publications.

Hecht, Leo, ed. 1983.*The Soviet Union Through Its Laws*. Translated by Leo Hecht. New York: Praeger.

Heidegger, Martin. 2010. *Being and Time*. Translated by Joan Stambaugh. Albany: State University of New York Press. Originally published in 1927.

Heidegger, Martin. 1997. *Kant and the Problem of Metaphysics*. 5th ed. Translated by Richard Taft. Bloomington: Indiana University Press.

Heidegger, Martin. 1977. *The Question Concerning Technology and Other Essays*. Translated by William Lovitt. New York: Harper & Row.

Heidegger, Martin. 1962. *Being and Time*. 1927. Translated by John Macquarrie and Edward Robinson. New York: Harper & Row.

Heuman, Susan Eva. 1990. "Perspectives on Legal Culture in Prerevolutionary Russia." In *Revolution in Law: Contributions to the Development of Soviet Legal Theory, 1917–1938*, edited by Piers Beirne, 3–30. M.E. Sharpe.

Heym, Stefen. 1959. *A Visit to Soviet Science*. Marzani & Munsell.

Hilferding, Rudolf. [1910] 1981. *Finance Capital: A Study of the Latest Phase of Capitalist Development*. Edited by Tom Bottomore. London: Routledge & Kegan Paul.

Hobbes, Thomas. 1991. *Leviathan*. 1651. Edited by Richard Tuck. Cambridge: Cambridge University Press.

Hudis, Peter, and Kevin Anderson, eds. 2004. *The Rosa Luxemburg Reader*. New York: Monthly Review Press.

Huttunen, Rauno, and Leena Kakkori. 2022. "Heidegger's Critique of Technology and the Educational Ecological Imperative." *Educational Philosophy and Theory* 54(6): 630–641.

Ioffe, Olympiad S., and Peter B. Maggs. 1983. *Soviet Law in Theory and Practice*. Oceana Publications.

Irwin, Ruth. 2008. *Heidegger, Politics and Climate Change: Risking It All*. London: Continuum.

Jameson, Fredric. 2009. *Valences of the Dialectic*. London: Verso.

Jameson, Fredric. 1981. *The Political Unconscious: Narrative as a Socially Symbolic Act*. Ithaca, NY: Cornell University Press.

Jennings, Jeremy. 2023. "Saint-Simon and Saint-Simonism." In *The Cambridge History of Socialism*, vol. 1, edited by Marcel van der Linden, 126–145. Cambridge: Cambridge University Press.

Kantorovich, Jacob. 1922. "The Civil Code of Soviet Russia." *Yale Law Journal* 32: 779.

Kapczynski, Amy. 2020. "The Law of Informational Capitalism." *Yale Law Journal* 129: 1460–1515.

Kaplan, Temma. 2014. *Democracy: A World History*. Oxford: Oxford University Press.

Kavass, Igor I. 1991. *Gorbachev's Law*. William S. Hein & Co.

Keene, Houston, and Brandon Gillespie. 2023. "Here Are the Top Moments from Trump's 'Hannity' Town Hall." *Fox News*, December 6. https://www.foxnews.com/politics/top-moments-trumps-hannity-town-hall.

Kelsen, Hans. 1961. *General Theory of Law and State*. Harvard University Press.

Kirkpatrick, David D. 2025. "The Senate's Age of Irrelevance." *The New Yorker*, April 7, 2025. https://www.newyorker.com/magazine/2025/04/07/john-thune-profile-senate-majority-leader.

Kornick, Lindsay. 2025. "CNN Presidential Historian Claims Trump Fulfilled 'Promise to Be a Dictator on Day One'." *Fox News*, January 21. https://www.foxnews.com/media/cnn-presidential-historian-claims-trump-fulfilled-promise-dictator-day-one-executive-orders.

Kramer, Larry. 2000. "Putting the Politics Back." *Columbia Law Review* 100: 215.

Krauß, Andrea. 2011. "Constellations: A Brief Introduction." *Modern Language Notes* 126 (April): 439–445.

Kropotkin, Peter. 1892. *The Conquest of Bread*. London: Chapman and Hall.

Krutz, Glen S., and Sylvie Waskiewicz. 2021. *American Government*. 3rd ed. Houston, TX: OpenStax. https://openstax.org/books/american-government-3e.

Kunkel, Benjamin. 2024. "The Art of Criticism, No. 5: Frederic Jameson." *The Paris Review*, no. 150, p. 31.

Kurlantzick, Joshua. 2016. *State Capitalism: How the Return of Statism is Transforming the World*. Oxford: Oxford University Press.

Lapena, Ivo. 1964. *State and Law: Soviet and Yugoslav Theory*.

Laski, Harold J. 1967. *A Grammar of Politics*. London: George Allen & Unwin, Ltd.

Lawrence, Frederick G. 1999. Editors' Introduction. In *Collected Works of Bernard Lonergan: Volume 15, Macroeconomic Dynamics: An Essay in Circulation Analysis*, xxxiii. Toronto: University of Toronto Press.

Leibniz, G.W. 1996. *New Essays on Human Understanding*. Translated and edited by Peter Remnant and Jonathan Bennett. Cambridge: Cambridge University Press.

Lenin, Vladimir Ilyich (Nikolai Lenin). [1919] 1977. "Introduction" to John Reed, *Ten Days That Shook the World*. London: Penguin Books.

Lenin, Vladimir Ilyich (Nikolai Lenin). [1917] 1964. *State and Revolution*. Moscow: Progress Publishers.

Lenin, Vladimir Ilyich (Nikolai Lenin). [1916] 1939. *Imperialism: The Highest Stage of Capitalism*. New York: International Publishers.

Lenin, Vladimir Ilyich (Nikolai Lenin). 1916. "Concerning a Caricature of Marxism and Concerning Imperialist Economism." In *Lenin Collected Works*, Vol. 23, 48. Progress Publishers.

Levine, Irving R. 1973. *The New Worker in Soviet Russia*. New York: The Macmillan Company.

Le Miere, Jason. 2018. "Donald Trump Says 'My Gut Tells Me More Sometimes Than Anybody Else's Brain Can Ever Tell Me.'" *Newsweek*, November 27, 2018. https://www.newsweek.com/donald-trump-gut-brain-climate-change-fed-1234540.

Le Point. 2016. "Fédorovski et le malentendu de l'histoire de la révolution russe." November 25. https://www.lepoint.fr/video/fedorovski-est-le-malentendu-de-l-histoire-de-la-revolution-russe-25-11-2016-2085791_738.php.

Li, Minqi. 2020. "Profit, Accumulation, and Crisis in Capitalism: Long-Term Trends in the UK, US, Japan, and China, 1855–2018." Unpublished manuscript or working paper. [Note: Add publication or institutional info if applicable.]

Linz, Juan. 2000. *Totalitarian and Authoritarian Regimes*. Boulder, CO: Lynne Rienner Publishers.

Locke, John. [1689]. *Second Treatise of Government*. London: Awnsham Churchill, 1690. https://www.gutenberg.org/files/7370/7370-h/7370-h.htm.

Lonergan, Bernard. 1988–2019. *Collected Works of Bernard Lonergan*. Toronto: University of Toronto Press.

Lonergan, Bernard. 1992. *Insight: A Study of Human Understanding*. Vol. 3 of *Collected Works of Bernard Lonergan*. Edited by Frederick E. Crowe and Robert M. Doran. Toronto: University of Toronto Press.

Lonergan, Bernard. 1992. *Volume 3: Insight: A Study of Human Understanding*. Toronto: University of Toronto Press.

Lonergan, Bernard. 1988. *Collected Works of Bernard Lonergan. Volume 5: Understanding and Being*. Edited by Elizabeth A. Morelli and Mark D. Morelli. Toronto: University of Toronto Press.

Lonergan, Bernard. 1957. *Insight: A Study of Human Understanding*. New York: Philosophical Library.

Lonergan, Bernard. 1941. "Review of M.M. Coady, *Masters of Their Own Destiny*." *The Montreal Beacon*, May 2.

Madison, James. [1788] 2003. "Federalist No. 51." In *The Federalist Papers*, edited by Clinton Rossiter, 320–322. New York: Signet Classics.

Madison, James. 1788. "Federalist No. 39." *New York Packet*, January 18. https://avalon.law.yale.edu/18th_century/fed39.asp.

Markovits, Inga S. 1968. "Civil Law in East Germany—Its Development and Relation to Soviet Legal History and Ideology." *Yale Law Journal* 78: 1–34.

Marx, Karl. [1875] 1938. *Critique of the Gotha Program*. Reprint. New York: International Publishers.

Marx, Karl. 1867. *Capital: A Critique of Political Economy*, Vol. 1. Translated by Samuel Moore and Edward Aveling. Edited by Frederick Engels. Moscow: Progress Publishers, 1965. https://www.marxists.org/archive/marx/works/1867-c1/.

Marx, Karl. [1852]. Karl Marx, "Marx to J. Weydemeyer in New York [Abstract]," March 5, 1852, Marxists Internet Archive, accessed September 8, 2025, https://www.marxists.org/archive/marx/works/1852/letters/52_03_05-ab.htm.

Marx, Karl. [1847]. *The Poverty of Philosophy*. Reprint. New York: International Publishers, 1963. Originally published in Brussels: Office de la Bibliothèque des Modernes.

Marx, Karl. 1847. *The Poverty of Philosophy*. Brussels: Office de la Bibliothèque des Modernes. https://www.marxists.org/archive/marx/works/download/pdf/Poverty-Philosophy.pdf.

Marx, Karl, and Friedrich Engels. [1848]. *The Communist Manifesto*. Rev. ed. London: Socialist Labour Press. 1888.

Marx, Karl, and Friedrich Engels. [1845–46] 1970. *The German Ideology*. Edited by C.J. Arthur. New York: International Publishers.

Michie, Jonathan. 2022. "Forms of Ownership for Sustainability and Resilience: The Need for Biodiversity and Corporate Diversity." In *Economic Policies for Sustainability and Resilience*, edited by Philip Arestis and Malcolm Sawyer. Cham: Palgrave Macmillan.

Mill, John Stuart. 1859. *On Liberty*. London: John W. Parker and Son.

Miller, John. 1997. *The Glorious Revolution*. Longman.

Montesquieu, Charles-Louis de Secondat, baron de la Brède et de. [1748]. *The Spirit of the Laws*. Translated by Thomas Nugent. London: J. Nourse. 1750.

Montesquieu, Charles-Louis de Secondat, baron de la Brède et de. 1733. *Considerations on the Causes of the Greatness of the Romans and of Their Decline*. Amsterdam: J. Wetstein.

Montesquieu, Charles-Louis de Secondat, baron de la Brède et de. 1721. *Persian Letters*. Paris: Prault.

Muller v. Oregon, 208 U.S. 412 (1908). https://supreme.justia.com/cases/federal/us/208/412/.

Munro, André. 2025. "Power." *Britannica*. Last updated January 14. https://www.britannica.com/topic/power-political-and-social-science.

Neacșu, Dana. 2025. "Against the Triumvirate of Common, Civil & Soviet/Socialist Law Systems. Lessons Learned from Foucault, Pashukanis & Vyshinsky." *Journal of Transnational Law & Policy* 34 (forthcoming). https://papers.ssrn.com/sol3/papers.cfm?abstract_id=4879851.

Neacșu, Dana. 2024a. *Tori Nor Is Sprouting*. New York: The Shortsighted New Yorker Press.

Neacșu, Dana. 2024b. "Essential Perspectives: Foundations of Capitalism." In *Sustainable Capitalism*, edited by Inara Scott. Salt Lake City: Utah University Press.

Neacșu, Dana. 2020. *The Bourgeois Charm of Karl Marx and the Ideological Irony of American Jurisprudence*. Leiden: Brill.

Neacșu, Dana. 2022. "Technology—Revealing or Framing the Truth? A Jurisprudential Debate." *Duquesne University Law Review* 60: 246.

Neacșu, Dana. 2013. "The Internet: Academic Foe or Friend." *AALL Spectrum* 17 (4). https://dsc.duq.edu/law-faculty-scholarship/28.

Neacșu, Dana. 2005. "Romania, Bulgaria, The United States and the European Union: The Rules of Empowerment at the Outskirts of Europe." *Brooklyn Journal of International* Law 30: 185–213. https://doi.org/10.7916/D8W09GF4.

Neacșu, Dana. 2000. "CLS Stands for Critical Legal Studies, If Anyone Remembers." *Journal of Law & Policy* 8: 415.

Nenni, Pietro. 1964. *Avanti!*, October 25, p. 7.

Owen, Robert. 1813–1816. *A New View of Society or Essays on the Principle of the Formation of the Human Character, and the Application of the Principle to Practice*. London: Cadell and Davies. https://la.utexas.edu/users/hcleaver/368/368OwenNewViewtable.pdf.

Oxford English Dictionary (OED). n.d. "Antithesis." https://www.oed.com/search/dictionary/?scope=Entries&q=antithesis.

Parekh, Bhiku. 1982. *Marx's Theory of Ideology*. Baltimore, MD: Johns Hopkins University.

Pashukanis, Evgeny B. [1924] 2002. *Law and Marxism: A General Theory of Law and Marxism*. Routledge.

Pashukanis, Evgeny B. 1930. "Speech on the Soviet State and the Revolution Law." Quoted in Conquest 1968.

Pasternak, Boris. [1957] 1958. *Doctor Zhivago*. Translated by Max Hayward and Manya Harari. London: Collins and Harvill Press.

Piketty, Thomas. 2014. *Capital in the Twenty-First Century*. Translated by Arthur Goldhammer. Cambridge, MA: Belknap Press.

Pistor, Katharina. 2019. *The Code of Capital: How the Law Creates Wealth and Inequality*. Princeton, NJ: Princeton University Press.

Plekanov, Georgi. 1895. *The Development of the Monist View of History*. Geneva: Library of the Russian Social Democratic Labour Party.

Plutarch. [*c*.100–120 CE] 2022. *Life of Pyrrhus*. In *Parallel Lives*, translated by Bernadotte Perrin. Loeb Classical Library. Harvard University Press.

Polanyi, Karl. 2008. *Economy and Society: Selected Writings*. Edited by Michele Cangiani and Claus Thomasberger. Cambridge: Polity Press.

Pozdnyakov, V.S. 1982. *USSR Contract Law*. Moscow: Progress Publishers.

Pradella, Lucia. 2022. "Marx and the Global South." In *The Cambridge History of Socialism*, edited by Marcel van der Linden and Magaly Rodríguez García, 1: 263–280. Cambridge: Cambridge University Press.

Prichard, Alex. 2023. "Pierre-Joseph Proudhon's Mutualist Social Science." In *The Cambridge History of Socialism*, vol. 1, edited by Marcel van der Linden, 286–307. Cambridge: Cambridge University Press.

Proudhon, Pierre-Joseph. 1840. *Qu'est-ce que la propriété?* Paris: Librairie Garnier Frères.

Proudhon, Pierre-Joseph. 2023. "Manifesto for Election." In *Property Is Theft!*, edited by Iain McKay, 372. Quoted in Alex Prichard, "Pierre-Joseph Proudhon's Mutualist Social Science," in *The Cambridge History of Socialism*, vol. 1, edited by Marcel van der Linden, 290. Cambridge: Cambridge University Press.

Reed, John. [1919] 1977. *Ten Days That Shook the World*. London: Penguin Books.

Resek, Carl, ed. 1967. *The Progressives*. Indianapolis: The Bobbs—Merrill Company, Inc.

Robinson, Joan. 1970. *Freedom and Necessity: An Introduction to the Study of Society*. London: Routledge.

Roosevelt, Franklin D. 1944. "State of the Union Message to Congress." January 11. http://www.fdrlibrary.marist.edu/archives/address_text.html.

Rousseau, Jean-Jacques. 1789. *Declaration of the Rights of Man and the Citizen*. Paris.

Roxborough, Scott. 2025. "Who Will Stand Up to Trump's Broligarchs?" *The Hollywood Reporter*, January 29. https://www.hollywoodreporter.com/business/business-news/trump-musk-zuckerberg-bezos-tech-bros-1236121204/.

Roy, Louis. 2016. *Engaging the Thought of Bernard Lonergan*. Montreal: McGill–Queen's University Press.

Russell, Bertrand. [1900] 1957. *A Critical Exposition of the Philosophy of Leibniz*. London: George Allen & Unwin.

Russell, Bertrand. 1920. *Bolshevism: Practice and Theory*. London: George Allen & Unwin.

Sadikov, O.N., ed. 1988. *Soviet Civil Law*. M.E. Sharpe.

Saint-Simon, Claude-Henri de. 1865–78. *Œuvres de Saint-Simon et d'Enfantin*. 47 vols. Paris: E. Dentu.

Sanger, David E. 2025. "President Blames D.E.I. and Biden for Crash Under Trump's Watch." *The New York Times*, January 30, 2025. https://www.nytimes.com/2025/01/30/us/politics/trump-plane-crash-dei-faa-diversity.html.

Schumpeter, Joseph A. [1942] 1950. *Capitalism, Socialism and Democracy*. 3rd ed. New York: Harper & Row.

Smith, Adam. 1776. *An Inquiry into the Nature and Causes of the Wealth of Nations*. London: W. Strahan and T. Cadell.

Solzhenitsyn, Aleksandr. 1973–1978. *The Gulag Archipelago, 1918–1956: An Experiment in Literary Investigation*. Vol. 1 translated by Thomas P. Whitney; vols. 2 and 3 translated by Harry Willetts. New York: Harper & Row.

Sonenscher, Michael. 2023. *Capitalism: The Story Behind the Word*. Princeton, NJ: Princeton University Press.

Sorkin, Andrew Ross, Ravi Mattu, Bernhard Warner, Sarah Kessler, Michael J. de la Merced, Lauren Hirsch, and Edmund Lee. 2025. "The Billionaires' Row at the Inauguration." *The New York Times*, January 21. https://www.nytimes.com/2025/01/21/business/dealbook/billionaires-trump-zuckerberg-bezos-musk.html.

Stalin, Joseph. [1936] 1978. *Constitution (Fundamental Law) of the Union of Soviet Socialist Republics*. In *Works*, vol. 14, 141–179. London: Red Star Press Ltd., https://www.marxists.org/reference/archive/stalin/works/1936/12/05.htm.

Stein, Gertrude. 1922. "Sacred Emily." In *Geography and Play*, 178–188. Boston: Four Seas Co. https://writing.upenn.edu/library/Stein-Gertrude_Rose-is-a-rose.html.

Stiegler, Bernard. 1998. *Technics and Time, 1: The Fault of Epimetheus*. Translated by Richard Beardsworth and George Collins. Stanford, CA: Stanford University Press.

Stiglitz, Joseph E. 2012. *The Price of Inequality: How Today's Divided Society Endangers Our Future*. New York: W.W. Norton.

Stiglitz, Joseph E. 2019. *People, Power, and Profits: Progressive Capitalism for an Age of Discontent*. New York: W.W. Norton.

Streeck, Wolfgang. 2016. *How Will Capitalism End?* London: Verso.

Sutherland, Keston. 2011. *Stupefaction: A Radical Anatomy of Phantoms*. New York: Seagull Books.

Taylor, Charles. 2003. *Modern Social Imaginaries*. Durham, NC: Duke University Press.

Thelwall, John. 1796. *The Rights of Nature Against the Usurpations of Establishments*. Quoted in Marcel van der Linden, "Introduction to Volume 1," in *The Cambridge History of Socialism*, vol. 1, 5. Cambridge: Cambridge University Press, 2023.

The New York Times. 2006. "The Decider." *The New York Times*, December 24, 2006. https://www.nytimes.com/2006/12/24/weekinreview/the-decider.html.

The New York Times. 1941. "29 Reds Indicted in 'Overthrow Plot.'" *The New York Times*, July 16, 1941.

Thompson, Clive. 2019. "How 19th Century Scientists Predicted Global Warming." *JSTOR Daily*, December 17. https://daily.jstor.org/how-19th-century-scientists-predicted-global-warming/.

Trotsky, Leon. 1937. "I Stake My Life"—Opening Address to the Dewey Commission. *Workers' International League*.

Trotsky, Leon. [1936]. 1987 *Polnoe sobranie sochinenii*, 1st series, vol. 38. Moscow.

Trotsky, Leon. 1925. "Towards Socialism or Capitalism." *The Labour Monthly* 7 (11): 20–25. https://www.marxists.org/archive/trotsky/1925/11/towards.htm.

Trump, Donald J. 2025. "Remarks on January 21, 2025."

Trump, Donald J., Executive Order No. 14160, Protecting the Meaning and Value of American Citizenship, 90 Fed. Reg. 8449 (January 20, 2025), https://www.federalregister.gov/documents/2025/01/29/2025-02007/protecting-the-meaning-and-value-of-american-citizenship.

Unger, Roberto, M. 1976. *Law in Modern Society: Toward a Criticism of Social Theory*. Free Press.

Unger, Roberto, M.1975. *Knowledge and Politics*. Free Press.

United Nations. 1966. *International Covenant on Civil and Political Rights*. 999 U.N.T.S. 171.

United Nations. 1966. *International Covenant on Economic, Social and Cultural Rights*. 993 U.N.T.S. 3.

United Nations. 1948. *Universal Declaration of Human Rights*. G.A. Res. 217 A (III), U.N. Doc. A/810.

United Nations. 1945. *Charter of the United Nations*. 59 Stat. 1031, T.S. No. 993.

U.S. Congress. 1980. *Patent and Trademark Law Amendments Act* (*Bayh-Dole Act*). Public Law 96–517, 94 Stat. 3015, enacted December 12, 1980, codified at 35 U.S.C. §§ 200–212. https://www.govinfo.gov/content/pkg/STATUTE-94/pdf/STATUTE-94-Pg3015.pdf.

U.S. Congress. 1965. *Voting Rights Act of 1965*. Public Law 89–110, 79 Stat. 437, codified at 52 U.S.C. §§ 10101–10702.

U.S. Congress. 1964. *Civil Rights Act of 1964*. Public Law 88–352, 78 Stat. 241, codified at 42 U.S.C. §§ 2000a-2000h-6.

U.S. Congress. 1938. *An Act to Provide for the Establishment of Fair Labor Standards for Employees*. Pub. L. No. 75–718, 52 Stat. 1060, codified as amended at 29 U.S.C. §§ 201–219. https://www.dol.gov/general/aboutdol/history/flsa1938.

U.S. Congress. 1890. *Sherman Antitrust Act of 1890*. Public Law 51–647, 26 Stat. 209, codified at 15 U.S.C. §§ 1–7. https://www.archives.gov/milestone-documents/sherman-anti-trust-act.

U.S. Constitution. 1787.

U.S. Constitution. 1787. Article I. https://constitution.congress.gov/constitution/article-1/.

U.S. Constitution. 1787. Article I, Section 2, Clause 3. https://constitution.congress.gov/browse/article-1/section-2/clause-3/.

U.S. Constitution. 1787. Article II. https://constitution.congress.gov/constitution/article-2/.

U.S. Constitution. 1787. Article III. https://constitution.congress.gov/constitution/article-3/.

U.S. Constitution. Amendment XIV. 1787. 1868. https://www.archives.gov/milestone-documents/14th-amendment#:~:text=Section%202.,State%2C%20excluding%20Indians%20not%20taxed.

United States Court of Appeals for the Eighth Circuit. 1943. *Dunne v. United States*, 138 F.2d 137, cert. denied, 320 U.S. 790.

United States District Court for the Northern District of California. 1944. *United States v. Dried Fruit Association of California*, 4 F.R.D. 1.

United States District Court for the Eastern District of Pennsylvania. 1910. *United States v. Reading Co.*, 183 F. 427.

United States Supreme Court. 1911. *Standard Oil Co. of New Jersey v. United States*, 221 U.S. 1.

United States Supreme Court. 1904. *Northern Securities Co. v. United States*, 193 U.S. 197. https://supreme.justia.com/cases/federal/us/193/197/.

United States Supreme Court. 1895. *United States v. E.C. Knight Co.*, 156 U.S. 1. https://supreme.justia.com/cases/federal/us/156/1/.

United States Supreme Court. 1803. *Marbury v. Madison*, 5 U.S. (1 Cranch) 137.

Upward, Edward. 1962. *In the Thirties*. London: Heinemann.

Veblen, Thorstein. 1904. *The Theory of Business Enterprise*. New York: Charles Scribner's.

Vyshinsky, Andrei Y. 1948. *The Law of the Soviet State*. Macmillan.

Vyshinsky, Andrei Y. 1951. "Fundamental Tasks of Soviet Law." In *Soviet Legal Philosophy*, 303–310.

Wayne, Stephen J., Richard L. Cole, John M. Rausch, and Donald M. Freeman. 1997. *The Politics of American Government: Complete Version*. 2nd ed. Boston: Houghton Mifflin, 1997.

Winnicott, D.W. (1963).1965. "Communicating and Not Communicating Leading to a Study of Certain Opposites." In *The Maturational Processes and the Facilitating Environment: Studies in the Theory of Emotional Development*, 186–87. London: Hogarth Press and the Institute of Psycho-Analysis.

Zhang, Sarah. 2019. "Trump's Most Trusted Adviser Is His Own Gut." *The Atlantic*, January 13, 2019. https://www.theatlantic.com/politics/archive/2019/01/trump-follows-his-gut/580084.

Zidek, Libor. 2019. *Centrally Planned Economies: Theory and Practice in Socialist Czechoslovakia*. Prague: Karolinum Press.

Zile, Zigurds L., ed. 1992. *Ideas and Forces in Soviet Legal History: A Reader on the Soviet State and Law*. Oxford University Press.

Zoninsein, Jonas. 1990. *Monopoly Capital Theory: Hilferding and Twentieth-Century Paeger*. Cambridge, MA: Harvard University Press.

Index

www.ingramcontent.com/pod-product-compliance
Lightning Source LLC
LaVergne TN
LVHW020938031026
849429LV00029B/338
* 9 7 9 8 8 8 8 9 0 9 0 4 1 *